THE BUFFALO TREE

Bobbie Sorich

ISBN: 1534993150
ISBN 13: 9781534993150
Library of Congress Control Number: 2016911078
CreateSpace Independent Publishing Platform
North Charleston, South Carolina

The writing of this book was very expensive.
Just ask my children, who paid for it
with their childhoods.

PROLOGUE

Institution-egg shell paint masked chipped stucco walls. Dreary beige linoleum endured heavy feet in ill-fitting shoes slogging and shuffling in predetermined circles. The mild aroma of beef cooking in some manner suggested that the faint clanging, clinking sounds came from a nearby kitchen. What air the beef didn't fill was consumed by the acrid odor of raw onions. The smell was, in fact, underarms unleashing the stench of suppressed desperation. Glazed eyes with drooping lids attempted to focus on the images flashing from the screen of a sorely scarred console television. They failed.

Dulled ears made a feeble effort to hear the dialogue despite the low volume. They failed as well, but it didn't matter. Lips moved, but no words came from the mouths they encircled. Inaudible conversations were held with invisible companions. Playing cards so worn they made no sound when shuffled by clumsy, unsure hands. Faces of varying ages portrayed no emotion. Sudden screams of protest intruded upon the already-surreal scene as a young woman who had just swallowed thirteen objects was dragged from the room. No one reacted. It didn't matter.

A mere five hours earlier, my mirror had reflected a young woman with blue eyes full of tentative hope. Not so now. There'd been a mistake. This wasn't the place for me. I was nothing like these people. I turned to leave, only to discover that the door into this room was for entry only. Five hours later, I was exactly like these people.

CHAPTER ONE

*There are as many worlds as there are kinds of days, and
as an opal changes its colors and its fire to match the
nature of a day, so do I.*

—John Steinbeck

"Why in the world is the alarm clock ringing so early in the morning?" I groaned aloud. A second groggy look confirmed it was only five thirty. *Wait till I get my hands on the kid who played with my clock.* As I reset the alarm for a more acceptable six thirty and turned over to go back to sleep, the new pale-blue skirt and matching floral-print blouse hanging on my bedroom doorknob caught my eye. The sight of them broke through my sleepy fog as it dawned on me: a child hadn't set the alarm for five thirty—I had.

Oh, yeah, my first day as an on-the-job-training employee at the Contra Costa County health department, I thought.

The program had been developed by the state of California to train single mothers on welfare to develop skills that would help them get mainstream, gainful employment.

Determination to put my general-education diploma to good use pulled me to a sitting position on the edge of my bed. It had taken four years of adult-education classes to earn it, and I wasn't about to let it go to waste. Self-respect and self-reliance were my goals. The office skills this training promised would surely land me a job that would pay enough to support my four children.

The need for caffeine got me to my feet and staggering down the hall to the kitchen. While referring to my to-do list, I deeply inhaled the aroma of the much-needed coffee as it percolated and made oatmeal for the children. My own breakfast was a mug of that coffee that I sipped on the way to the bathroom. There was no time for anything more. After a hurried bath, I threw on my new duds and applied makeup in a manner I hoped looked business-like. Time to wake the brood.

The door of the girls' room creaked as I opened it and peeked in. Eight-month-old Joanie was awake and peering through the prison bars of her crib at Binky, her sleeping four-year-old sister. Her face expressed delight at the sight of my head poking in, as if to say, "Yay, the rescue team has arrived. I'm outta here." She rewarded my smile with one of her own.

"Good morning, sweet cheeks," I said softly.

"Mum-mum-mum," she replied.

The changing table stood ready to receive her. A severe case of overnight sogginess prompted me to carry her to it at arm's length. There would be time for cuddles after she was dry.

While stripping her down and pinning a dry diaper in place, I rhetorically asked her, "Guess what today is?"

"Mum-mum-mum," she replied, her dark eyes twinkling as I slipped a fresh gown over her little head.

"Right, Mommy goes to work today. Know what else?"

"Mum-mum-mum."

"I'm so nervous I've nearly bitten off all my fingernails. How 'bout I chew on yours?"

Trying to pat my cheeks, Joanie waved her tiny hands in the air. Leaning over, I buried my face cautiously in the dark curls behind her ear. Concern about my makeup made it difficult to do any serious nuzzling. Doing my hair and makeup last from then on seemed a good decision.

After plunking Joanie on the floor with some toys, my attention turned to Binky. Feeling my weight on the edge of her bed, she pulled the covers over her face.

"Oh, no, you don't. Don't you hide your dimples from your momma. Come on out of there."

"Don't want to," she mumbled. "Me want to sleep more."

We played tug-of-war with the blankets until I offered her a friendly challenge. "It's morning! What happens when it's morning?"

"Sunshine happens," replied her voice, muffled by the blankets.

"And what are you?"

She came out from under the covers and reached for my neck. "I'm Mommy's sunshine."

We both giggled as I gathered her in close for a hug. "That's right. Every morning and every mommy needs sunshine, so you need to get up."

In the kitchen I put Joanie in her high chair with a piece of toast and fixed Binky a bowl of oatmeal. Time to wake up the boys.

Stepping into their room required caution. Not in fear of disturbing them but in fear of tripping over one of two thousand and four secondhand toys strewn about the floor.

Butch was my first target. Removing the blankets off his little two-year-old body turned into a game of hide-and-seek. As I inched the blankets down, he scooted toward the foot of his bed and found his way under them again. Laughing, I tried again while he kept up his inchworm impersonation. Finally I just uncovered his face and saw that despite his closed eyes, he was awake and grinning.

"I think I've finally figured out why you look like a chipmunk. It's because you were born on Groundhog Day. With those chubby little cheeks, you look like you're smuggling acorns."

His goofy grin turned into a laugh, and he jumped up to grab my ears. With his small hands, he pulled my face to his and planted a sloppy kiss on my nose. The makeup definitely had to go on last.

After sending him to the bathroom, I turned to wake five-year-old Ricky. That child slept the way he did everything—frantically! His blankets were everywhere but on him. At my touch on his shoulder, the red-haired, freckle-faced tornado bounded out of bed and charged down the hall.

"Hey!" I cried after him. "Where's my kiss? And you! Take a left at the end of the hall. No cartoons until after you eat."

He pretended not to hear me, of course, and mumbled something about, "Just old oatmeal anyway," as the voice of Yogi Bear invaded the living room.

Listening to the sounds coming down the hall, I began to wonder if going to work was the right thing. Leaving them was hard, and I would miss those little characters. My eyes took in the chipped dark-chocolate-tiled floor under my feet and the shabbiness of our furnishings. Yes, going to work was the right thing. My children deserved a better home than this cockroach-infested place.

Laura, the babysitter, knocked at the door, and I let her in and handed her the list I had made out on the care and feeding of the Elling bunch. After hugging and kissing the gang good-bye, I went on my way, with a stomach full of anxiety mixed with excitement.

Driving to work that June day in 1965, I hoped this job would indeed change our lives. That they would ultimately change so drastically and dramatically was something I neither would have hoped for nor could have known. If I had, I'd have turned off that alarm, gone back to sleep, and given up my goals.

CHAPTER TWO

It's no wonder that truth is stranger than fiction.
Fiction has to make sense.

—Mark Twain

Upon arriving in Martinez, I parked my 1952 Chevy two blocks away from the employee parking lot. The walk to the county office building in the heat of summer's sun was preferable to claiming ownership of that car. A few weeks prior, some hapless individual had run into and dented the front right fender. He had then nonchalantly stepped out of his car, whipped out a can of black spray paint, and written out the word "ouch" on the damaged fender. Laughing hysterically, he and his buddies had driven away while I'd stood staring after them in shock.

The huge, old, Spanish-style building had as many chips and cracks in its plaster as the tile on my kitchen floor. In reality, it hadn't known style, Spanish or otherwise, in decades. Up the many flagstone steps, I trekked, and after pushing through one of six thick glass doors, I found the bank of elevators and boarded one. It felt strange not manipulating one child, two toddlers, and a baby, along with all the paraphernalia that accompanies those ages, through the door before it closed on one or more little fingers. No one in the crowd of business professionals who joined me in the elevator needed to cling to my knees or hang on to my skirt. They were just adults, hurrying to their workplaces.

While they appeared to feel confident and at home there, it was foreign territory to me, and I would gladly have traded two of those self-assured-looking grown-ups for one frightened-faced child. Children were people I understood, felt secure with. Hopefully there would be a spot somewhere I could place their pictures. I missed them already. The sight of their precious faces would encourage me.

Traveling to the health department on the ninth floor, the elevator stopped at each floor, letting people off and taking others on. It amused me that the chatter among people stopped the minute they set foot inside. We ascended silently, save for the occasional clearing of a throat or small cough. This frequent change of passengers gave me a chance to check out the attire of the women. My appraisal reassured me that I was dressed appropriately. Each stop also brought a new mix of cologne and aftershave scents, which hung heavy in the air. During these frequent stops, I noticed that even when the elevator ceased moving, I experienced an upward floating sensation. *Hmm, this building must have a sway to it.*

Stepping out of the elevator into a dull, nondescript hall, I looked around for the right office. The floor rolled slightly under me, as if I stood on a conveyor belt. Taking a deep breath, I opened the door marked "Health Services," where a variety pack of clerical workers greeted me warmly. Frieda, tall and mannishly tailored in her attire, seemed to be the leader of the pack; she came forward and offered her hand.

"You must be Barbara," she said. "We're so glad you're here."

Doris, a young, chubby blonde, chimed in. "Yes, I'm especially glad because I understand you're here to learn clerical skills, and, boy, I've got a lot of clerical for you to learn so you can take over some of my load."

Full-figured Jennifer gave Doris a playful shove. "Don't let her scare you off. We'll go easy on you. Welcome aboard."

A mousy, dowdy-looking woman shyly offered, "Hi, I'm Patricia. I'll be showing you where and how to place the books in the library." She pushed at the nosepiece of her thick glasses and said toward the floor, "There's a certain order, you know."

Frieda resumed control. "Well, I'm thinking I'll be your favorite coworker because I'll be the one showing you where the lunchroom and your desk are." She smiled broadly.

My very own desk! I whipped out the picture I'd brought of the kids and placed it prominently where I, and anyone else in the building, could easily see it. Who knew? Other people might want to ooh and ah over my beautiful children, and who was I to prevent them? A scan of my new surroundings brought a smile to my face. Typewriters, copiers, and other assorted office equipment filled the large room...not a diaper in sight.

That first day was educational, and I loved functioning as a responsible adult outside the familiarity of my home and my role as Mommy. My fellow workers exposed me to various aspects of clerical work. Poor Frieda was elected to teach me the complexities of the mimeograph machine; she was amused that I loved the smell of the ink. Doris taught me the complex filing system. Jennifer walked me through the idiosyncrasies of the copier, and Patricia familiarized me on how and where to put the many medical books in their proper places. It was fun learning how this new world worked, and I enjoyed the friendly atmosphere.

The only blemish on an otherwise-smooth day popped up whenever I stood in one spot after taking the elevator to another floor. Whenever the elevator stopped after an upward climb, I floated. A descent caused a falling sensation even after I exited. Bewildered, I tried to just shrug it off and keep going, but it was, at the very least, unpleasant.

Being a part of this new world pleased me. The gals obviously liked me and appreciated my efforts to become a part of the team. At the end of the day, Frieda came up behind me and laid a hand on my shoulder. "Good first day, Barbara. You're going to work out fine."

Elation and a tremendous sense of satisfaction followed me home. The kids squealed with delight when they saw me and didn't seem at all traumatized by my absence. They could hardly wait to share all the events of their day with me. We gathered on the sofa to exchange full reports, and as I sat with them and listened to their chatter, I realized how much I'd missed them. It felt great to nuzzle and hug them all. For the rest of the evening, while I cooked dinner, bathed all the little bodies, and did a bit of housework and laundry, I reflected again. *Boy, this is going to be great.*

For the next few weeks, things *were* great as we settled into a hectic but satisfying routine. The floating and falling sensations hadn't gotten any better. But they hadn't gotten any worse, either, so I grudgingly accepted them.

Then one day at work, one of the home nurses asked me to deliver some child-abuse reports to the district attorney's office on the fourteenth floor. The elevator was empty when I got in on my floor, but at each stop on the way up, more people boarded. Every time the elevator stopped to take on additional passengers, I became so dizzy I nearly passed out. Shaken, I asked a copassenger, "Does this building sway?"

Cocking her head and raising an eyebrow, she answered, "No."

Feeling foolish, I gazed at the floor. Breathing became difficult. The idea of fainting in front of all those professional people embarrassed me, so, unable to stay in that confined space with them, I escaped after the third stop. Rather than call attention to myself by telling anyone how I felt, I got off and walked down the corridor as quickly as my wobbly legs would carry me. Possible ridicule or rejection concerned me more than the idea of choking to death.

Oh, God, what am I going to do? My thoughts raced. *I have all these reports to deliver. I can't let these people down.* I ducked inside the door marked "Stairs" and collapsed on the first step. My face numbed, and needles replaced the hairs in the pores of my entire body while my leg muscles and kneecaps did a crazy dance. My heart pounded so hard that the importance of delivering those reports paled in comparison to the fear of it bursting out of my chest and onto the floor.

If that happens, what will I carry it in? That silly thought made me feel a bit better, but still frightened. When my lungs could finally get their fill, I continued on to the district attorney's office via the stairs in order to avoid another episode.

Walking eased some of the dizziness, but climbing those stairs made the breathlessness worse. By the time I got to the fourteenth floor, sheer misery and panic threatened to take over my whole body. Still unwilling to reveal my problem to anyone, I masked my internal distress with a forcibly fixed smile and triumphantly delivered the reports.

The return trip to my office filled me with dread. What I *wanted* to do was go home, where I'd feel safe. But I was a working woman now and couldn't just run out on my responsibilities. No way was I giving the elevator another chance, so I opted for the steep stairs again.

Boy, stairwells are dismal at best, I thought, fighting back tears. *Some music would be nice, and a few colorful pictures would certainly be in order.* But then, I supposed, not many people were reduced to using this gray spiral unless an emergency arose. Well, this was my definition of an emergency. I decided it was time to see my doctor.

CHAPTER THREE

If you don't know where you are going, any road will get you there.

—Lewis Carroll

D r. Fisher knew me better than any other living soul. He knew my desperate need for more than a good physician and allowed me to use him as a father figure as well. My doctor-patient relationship with him began when I was seventeen, unmarried, and pregnant with Ricky. In the six years since, he had always been there for me, and I had often run to him with emotional as well as physical issues.

Walking into Dr. Fisher's waiting room usually amused me, but that day I inwardly lamented when I saw the number of people already there. It was going to be a long wait, which put a damper on my eagerness to see him. It certainly wasn't the way one expected a medical office to look or smell. Seated uncomfortably in hard wooden chairs, patients lined each side of the narrow room. The air stank of the ever-present cigarette smoke filling the small space. The primary decor consisted of a water cooler in the corner next to the reception window and a large metal ashtray that was pulled back and forth across the threadbare burgundy carpet by the smokers. The customary antiseptic odor of a doctor's office didn't stand a chance there. No one ever seemed to mind the crowdedness or shabbiness, though. Like me, they knew he was a good doctor and, more importantly, a good and compassionate man.

His Jane-of-all-trades lifted her head from the stack of files that she shifted from one pile to another to greet me. That she put up with working there filled me with wonder. Dr. Fisher attended to anyone who walked through the door, even if that person had no appointment. This created a real juggling act for her. Anne was a beautiful, buxom, dark-haired young woman who always dressed stylishly, albeit a bit provocatively. Her looks clashed with her surroundings.

"Hey, Bobbie, how's it going?"

"Going OK, I guess," I replied. "About how long is the wait today?"

She rolled her heavily mascaraed eyes. "Not too long, I hope. Since you actually have an appointment, I've moved your chart to the top of the pile."

A small space beside the water cooler offered the only place to stand while waiting, so my feet claimed it. Several minutes passed before the inner door opened and a woman with her three children walked out.

"Bobbie," Anne said, "you can go on in. Take the third room on the left. He'll be right with you."

The room to which she directed me was almost as small as the waiting room and equally as sparse in furnishings. Since there was no chair, I perched on the end of the examination table and looked around the familiar room. Nothing had changed since my last visit. The same old metal tray stood ready to serve on its wheeled feet; next to that was the chipped white-enamel cabinet, housing remedial instruments of healing in its drawers. Unframed posters of internal organs still blemished the walls, and these were what I contemplated while waiting and wondering which of these organs was creating havoc in me.

As he entered the examining room, Dr. Fisher threw up his hands in mock despair and then bopped me on the head with my chart. "You again!" he exclaimed.

He was an immense man—way beyond overweight and on to obesity. The stool he wheeled over to sit on completely disappeared beneath his girth.

"What do you need from me today?" he teased.

"Whatever you've got," I shot back. "I've been having the strangest dizzy spells and can't figure out why. They're getting more frequent and severe."

"Hmm, OK. Any headache pain with these dizzy spells?" he asked.

"Ha, you must be kidding. You know I can't allow myself to have headaches. With my four little ones, I'd be in pain all the time."

At that, he laughed; he knew my kids. It cheered me to hear him laugh.

"Smarty," he said, "you're like a rubber band. No matter how bad you feel, you always snap back to your sassy self. OK, no headaches." He scribbled in my chart.

"No, whenever this dizziness starts, I feel like I'm going to fall over. I feel the floor moving, only I know it's not. Then I feel sick to my stomach. At first this only happened at work, but now even at the grocery store, I sometimes have to sit down in the aisle because I'm afraid I'll drop Joanie. A few times while driving, I've gotten so dizzy while stopped at a red light that I've had to pull the car over and wait for the dizziness to pass. It's seriously scaring me."

"How long has this been going on?" he asked. More scribbling.

"About three weeks."

"What! Three weeks? It can't scare you too much if it's taken you this long to come see me about it," he chuckled.

"Well, you know how it is." A touch of embarrassment made me squirm. "I owe you so much money already. If these dizzy spells turn out to be fatal, I don't want to die with you on my conscience."

"Very funny. Dumb but funny. Why don't you let me worry about my finances, and you just write a book about your fascinating life and cut me in on the royalties?" he joked.

"Come on. You know darn well I'd never write a book. I'd be too ashamed for my kids to know about their mother and all the foolish choices she's made in her life."

"Oh, cheer up," he admonished. "It's been a short life, so you have plenty of time to make a comeback. Now back to your dizziness. I'll run a blood test, but I'm pretty confident that the problem is that you just don't know how to handle your own successes. You've faced some bad times for someone your age, and now I don't think you comprehend the reality of your present circumstances. You finally have a decent, affordable place to live; you're doing a fine job of raising your children and doing it alone, at that. Despite some pretty significant obstacles, you got your high-school diploma, and in spite of the dire predictions of your family, you're working toward being financially self-sufficient. You've slain a lot of external dragons, but I'm afraid you've replaced them with internal ones. Honey, I think your emotional stresses are taking their toll on you."

"So now what? Just keep going on like this and hope for the best?" I demanded.

"Well, I think we can try one other thing," he replied. "I want you to contact mental-health services. Ask them to recommend a therapist for you to see. I'll let you know if anything shows up in the blood test. Since we don't know what the problem is, I can't prescribe any medication to help you. Keep in touch, and come back if there are any changes in the symptoms."

We said our good-byes, and he left the room. As I headed for the door, I overheard him telling Anne, "Do not—I repeat, do *not*—ever send that girl a billing statement again. As far as I'm concerned, she doesn't owe anybody anything."

Love and gratitude filled my heart as I waded through the overflowing waiting room to leave. What a rare person. Knowing him, he'd be embarrassed if he knew I'd overheard, so I vowed never to mention it. However, I did promise myself I'd try to send some small payment each month because—I smiled to myself—*Really, Dr. Fisher, I'm never going to write that book.*

While driving home, I mulled over what he'd said about creating an internal dragon. How could it be that a person could bring on physical symptoms by an inability to accept success? It didn't make sense to me, but as far as I was concerned, if Dr. Fisher said it, it must be true.

A glum feeling settled in on me as I mulled over all the weird symptoms and wondered if I'd forgotten any. All pondering ceased as I neared a stoplight on the expressway. The world flipped upside down and around. Panic hit as I frantically tried to find where *up* was. My entire body tensed, and an urge to jump out of the car seized me; I wanted to run. Pressure grabbed the top of my head, and I couldn't feel my face. My arms and legs numbed. Air refused to enter my lungs, and I knew I was passing out. A scream formed in my gut as the world started fading away. I floored the gas pedal and aimed the car toward the side of the road. Horns blared, and unfriendly hand gestures flew my way as I sped across the adjacent lanes of traffic and screeched to a stop on the shoulder. As I sat there, fighting nausea, I became aware that all sound was distorted, as if I were sitting in a tunnel. When I could catch my breath and my heart rate slowed, I got back on the road and drove home cautiously, taking pains to stay in an outside lane.

When I arrived, Ricky and Binky were outside playing with their friends, and Butch and Joanie were napping. After paying Laura, I called Dr. Fisher's office and left a message about the episode during my drive home. Looking around at the assorted debris, known as toys, hiding most of the floor, I decided to straighten up a bit before starting dinner.

I came upon a phone message taken by the sitter earlier. It read, "Please call the guy who got cheated out of his *K*." The phone number was unfamiliar. The strange message made me laugh as it dawned on me who it was. When I was fourteen, my mother and I had frequently visited a friend of hers who had a sixteen-year-old son named Don Clar—not Clark or Clarke, just Clar. He had always maintained he'd been cheated out of his *K*. I picked up the phone and dialed.

CHAPTER FOUR

Your children are not your children. They are the sons and daughters of Life's longing for itself. They came through you, but not from you, and though they are with you, yet they belong not to you.

—Khalil Gibran

"Hello?" came a man's voice.

"Hello, I'd like to speak to the guy who got cheated out of his *K*."

"Bobbie!" he yelled. "Is it really you? Is it really my other two and a half pounds of wire coat hangers?"

The coat-hanger bit was from when we had known each other long ago. We had both been so thin that he used to tease that if we ever hugged each other, it would sound like five pounds of coat hangers clashing together. Hearing him recall that made me laugh. Apparently neither he nor his jokes had changed much in nine years.

"Well, let's get all caught up," he continued cheerfully. "Are you married? Any kids? Still skinny? Hair still red? Is it still long? I want to see any other vital statistics for myself, so I won't ask."

Yep, he is still a loony tune.

"OK, in order. No, four, yes, yes, yes, and it's none of your business anyway. Now it's my turn. Are you married? Any kids? Still skinny? Have any hair at all? And if the answer to my first question is no and we go out on a date, I won't even ask to drive your car, cuz these days I have my own."

He laughed as he answered. "No, no, yes, yes, and you're a creep for even suggesting otherwise. I still have plenty of that black hair for you to run your fingers through if you're so inclined. If your bony frame is available Friday night, we'll have that date, now that I've tracked you down. And don't worry; I don't hold that crunching-my-car thing against you, so you could drive it if you wanted to."

We both laughed at that memory; I had asked him if I could drive his car, and he'd agreed on the condition that I let him kiss me. At sixteen, he had never kissed a girl before, so I was his trial run at it. After a nondescript smooch, I got behind the wheel of his beloved '49 Ford and promptly drove it into a ditch.

It was great hearing from him, especially considering my currently nonexistent social life. Having four children usually caused the men I met to vanish, no matter how they felt about me. They just weren't at all eager to get involved with a ready-made family. Most of the time, I was fine with that, but other times, when the kids played outside or slept, I bore a deep loneliness and longed for adult companionship. Beyond that, I needed to look into a man's eyes and see a woman reflected there instead of a mom or employee. In a sense, I was married—married to a house and kids. That loneliness led me to fancy myself in love often, easily, and falsely. It would be different with Don, though, no romance but some much-needed fun.

Don and I set up a date for the next Friday. We planned an evening of dessert, coffee, and a lot of catching-up conversation that would undoubtedly begin with, "Remember the time…?"

Dinner that night was the usual noisy affair, and as always, I struggled to keep a straight face while listening to the children's chatter.

Based on being the oldest and in school, Ricky considered himself superior to his brother and sisters. He was at that conflicted age between being a baby and a big boy, staunchly demanding his independence while clutching my skirt.

"Mama, would you *please* help that baby eat his peas? He's makin' a mess," he demanded and then returned to his drum accompaniment to the music playing on the radio, slapping his hand on the tabletop. In an attempt to dissuade the clatter, I laid my hand firmly over his.

Binky, so cute, with big brown eyes often filled with an expression of unexplainable insecurity, played the dual roles of Ricky's shadow and Butch's little mommy.

"Me help you, Butchie," she said. "This how you do it." She put her mashed potatoes on top of her peas, which made them unable to roll away from her fork.

Amusement at her clever solution brought a smile to my face, which turned into laughter as Butch giggled and put his peas on *top* of his potatoes and declared, "This way more gooder."

Butch was a charmer. If a person needed cheering up, a few minutes with him did the trick. He was spring sunshine and fresh mountain air, which made him a difficult child to discipline. After occasionally busting through his two-year-old boundaries, he would look at me with an impish grin, and I'd think, *Oh, what the heck. What he did wasn't really important.*

Again, I laughed when I turned to Joanie to see how she was faring with *her* peas. She was so tiny and delicate looking. Instead of grabbing a handful of peas like most babies her age, she daintily used her thumb and forefinger to pick up one at a time and place it in her mouth. She hadn't yet mastered a spoon and detested messy hands, so I handled the potatoes for her.

Listening to their silly exchanges sent a surge of renewed love through my heart, much like the first time they were laid in my arms when they were born…so precious. As I looked at those four pairs of brown eyes, I began to feel a great fear, a fear almost as great as the feeling of love.

What if Dr. Fisher was wrong? What if I had a brain tumor or a heart problem? Who would take care of these children? What would happen to them if something happened to me? I was all they had. Not for the first time in their lives, I felt inadequate. The aloneness lay heavy on me.

"Well, Bobbie," I mumbled to myself, something I did often since there was no other adult around to discuss things with, "find the bright side, and concentrate on it. There are only two sides to consider: physical sickness or psychiatric counseling. Counseling looks the brightest."

With that thought in mind, I eagerly looked forward to my first appointment. Naïveté had me believing that for every ailment, there had to be a cure. You only had to identify the problem and then fix it. If Dr. Fisher said I had an emotional problem, then counseling should put everything right again in no time.

CHAPTER FIVE

Never go to a doctor whose office plants have died.

—Erma Bombeck

After a restless night of tossing and turning, I found my way to the mental-health clinic. The office complex resembled a grade-school corridor, with all its gray cement walkways and a long line of heavy metal doors, each with a bold brass number. Spotting the one I needed, I eased it open and entered. The rather-cool temperature in the waiting room suited me. Anxiety always made me uncomfortably warm.

After checking in with the receptionist, I selected a magazine from the tall metal rack and took a seat. Unable to concentrate, I laid the magazine aside and looked around the room. It seemed that all office waiting rooms had the same interior decorator, who must have purchased a surplus of blond, wood-framed chairs with only the seats and backs upholstered in dark blue, burgundy, or beige. The selection for this office was beige, a nice, neutral color for all us excitable types.

A door next to the receptionist's window opened, and the appearance of the woman who came through it startled me. Several strands of gray hair had escaped the bun on the back of her head to fall around her face and across her eyes. Her peach floral-print blouse had snuck out of places from the waistband of her off-white skirt. In short, she embodied dishevelment. A broad smile, however, was intact, and she flashed it my way as she identified herself as Mrs. Dill, the therapist I'd been assigned.

She motioned me to follow her to her office, which reflected more of her dishevelment. The browning plants crowding the windowsill offered no cheer, contrary to the randomly tacked-up posters with cutesy sayings. Once seated, she aimed a few gusts of breath toward the wayward hair strands and grabbed a pen and clipboard. She listed the types of therapy on the menu: group or individual, with either a male or female therapist.

"I don't know anything about psychiatric therapy," I confided. "So I don't know the difference between group or individual. I do know I'd rather have a female therapist, though."

Her slight raise of an eyebrow at my adamancy for a female therapist didn't escape my attention. But I didn't comment, and neither did she.

"Well, Barbara, why do you feel you've been referred to us?" she asked, with her pen poised.

A frown replaced my smile. "My doctor suggested it. I've been having dizzy spells, and he feels they're emotionally induced."

"So," she said, "anxiety attacks, huh?"

Wow, she zeroed in on that quick enough. This is going smoother than I thought it would.

"I don't know what an anxiety attack is," I admitted.

She set the clipboard aside. "An anxiety attack is the physical manifestation of emotional tension triggered by certain situations. For example, people who are nervous when they go to the dentist can become nauseated. Or tension at work can cause headaches. In your case, I'm guessing your doctor feels tension is expressing itself as dizziness. Once you identify what makes you so tense, you can deal with it."

"Well, OK. I'm willing to try anything at this point, because this dizziness frightens me. I don't think I'm tense about anything, except these spells or attacks—whatever you'd call them. I'm usually a pretty relaxed person. Not much gets to me."

Except those dying plants.

She gave me an encouraging smile and said, "Good. Let's get started. Tell me a little about yourself. Are you married?"

"Not anymore. I've been separated from my husband for four years."

A puzzled expression came over her face as she shuffled through the client-profile forms I had filled out earlier.

"Uh, I see on these forms that you have children ages eight months to five years," she said. "And yet you say you've been separated for four years?"

The smile I'd pasted on my face faded. "Yes, that's correct. I've had two children by two different men since my separation." Embarrassment burned through me.

She merely nodded and asked, "Do you feel guilty or ashamed about that?"

"It's hard to say *how* I feel about it. I *feel* all kinds of things. To tell you the truth, I actually *try* to feel guilty but can't quite manage to. I mean, I underwent guilt and a bit of shame through my pregnancies with those two children, but once they were born, those feelings were replaced with love."

Her question about guilty feelings had caught me off guard, and it took me a moment to answer it further. As I averted my eyes, my hand moved to the plant nearest to me, and my fingers absent-mindedly picked at its dead leaves. She was there to help me, so her understanding and approval were important to me.

"Uh, do you mind? I asked.

"No." Her eyebrows rose a bit, and she grinned a little self-consciously. "Please help yourself."

"I really love babies," I attempted to explain further. "For the first time in my life, I go to bed at night and get up in the morning knowing someone in this world loves me. More importantly, the kind of love my kids have for me is so pure and accepting. They don't care if I'm pretty or smart or have a lot of money. They simply love me."

She leaned toward me and asked, "Why is that so significant to you, Barbara? Haven't you ever got that kind of love before? What about your parents? Didn't they express that same unconditional love for you?"

"No, uh, yes," I stammered, searching for an answer. "It's hard to explain. I doubt that my father ever loved me at all. My mother probably loves me but hasn't always shown it very well. She's never treated me the way other mothers treat their children or like I do mine. Maybe she just loves differently than other people."

"Well, it seems we've found our starting place," Mrs. Dill offered. "Why don't you begin wherever you want and just tell me a little about your childhood?"

"I don't mind telling you about my childhood, but I came here because of dizzy spells. I don't see what one has to do with the other."

Her expression lost some of its former intensity as she answered. "I know; I know, but sometimes we carry a lot of painful things in our subconscious minds, until one day they start to nag at our conscious minds, wanting attention and resolution. So if childhood memories are painful to you, let's just look at them and see what we find."

Her words frustrated me. Strong skepticism filled my mind. But she and Dr. Fisher were the experts. If they agreed that this therapy was the solution, I needed to cooperate, so I embarked on the painful trip down memory lane.

CHAPTER SIX

It is not observed in history that families improve with time.

—George William Curtis

"Well, I'll try not to bore you to death," I said to the therapist. "My parents divorced when I was three years old. My father had custody of my brother, and my mother had custody of me. She and I moved from Oklahoma, where I was born, to California. She took me to her parents' home, and I lived with them until I was seven."

"You say *you* lived there," Mrs. Dill questioned. "Didn't your mother live there as well?"

"No, and I always looked forward to seeing her on weekends. Her youngest sister, Billie, lived with me and my grandparents in a regular house, and her oldest sister, Opal, lived with her husband and two kids in a little place in the backyard that was once a chicken coop. My grandpa saw any structure as a potentially moneymaking dwelling. He once rented a water-tank house to a guy for a hundred dollars a month."

Mrs. Dill and I had a good laugh about that, which eased a bit of the tension that had built up in my gut.

Having sufficiently plucked one plant clean of dry leaves, I turned my pruning attention to another.

"No one ever mistreated me exactly, but they referred to me as 'Chris's kid' instead of my name and had nothing good to say about my mother. They disapproved of her makeup, the way she dressed, and her fondness for nightclubs. All I knew was that when she came to visit, she brought with her a…well, I guess you'd call it a brightness. She was a tall and slender, blond Hollywood beauty, with a loud, raucous laugh. And she didn't just bring me a candy bar; she'd bring a *box* of candy bars. Not one or two dresses, but five or six. No hugs or kisses ever came with her, though. My love for her nearly made my chest burst with its hugeness. The real heart buster, though, was when she would leave. Children were supposed to live with their parents, and I didn't understand why I couldn't. More than once I screamed and cried for her to take me with her, but instead she would threaten that if I didn't straighten up, she wouldn't come back. I'd be upset for days after she left. My cousins teased me and called me a crybaby."

"What about now?" Mrs. Dill pressed. "What's your relationship like with your mother today?"

"Oh, it's OK, I guess, but I don't think of her as Momma. A momma is someone like Grandma or Aunt Billie, someone who reads to you, or teaches you arithmetic, cooking, sewing, and other kinds of life skills. Mother just never invested that kind of time in me."

Tears suddenly ran down my cheeks. Feeling embarrassed and foolish, I swiped at them.

"So what are the tears about?" she asked gently.

"It's just—well, I get confused about what kind of woman I should be. Sometimes I think I should be like my grandma: an old-fashioned, stay-at-home woman who takes care of a husband and has lots of kids. Other times I'm impressed with my modern-thinking, beautiful mother, who claims that kids are just a messy nuisance and that all men are worthless. Grandma says I shouldn't work, stay home to take care of the kids and remain on welfare until I find a man to take over. She thinks that to do anything else is just foolishness. My mother has been married and divorced three times and believes I should work if only to get *away* from the kids. They're so different. There seems to be a wrong or right one to pattern myself after, and I don't know which model to pick. Mother also tells me that I've ruined my life by having the children in the first place and now no man will ever want to marry me because of them."

"And how about you, Barbara?" she queried further. "Do you agree with her that you've been so bad that no one will want to marry you?"

A gray, metal trash basket accepted the dry leaves from my hands. With head hung down, I searched my mind for an answer.

"Ha, based on my current experiences with men, I'd say she's right. So it doesn't matter how I behave. My old-fashioned heart, with its old-fashioned desires, is beaten down by a defeated spirit. Men are easy to get but impossible to keep, given my circumstances. I take what they offer without expectation of anything permanent and then let them go.

"Yeah, I guess I've done some 'bad' things, but I don't think that I, myself, am bad. And I just *know* I can make up for anything bad I've done. I'm trying to be a better mother than either my grandma or mother. My kids don't have to wonder if I love them because I show them I do every day. I tell them I love them and hold them close while I read to them. We play and dance and have fun together. People may disapprove of how my little family was created, but we're fine. I gave birth to them, and they're my joy and my responsibility. That's why I'm desperate to find out why I'm having these dizzy spells. I can't afford to be sick. My kids need me. If anything happens to me, they have no one."

"OK." Mrs. Dill put down her pen. "I think that's enough for today. Will you come see me next week at this same time?"

Protests rushed from my mouth. "But what about the dizzy spells? Aren't you going to help me with them?"

"I'm certainly going to try," she replied, "but surely you didn't think we could solve this in one session, did you?"

"I didn't *surely* know what to think. I'm just acting on Dr. Fisher's advice. Do you mean to tell me that coming here and telling you about things in my life that have made me unhappy will explain the dizzy spells?"

"Trust me, dear," she assured. "When we gather enough information about your background, we'll be able to piece together a reason why your suppressed anxiety acts out as dizziness."

The next three weeks proved her wrong. Well intentioned but definitely wrong.

CHAPTER SEVEN

The aim of the wise is not to secure pleasure but to avoid pain.

—Aristotle

Every day that passed with no explanation or solution for my dizzy spells increased my level of tension and anxiety. The constant but necessary pretense that everything was fine became a nerve-racking strain. Routine activities required enormous effort. My body wanted to move constantly. Entering a store brought on a shortness of breath and an insistent urge to run away, although I didn't know from what. That's what frightened me so—not knowing. Having a window or an exit within sight, which wasn't possible at my job, became mandatory. Dr. Fisher continued to answer my frantic calls with, "It's only nerves. Be patient." I had heard the term "nervous breakdown," but I didn't know exactly what it meant. It occurred to me that this might be what was happening to me.

Don Clar remained a frequent visitor, and I thoroughly enjoyed our times together. His humor lightened my heavy days. He helped me forget, if only for an hour, that each day I was growing dizzier and more anxious and losing control of my life. He knew I loved music and had even hoped to be a rhythm and blues backup singer when I grew up. So he always brought over the latest album, and we'd listen to it after the kids were in bed. Embarrassment prevented me from discussing my problem with anyone, especially him.

When at long last I *did* need to talk about it, no one wanted to hear. My efforts to explain my situation to family members were met with vague verbal responses, such as "uh-huh" or "hmm, how 'bout that?" Then I could feel them emotionally take one giant step away from me. In their defense, I hardly expected them to understand something so difficult I couldn't explain it to myself. Emotional illness, crouching under a cloud of question marks, was far worse than a physical ailment that people could see.

Fear of the next spell and feelings of rejection by family and friends kept me isolated at home. Other than to the smallest of stores and work, I went nowhere. No longer was I the mom who taxied all the neighborhood kids to school; instead, I stood at the back door of our duplex and waved good-bye to Ricky as he trudged across the field with the other children.

Another intense elevator episode brought on the worst bout of dizziness I'd experienced thus far. As was usually the case, it came with the accompanying nausea and panic. Its severity sent me rushing and gasping for air, and I had to hide out in the ladies' restroom until it passed. While I paced in circles and frantically rubbed my face with a damp paper towel, Doris came in.

Surprised by what she saw, she asked, "Bobbie, what's the matter, honey? You're shaking like a leaf. Can I help you?"

My facade shattered, and I slumped down on a cot, sobbing, overwhelmed by defeat. Pretense became too heavy for me to carry any longer.

"Thank you, but I wouldn't even know what to ask you to do," I whimpered. "I've been having bouts of dizziness for weeks, and they're steadily getting worse. I think I must be going crazy. I'm in therapy, and the therapist says this is all because of emotional problems that sometimes have to get worse before they can get better. But I can't take *worse!*"

The dam had broken, and poor Doris looked as though she'd rather be *anywhere* other than there with me, a crazed, crying woman. She took a tentative step toward me, gingerly sat beside me, and placed a hand on my shoulder.

The babbling continued. "I have to take care of my kids, and I need this job. But I'm barely able to drive and can't even shop alone because I'm afraid I'll faint and drop the baby. If that happened, what would the other kids do? It would scare them to death."

"Oh, honey," she said soothingly. "Why don't you just go home for the rest of the day? I'll let Frieda know you're ill and needed to leave. Do you need someone to drive you home?"

"No." Feeling calmer, I blew my nose and assured her. "I'm pretty sure I can make it. Thanks for letting me cry all over you, and don't worry; I'll see you tomorrow."

The walk to the car made me feel a bit better, but I knew I'd never go back. Now that my secret was out, facing them would be too hard.

When I got home, I called Mrs. Dill and told her about the episode at work. And since I wouldn't be working, I asked if she could see me every day to speed things up. She said she would rearrange her appointments to accommodate daily sessions. She understood my growing desperation for answers and saw me daily for two weeks. It didn't help. The dizziness and anxiety increased.

On my drive home after the last session of those two weeks, I spotted a Catholic church to my left. It had a look of tired splendor, and it beckoned me. Impulsively, I bent a few traffic laws and maneuvered my car into the church parking lot.

I'd been baptized in the Catholic Church to please my first stepfather, but I hadn't attended mass since he and my mother had divorced. That day, though, I had a strong urge to seek help from someone in touch with God. I wondered if God even remembered me.

I ransacked the back seat of the car for something to cover my head, but only a yellow cardigan sweater of Joanie's turned up. Since that didn't seem suitable, my concern about entering the church with a bare head was quickly set aside. Once I was inside the cavernous, silent sanctuary, the scent and flickering light of candles infused me with a sense of peace. Even the numerous statues seemed to nod their approval.

The swishing sound of the priest's cassock startled me. He had quietly come out of a small room off to the side of where I stood. The black skullcap on his head hid most of his light-brown hair, while his black horn-rimmed glasses hid most of his face. Tightly closed lips hid his teeth and left me with a visual impression of nothing more than a black robe and hat. He bade me follow him down a dimly lit hallway. He moved silently, while my own steps made a click-clack sound magnified by the vastness of the building.

Once seated in his office, I poured out my heart and bared my soul to him about my failed marriage, the two babies born outside of marriage, the dizziness, and the general rottenness of my life. Sitting across from me, he listened and nodded without comment, his hands folded on the dark wood of his desktop. Once finished with my tale of woe, I tearfully begged him to offer up any explanation or help with the anxiety attacks. His answer was a sorrowful look and the offer of a ten-dollar bill, along with the suggestion to light a candle on my way out. Absolutely crushed, I looked at him and dumbly held out my hand to accept the money before I skulked out the door. Ten dollars richer monetarily but a fortune poorer emotionally.

Well, that's it then. The answer is there is no answer. That priest could not have known that this type of giving robbed me of what little strength I'd had left.

I returned home and, to Laura's surprise, handed her the ten dollars. My mind was numb and wanted to stay numb, but the kids needed an on-duty mother. Ricky was upset about some trouble at school; Binky had a list of grievances about Ricky; Butch wanted a snack; and Joanie wanted some cuddle time. Looking at them, it hit me: love and a working knowledge of PB-and-J sandwiches alone weren't enough to parent these children; parenting them required clothes, food, toys, a decent place to live, and, most importantly, a healthy mother. For the first time in their lives, I was convinced I could no longer take care of them.

A little voice in my head protested, *Aren't you scared? Aren't you going to cry? Don't you want to take care of them anymore?* Something inside me broke.

After the draining, fruitless therapy session and the emotional encounter with the priest, there was only one answer. *I can't think about it anymore today. I keep going into battle unarmed, and I'm failing these kids.*

And so, throwing a few things into a small suitcase, I mechanically doled out graham crackers and milk, cuddled Joanie a bit, and then called Laura to come back over. When she arrived, I asked if she could stay with the kids overnight. She said that was perfectly doable since she just lived across the driveway from us, so her mom would be close by. After giving her the phone number to where I'd be and kissing all the confused little faces good-bye, I did what Ricky threatened to do on occasion.

I ran away from home.

CHAPTER EIGHT

Never keep a line of retreat: it is a wretched invention.

—Fridtjof Nansen

Don looked surprised when I showed up at his door, suitcase in hand. Apparently I had interrupted one of his endless race-car-engine fix-it sessions. His straight-as-a-stick, black hair stood up in random tufts, and his brown eyes were nearly hidden under a thick layer of engine grease.

Scrubbing at his hands with a red rag, he greeted me by the latest nickname he had given me. "Hey, Slick, where you off to with the suitcase?" Seeing the look on my face, he asked, "What's wrong? You look pretty shook up."

"Oh, Don, can I stay here tonight? I promise to stay out of your way. I just need a time-out to figure out what to do. If you don't mind me crying all over you, I'll tell you all about it, or I can spare your shoulder, hide in a bedroom, and just keep it to myself. But please let me stay; I can't think of anywhere else to go." Tears of pure misery streamed down my cheeks, and I made no attempt to control them.

"Hey, hey," he said as he reached for my suitcase and pulled me in for a hug. "Nothing can be that bad. Come on in, and tell me what the problem is. I suspected something was wrong days ago. You just haven't been your usual sassy, creepy, little self. You haven't insulted me for weeks. And, hey, if tears are good for stain removal, cry on my left shoulder; I slopped some spaghetti sauce on it."

The smell of hamburger, spices, and tomatoes lent a homey, welcoming feel to his house that was comforting, and I inhaled it deeply.

The tears continued to flow but didn't stop me from laughing. With the kids, laughing was frequent, but out of fear of upsetting them, crying was not a thing I allowed myself to do.

After collapsing on the brown-and-orange sofa smudged with car-engine grease, I continued with my request. "I'm so sorry to burden you with my problems or take advantage of our friendship, but I don't know who else to turn to. I've been having some sort of crazy dizzy spells for a while. At first they didn't bother me, because I figured there must be a logical explanation for them and were fixable, so I never mentioned them."

"There *is* a logical explanation," he insisted with a smirk. "You're not really a redhead after all. You're a blonde!"

His attempt at humor hit a wall with me this time.

"No, the logical explanation seems to be I'm going crazy. Something is going on inside me that I can't control. The best description I can offer is to tell you to imagine that you live in a small town where a murderer is on the loose. He's killed many people in your neighborhood, and the police are completely baffled. Imagine being so terrified that you're afraid to step outside your front door because you're sure he's hiding behind a tree or bush, just waiting for you. You're convinced that at any moment, he'll jump out and attack. Your fear finally reaches such proportions that you decide not to go out at all rather than risk facing him.

"That's how it is with me and the panic that comes with the dizziness. Every day that passes with no explanation or solution for how to stop it makes me *more* fearful. I'm carrying around my own bogeyman. He simply waits, ready to pounce on me when I step out my front door. I can't rest; I can barely eat; and I can't go to the store without having Ricky to cover for me if I have to run out. He's only five, for God's sake! I'm the mother! He shouldn't have to take care of me!"

Listening intently, Don sat motionless. By the time I finished, the twinkle of all humor had left his eyes. He gave me a small smile and said, "Tell you what, Slick; first we call your doctor. I'll talk to him if you want, and I'll ask if there is some kind of medication to help you rest. You can stay here until you're able to start dealing with this, because I agree that you need a rest from it for a while. But you can't just give up. Nope, not allowed. Your kids need you, and, what's more, you need them. What the heck, it'll be nice to have a woman's touch here. You *do* do windows, don't you?"

"Not to be rude, but this place needs more than a touch," I countered. "You need a heavy-machine operator to clean this place up. Carburetors and crankcases in the living room? Really? No wonder you're still single."

Relief washed over me the next day as Don called Dr. Fisher, who prescribed phenobarbital. Taken as prescribed, it made sleep possible but did nothing for the tension and anxiety.

That first day passed quickly, as I threw myself into cleaning some of the bachelor life out of Don's house while he was at work. A call home to check in with Laura and talk with the kids brought on choking tears.

"When you coming home?" they wanted to know.

Just that simple question made my skin prickle. I wasn't ready. Hearing me cry, the ever-compassionate Laura assured me she could stay with them another day. She knew I'd been struggling and agreed that some time and distance from the struggle would allow me to think things through more clearly. Her mother even agreed to bring the kids to Don's for a visit if I needed more time.

My heart nearly exploded with joy at the sight of them. I couldn't get enough of touching them, feeling their hair, or massaging their small backs. But even then I couldn't force myself to return home. The very challenge I'd once so loved had become a knockout punch in the gut. When Laura told them it was time to go, the looks in their eyes reflected two things: confusion and expectation. The expectation was the fist delivering the punch.

Vivid recollections played a slide show in my mind. Through my brain burned images of being so dizzy and panic-stricken inside a grocery store that I had to lay Joanie on the floor while I sat down beside her, mumbling halfhearted threats to the other children about what could happen to them if they wandered away from me. I remembered feeling the need to pull the car off the road for fear we'd all be killed when vertigo impaired my judgment. The lack of an explanation to soothe their confusion made it worse. No longer did I feel worthy of their love and trust. Doubts about my capabilities waged war with homesickness and a tortured longing to be with them.

Over the next six days, I talked to the children daily by phone, but there were no more visits. While we were having coffee the morning of the seventh day, Don reached across the table and took one of my hands in his.

"Slick, I've really enjoyed having you here, but I think it's time for you to go home. Staying here isn't doing you any good, and it just isn't reality. As much as I care about you, I can't provide you with the help and care you need. You need to get back on track, and today is as good a day as any to start. If you don't think you can make the drive, I'll take you."

The thought of giving up this safe haven made me tremble with anxiety, but he was right. I gathered up my things, gave him a brief hug, and drove home, all the time wondering, *What now?*

CHAPTER NINE

No one is so brave that he is not disturbed by something unexpected.

—Julius Caesar

The kids jumped on me before I even cleared the door. It was so good to be home with them, where I belonged, no matter what life and dizzy spells might bring.

"Mommy, I didn't get in no trouble at school all the days you was gone," Ricky announced.

"Ricky a good boy," chimed in Binky. "Butchie a good boy, too."

Smiling, I turned to Ricky. "And how 'bout Binky? Was she a good girl?"

Ricky looked at me like I'd asked the dumbest question he'd ever heard and then gave Binky a look of consideration. "Yeah, she was OK."

Handing me his favorite book, Butch looked at me quizzically. "Read a story?"

Joanie just patted each of my cheeks with her little dimpled hands and warbled something unintelligible.

After being thanked profusely, Laura eased out the door, and the five of us settled together on the sofa to find out if the little engine really could. As I read, Butch, as usual, played with my hair, and I experienced a glimmer of hope. Maybe I *could* start over again. Surely there was still a way to get over, or through, this thing together. Maybe if I just took it easy, everything would be OK again.

After all, I have friends who might do the shopping for me or at least go with me. I don't have to go anywhere alone if I don't want to.

For the next few days, I enjoyed catching up on laundry, cleaning the house, and playing with the kids. Then Mrs. Dill called.

"Hello, Barbara," she said. "I've missed seeing you. Have you been away?"

"Yes. I spent a few days with a friend."

After I explained my stay at Don's and expressed my good feelings about being home, we set up an appointment for the next day to resume work on my problem.

Walking down the corridor to Mrs. Dill's office, I spotted a man and woman standing just outside her door. Even with their backs toward me, I easily recognized the six-foot-four-inch man as my brother, Donnie, whose height made him stand out in any crowd. His long, khaki-clad legs were topped with his signature cotton plaid shirt tucked in tightly and held in place with a thin, brown belt that matched his freshly shined shoes. No one but my aunt Mary had that full and luxurious copper-red hair that cascaded down her back in waves. Looking at her from behind, one expected a foxy lady, but when she turned around—it was not so.

What on earth are they doing here? How do they even know about here?

As I approached them, Mrs. Dill came out of her office and asked my brother to come in. She looked startled when she saw me, which I thought was odd, since we did have an appointment.

"Barbara," she said, "would you mind waiting out here for a moment while I talk to your brother? Mr. Everett, won't you come in, please?"

They disappeared behind her door without Donnie saying a word to me. Turning to Mary, I asked, "Why is Donnie here? For that matter, why are *you* here?"

She shifted her body around uneasily and looked at the floor as she answered. "Donnie axt me to ride over here with 'im. I got no idee what's going on. Yew know me; I don't git in nobody's business."

Mary was married to my mother's only brother, Bud, which couldn't have been easy. None of my mother's five sisters or my grandma cared much for her. Their dislike stemmed from the fact that she was his second wife and they had adored his first one. The rest of their negative reaction to her was because Bud had met her in Southern California and had moved there, taking away my grandmother's favored baby boy.

Being an outsider in this family was tough, and I sympathized with her. Before they moved back to Concord, I'd made every effort to befriend her when they visited. She was only eighteen, and Bud pretty much neglected her. A strict teetotaler, she stayed home while he went out at night. He partied hard and drank harder.

Her facial features sharply contrasted her beautiful hair. Devoid of any makeup, her pale-green eyes peered out of a pinched, drawn face that looked like she had just sucked on a lemon or bitten into a persimmon. Any attempt at beautification was further thwarted by her mode of dress—rumpled, baggy denims and shapeless shirts.

The woman had two saving graces, however; she was the wife of Grandma's only son, and she baked a mean German chocolate cake. Those two facts kept her from being eaten alive by her sisters-in-law. Seeing her there was surreal, since I rarely saw her anywhere other than Grandma's.

Several minutes passed before Mrs. Dill opened her office door and asked me to come in. Once inside her office, I turned to greet my brother, but the look on his face stopped me short. His expression was one I knew well: thin lips tightly pressed together, blue eyes narrowed, and facial muscles tensed. Donnie's long, thin face was confined to two expressions: pouting or fury. That day it wore fury and was so flushed with anger that even the scalp under his light-brown crew cut had reddened. He spoke fluent sarcasm, our family's native tongue, accented with bitter wittiness. In short, he was not by nature a happy man.

My intended words of greeting changed course. I said, "I don't *mind* that you're here, but I have to say I don't understand *why*. How did you even know about here?"

"I'll tell you how," he sneered. "Don's mother called *our* mother, who called me. I'm here because—"

Mrs. Dill held up her hand to interrupt him. "Barbara." She turned to me. "You've been eager to rid yourself of the dizziness and anxiety attacks, and your brother and I have come up with a possible solution. We've been discussing the possibility of a hospital stay for you."

"A hospital stay! What kind of hospital and for how long?"

"Well, I've had a high success rate with clients such as yourself at Stockton State Mental Hospital," she said. "They're more than equipped to meet your needs. I imagine you should plan on a three-month stay."

"Three months," I cried. "I can't leave my children for three months! What about *them*?"

"Your brother has graciously offered to take Ricky and Binky to stay with him and his wife," she replied. "You only need places for Butch and Joanie. Perhaps you have other relatives who would be willing to take them."

"Wait, wait," I demanded. My brain threatened to short-circuit. "Do you really think this is necessary? Isn't there something else I can do?" My hand flew to my chest, grabbed a fistful of blouse, and twisted it into a knot. "Will they *really* be able to help me? Three months is such a long time!"

The air in the room thickened and pressed in on me.

"Actually three months in Stockton would work out to be a shorter treatment time than if we continue on as we have been," she offered. "Treatment would be more concentrated, and you would be free of distractions and worries about your children. No, you don't *have* to do this, but I do recommend it as the solution."

Turning to Donnie, I choked out, "How does Sally feel about this? She's expecting your baby anytime now. Would she be able to take care of Ricky and Binky, too?"

"She feels a lot better about this than she does about you deserting them." He snorted. "You've been crying that you need help, so, OK, go get it."

Stung and outraged, I balled my hands into fists and beat them on an invisible surface as I yelled, "How dare you say I deserted my children! I did no such thing. The sitter knew where I was, and she was perfectly willing to take care of them while I stayed at Don's for a time-out."

"Please, please," Mrs. Dill intervened, "let's stick to the issue at hand. Barbara, what do you want to do?"

Confusion tore my insides. The concept sounded hopeful on the one hand, frightening on the other.

"Can the kids come to see me while I'm there?" I asked.

"It's not like Stockton's just around the corner," Donnie replied sarcastically, "but we'll bring them when we can."

Unable to stand for the rest of this exchange, I sank into a chair and took a deep, ragged breath. "If you really think it will provide an explanation and a treatment for all this, I'll go. I'll call my aunt Billie and see if she can take Joanie. I have a neighbor who used to watch the kids when I had a dishwashing job, and she just loves Butch. She knows I'm having problems and would take him if I explain all this to her."

And so it was decided. As soon as all the necessary arrangements were made, I would sign myself in as a voluntary patient.

Is this really the best way to fight back at the strange dizziness and fear that have taken over my life? Will hospitalization finally provide the answers I need?

Racked with misgivings, I left Mrs. Dill's office.

CHAPTER TEN

Courage is being scared to death...and saddling up
anyway.

—John Wayne

My head ached with the momentous course of action I was about to embark on. Maybe it wouldn't be so bad. I'd miss the kids, but wouldn't have to worry about them. I'd be able to concentrate on getting cured. Since Mrs. Dill was the expert on mental issues, doing as she recommended seemed only logical.

Why Donnie had decided to get involved in my life after the long-estranged relationship we'd had was curious. I thought maybe he was finally ready to attempt a new beginning for us as brother and sister. Even more surprising was that he and Sally were volunteering to keep Ricky and Binky.

Sally had never been my favorite person. She was raucous, snide, and sneaky. Stirring up dissension between people seemed to be a hobby for her. With a personality as black as her bouffant hairdo, she would sidle up to people and drop unwelcome gossip like hot coals in their ears. Her type was distasteful to me, and this caused me no small amount of apprehension at the thought of my children being in her care for three months.

Telling Ricky and Binky I was going away again so soon was hard. The matter-of-fact tone I tried to affect was nearly impossible. They sat on the couch with me, one on each side, with Butch snuggled in close on my lap. Joanie, the little sleepyhead, was in her crib and wouldn't have understood anyway.

My throat hurt and nearly closed up from the pain of locked-in tears. "I love you all very, very much, and I really like being your mommy. You know how I take care of you when you get sick?"

They nodded their heads and recalled various bouts of ear infections, sore throats, or upset tummies.

"Well, sometimes mommies get sick, and we don't have anyone to take care of us," I told them. "When that happens, the mommy has to go to a hospital so doctors can make her well again. Right now I'm a little sick, and *I* need to go to a hospital. We're lucky, though, because while I'm there, you all will have *other* people to take care of you."

Ricky, ever the pragmatist, asked, "How long will you be gone? Does your tummy hurt?"

"I'll be gone for about ninety days." My tummy *did* hurt. "You and Binky get to stay with Uncle Donnie and Aunt Sally. That OK with you?"

"Yeah, I guess," he replied. "Where're Butchie and Joanie gonna be?"

"I'm going to ask Gloria if Butchie can stay with her," I told him, "and I'm going to see if my aunt Billie will take care of Joanie."

"Oh, man, they're lucky!" he muttered.

Binky had remained silent through all this and stared up at me with a solemn look while Butch made engine noises and pulled my ponytail like a train whistle. Not knowing what else to say, I gave them each a squeeze and kiss on the top of the head. Reluctantly I released them to watch cartoons while I called Aunt Billie.

"Hi, it's just me," I began. "I'm calling to ask…Well, you've done me some big favors in the past, but the one I'm about to ask for now is a doozy."

After that ominous opening, I dropped any attempt to make light of the matter and broke down, telling her all about the dizzy spells and the fear that seemed to be a result of them and the doctor's diagnosis, the therapy, and the decision to enter the hospital. "I'm not sure how to get her to Oregon, but would you keep Joanie while I'm away?"

Without question or hesitation, Billie assured me, "Well, sure I will. After four boys, I'd love to have a little girl to fuss over and spoil. Bud and Mary are coming up to Medford for a visit, so they can bring her to me. I heard you were going through a rough time. I'm so sorry. Don't worry about Joanie. Just do what you need to do."

Warning flags waved furiously in my mind as I heard her say that Bud and Mary would take Joanie. Family members had said many times that Joanie resembled Bud, and more than once Mary had asked in a teasing voice if they could adopt her. *What if…?* I stopped the thought before it completed itself. Foolish suspicions shouldn't hamper my search for a cure.

With plans for Joanie taken care of, I called my neighbor Gloria and told her of my impending hospital stay. She said she would be delighted to keep Butch. The whole family had enjoyed him when she'd babysat him previously.

Having made sure all the kids would be taken care of, I reported back to Mrs. Dill that I could go within two days. She said that would be fine. The hospital was expecting me.

After we hung up, I called a few friends to tell them where and when I was going and to ask them if they'd keep in touch, since I knew I would be lonely and homesick.

JoJo, my dearest friend since high school, was so distressed about my decision that she showed up at my house the next morning. She charged through the front door so forcefully that I backed away from her and sat suddenly into the worn, green, leatherette club chair that caught me. She looked a mess. Her black hair was thrown back in a haphazard ponytail, and she apparently hadn't cared how she dressed. She looked like someone had thrown a worn flannel shirt and jeans into the air and her body had accidentally caught them. Her long, narrow feet were sockless and thrust into slippers. The intensity shooting from her dark-brown eyes pierced my gut. Grabbing the dark-wood arms of the chair, with my mouth gaping in shock, I waited to hear what she had to say.

Her face twisted with emotion, and one hand was planted firmly on her hip while the other shook a finger in my face. "Bobbie, I am not going to leave this house, and neither are you, until you make me understand how going into a mental hospital for three months will accomplish anything."

"JoJo," I pleaded, "please, don't make this any rougher than it is already. I can't go on this way, so if that place can help, then I have to go. I've gone over and over it until I'm about to lose my mind."

With that said, all former ferocity left her, and her shoulders slumped. She fell to her knees at my feet and wrapped her arms around my legs. Laying her head in my lap, she moaned, "No, no, no. Please don't do this. I can't let you go. I can't explain it, but I have a bad feeling about it. Don't you understand? This is a mental institution! You don't belong there. You're not crazy. You just have too many responsibilities. You're just tired. You'll be so far away, and I don't drive. I won't be able to get to you if you need me. And what about the kids? You know you can't leave them for that long!"

JoJo's long, black hair emanated an herbal fragrance as I stroked it in an attempt to soothe her. "My little JoJo," I said, trying to introduce some humor into the tearful exchange, "you know it's really a shame. I love you so much and you don't seem to like me at all."

That didn't get the response I was after. Her slender body began to shake with sobs, which caused me to break down and beg, "Oh, honey, don't do this. Let me go with your approval about my efforts to get rid of this thing, whatever it is. The therapist says that she really believes this hospital has the answer. I have to give this a try. If I don't like it there, I can always come home. JoJo, the truth is I *will* be crazy if I don't get this dizziness and fear under control. I can't take it anymore. Yeah, you're right; I am tired—tired and beaten. Feeling faint with Joanie in my arms scares me to death. Hiding at home and asking people to shop and run my errands can't go on forever. I'm tellin' ya, kiddo, whatever this thing is, it's for rich people with lots of hired help, not for poor folks like me."

A horn honked outside and signaled that whoever had driven her was ready to go. JoJo slowly stood, hiccuped a few times, and then dried her eyes on her shirttail. After giving me a long, hard hug, she left, her thin shoulders sagging in defeat.

After such an emotional visit with her, I was glad I had a lot to do. Inhaling the smell of the kids' clothes, I folded them and put them into paper sacks. Tears dripped on their favorite toys and books as they were added as well. All too soon it was time to go.

The first stop was Gloria's kid-friendly house. She was already up and out working in her yard, surrounded by her four children. It always amused me to watch her with her kids, because she looked like one of them rather than their mother. Not much taller than her eight-year-old, she was so diminutive it was hard to believe she could keep her four kids in line. With all the toy trucks, wagons, and doll carriages strewn among the growing herbs and flowers, her house screamed fun. The kids all ran to greet us, hauled Butch out of the car, and dragged him to the swing set. Ricky and Binky didn't need to be hauled or dragged; they jumped out of the car to join in on the fun.

With Joanie on my hip and Butch's belongings in hand, I solemnly made my way to stand beside Gloria. Wordlessly, we stood and watched the kids. My mouth opened several times in an attempt to express even a small part of what I was feeling and my gratitude toward her. But my throat closed up, and I couldn't get a word out. She reached up and drew my face to hers to kiss me firmly on the cheek. We clutched one another in a long, pained embrace before I handed Joanie off to her and made my way over to Butch. Kneeling down beside him as he pushed a toy dump truck through the dirt, I pulled him close and hugged him tightly.

"Mommy has to go now," I squeaked hoarsely. "Be a good boy for Auntie Gloria, OK?"

"Butchie a good boy," he assured me, nodding his head emphatically.

"Yes, yes, you are. You're the best little boy ever, and Mommy loves you very much. I'll be back pretty soon."

The happy expression on his face about being there simultaneously encouraged me and wrenched my gut. Another quick hug, and I hurried away. After loading Ricky, Binky, and Joanie back into the car, I drove them to Grandma's house. Donnie and Sally would pick Ricky and Binky up and Mary would get Joanie from there. They didn't appear to realize what was happening, even though I had gone over the plan a dozen times. The thought ran through my head that ignorance really was bliss. As I drove up the gravel driveway between the rose beds and plum trees, a wide band wrapped itself tightly around my chest, making my heart hurt. As soon as I parked and turned off the engine, Ricky and Binky were halfway out of the car.

"Hey, aren't you even going to hug me good-bye?" I admonished.

"Huh? Oh, yeah, bye, Momma," Ricky answered hurriedly. He grabbed my neck in a rushed stranglehold, planted a sloppy kiss on my cheek, and then took off, running to his favorite climbing tree.

"Me sorry, Momma," Binky said. "Me loves you. Bye." She treated my other cheek to a mushy kiss, accompanied by a gentler hug, before running after her brother.

As I watched them race away, it occurred to me that for them this was like any other visit to Grandma's house.

Turning back to the car, I opened the door to gather up a sleeping Joanie. She stirred a little and gave me a foggy look and grin before returning to her slumber.

The back screen door squeaked open, and I looked up to see Grandma standing on the concrete steps. The sight of her was always comforting: the stained, blue-gingham apron that barely covered her round belly; the hair, more pepper than salt, pulled back and rolled into some sloppily fashioned bun; the panty hose always sagging at the knees somehow; and the feet shoved into the shaggy slippers she called house shoes. Her face defined the term "grandmotherly," with her rosy cheeks, soft smile, and dark-brown eyes that twinkled with amusement. Or was it mischief? Either one, it was a lovely face, wrinkles, flour smudges, and all.

"Git on in here, Bobbie Jo," she commanded, holding the door open. "Git that young 'un outta the heat."

Once we were through the square wire gate, a pebbled sidewalk led to the back door. A variety of rosebushes hemmed both sides of the walkway. The enclosed porch was a riotous mix of a deep freezer, a refrigerator, a wringer washer, and two laundry sinks. Both sinks were filled beyond health-regulated capacity with pots, pans, and baking dishes waiting to be washed. The crown to all this glory was a throne—an enclosed toilet the size of a Porta-Potty. These all sat on linoleum printed with red roses on a gray background, which had chunks and pieces worn through to black backing. Grandma would never be nominated for housekeeper or interior decorator of the year, but as I passed through the kitchen door and the aroma of fresh, made-from-scratch biscuits pleasured my nose, I would have nominated her for best cook. When Ricky and Binky took a break from tree climbing, they would be treated with their favorite—Grandma's warm biscuits and jelly.

With my nose pressed to the top of her sleeping head, I breathed in the fragrance of Joanie's curls. Gently walking her through the kitchen, I reflected on the oddity of having a bedroom adjoining the dining room, but there it was. A comfy double bed decked out in a chenille bedspread, directly in line with the large, dark-wood dining table. After carefully laying her down, I stood for a moment, just taking in the sight of her, and committed her peaceful countenance to memory. Only when my throat began to ache with unshed tears was I able to turn and walk away.

When I walked back into the kitchen, I saw that Grandma had assumed her no-nonsense pose: one hand on a hip and the other wagging a finger my way. "Now don't you be frettin' none, Bobbie Jo. You jes' git yerself well and git on back to yer young 'uns. They'll be jes' fine. And so will you, so go on now."

A wordless nod and brief hug were all I could manage in reply before heading for the car. Thankfully I didn't encounter Ricky or Binky in the yard for another strained good-bye. An unfamiliar silence filled the car. No giggling, no back-seat wrestling matches, no whimpering for a lost pacifier accompanied me while heading down the driveway, only the sound of tires crunching on gravel as I drove home to await going to the place that was my hope for restored mental and emotional health.

Will this hospital stay be worth all this pain and upheaval? I certainly hoped so.

CHAPTER ELEVEN

"But I don't want to go among mad people," said Alice.
"Oh, you can't help that," said the cat. "We're all mad here."

—Lewis Carroll, Alice in Wonderland

That night passed filled with loneliness and empty of sound. Wandering down the hall, I looked into each bedroom. All the happy mess that defines children had been packed up; there was no trace of them ever having been there. Silent tears streamed as I closed the door to the boys' room and then escalated into strangling sobs as I closed the door to the girls' room. Lost. I felt so lost as I cried until my stomach muscles cramped in protest. No baths to give, no diapers to change, and no giggles to hush at bedtime. There was no point in staying up, so I went to bed.

Lying in the dark, deafening silence, I reflected on all the effort I had put into obtaining this place to live. It would no longer be our home, and I needed to get past the sorrow of that fact. Not liking that sad place in my heart, I tried looking to the future with hope and knew that this would pass, as all things did. Telling my-self it would be better, I eventually fell asleep.

Sally arrived early the next morning to drive me to the hos-pital. As I stood at the front door, I looked back into the house I had fought so hard to move into. It was unsettling, at best, to know I'd never return. The housing authority couldn't hold it for us for three months. Donnie would pack and store what little furniture we had at Grandma's.

Locking the door, I thought of JoJo. *Don't worry, my friend. Everything is going to be OK. The rubber-band lady is going to be fine.*

The ride to the hospital was dismal. For months, my best friend had been familiarity, and now I was leaving it. On top of that, the long ride in the car held me captive to Sally's assessment of my life, which she described as wasted and shameful. Her snide tone of voice grated on my nerves like an out-of-tune piano. The holier-than-thou attitude and sermon *really* wore on me, but in my posi-tion, I could hardly say or do much other than stare silently out the car window.

Sally was grossly overweight and grossly overesteemed by the family. Her cynical personality made it hard to believe she was a social worker, a huge deal to physically hardworking rednecks. She was also grossly inappropriate, imparting unsolicited and unwel-come information about her sex life with my brother.

Sally had been adopted at birth, and her parents were angels on earth: soft-spoken, kind, and loving. Spawned by the devil and adopted by saints was how I thought of her. She made me think of snakes, which were always loathsome to me. In a room full of people, she'd single one person out and slither over to that person to whis-per in his or her ear as though she were sharing some scandalous secret, when, in fact, she might just be telling them it was raining. To the observer, however, her actions looked as though she were con-spiring to eat a puppy for lunch, which wouldn't have surprised me.

The upside of the distasteful trip to the hospital was that by the time we got there, my sadness had turned into an eagerness to get out of that car. My dread became a sense of relief and then rapidly changed to awe as I took in the size of the building. The grounds were larger than most of the parks where I'd taken the kids to play. Guessing the dimensions of the building was beyond me. It resembled a giant octopus: a huge middle building, with smaller buildings branching out the sides like long arms. A wrought-iron fence surrounded the imposing structure and followed the natural lines of grassy dips and knolls. The vastness of the grounds was made all the more noticeable by the scarcity of trees; they were few and very far between.

We entered the body of the octopus, and Sally hung over my shoulder while I filled out the lengthy admission forms. Once she was satisfied that I was indeed signed in, she left. That this detestable woman would have two of my children in her care left me staring after her for a moment—irony defined. A sharp pang of renewed concern shot through my heart and was followed by a sigh of gratitude that I was out of her verbal-barrage range. The sound of a man calling my name interrupted my fretful thoughts. He was an orderly, dressed, as most of the staff members were, in regular street clothes with an identification tag clipped to his pocket. No proverbial white coats in sight.

"Barbara, would you come this way, please? I need to take your picture."

I stepped into a little alcove behind the admissions desk and gave the camera a tentative smile. "My picture? Why?"

"In case you wander off, we'll be able to find you," he replied, nonchalantly. "Wanna see it?"

Horrified, I stared at him until my thoughts shifted to what I thought was the absurdity of his answer, and I laughed. "Best photo of me I've ever had. If I could afford it, I'd hire you as my personal family photographer." That laugh had to last me a long while.

Stepping out of the photographer's alcove, I was confronted with another staff person, this one a woman, holding out two small, white paper cups. "If you'll just take this pill for me," she said, "I'll take you to the dayroom with the other patients."

"Oh, no, thank you," I replied blithely. "I feel fine. I don't need any medicine. I'm just eager to get started on whatever treatment I'm here for so I can go home as soon as possible."

Tilting her head to one side, she advanced a step closer to me, and her voice took on a firmer tone. "Hospital regulations require you to take this medication to help you relax," came her reply. "I'm afraid you don't have a choice in the matter."

Not wanting to appear uncooperative, I took the pill and followed her farther into the bowels of the octopus.

As I walked through electronically locking doors, I carried with me my fears and my dizziness and my hope to get rid of them. My hope lasted until the end of the first day and then fled to join my pride and dignity on the free side of those doors.

All my personal belongings were confiscated, and I was dressed in hospital-issued garb: a dress three sizes too big and flat slip-on shoes so large they fell off my feet with each step. Despite the misgivings already besetting me, they could have stopped worrying about me wandering off right then. Venturing anywhere dressed like that was out of the question. Sensing that protest about the taking of my things was a bad idea, I stifled it.

She escorted me into a large room smelling of apathy and painted in gray despair. Twenty or so other patients rocked, hummed, paced, or mumbled to themselves. A few held muffled, nonsensical conversations with a large television placed strategically in the room, which was otherwise furnished with worn wooden tables and chairs of varying size and design.

Matches weren't allowed, but they let me keep my cigarettes. For lighting up, there was a small, cylindrical hole with coils recessed into the wall, much like a cigarette lighter in a car. That amused me at first, but I later realized the logic behind it.

Looking around at the condition of the others, I was deeply moved with compassion for these poor people. Sure, I had my problems, but I was optimistic and eager to get going on treatment, confident I'd be home in no time, since I was nothing like them...until the pill took effect.

That introduction to the hospital convinced me that any sane person could be *driven* crazy after spending one day in there. I wondered what condition I'd be in at the end of three months. A staff member later told me that all incoming patients were given medication to keep them manageable, and true enough, I was certainly sedated to the point of manageability by the staff but had trouble managing myself. My mind grew fuzzy, which caused my general anxiety to increase. The drugs caused all of us to be sleepy and groggy, but sleeping during the day was not permitted. Only the staff walked normally, while the rest of us shuffled. I was living out a scene from a bad movie about zombies.

Each day started with group therapy sessions. At the first meeting, I thought, *Oh, good. Now we talk and get everything out in the open. They'll decide what's wrong, and treatment will begin.* Wrong. Most of the patients were drugged to a state of apathy and didn't appear to feel the need to communicate. Frustration overtook the fuzziness of my brain, and I turned to the nurse in charge to ask, "Well, what do we do? I mean, aren't we supposed to share why we're here?"

She flatly responded with a question of her own. "Why, Barbara? Is that what you want to do?" Her tone of voice told me that she really couldn't care less about what I wanted to do.

Indignation climbed atop my frustration. "Well, I want to do more than just sit here, staring at the floor. I want to do whatever it's going to take to speed up getting well and going home."

She didn't respond to that other than to scribble in a notebook she held on her lap.

Every day continued pretty much the same: dead-on-their-feet people just wanting to go to bed.

We newcomers slept in back of the nurses' station, with thick windows running the length of the room so that the nurses could observe us. The constant light from the observation deck was appreciated. Several severely disturbed people slept in that area with me, so I felt the need to watch out for them. Considering how drugged everyone was, I probably worried for nothing.

Upon awakening each morning, I hoped the day would bring something different and effective. All that happened though was the steady growth of my fear and concern. Each day brought new things to fear and would get me so worked up internally that I couldn't keep anything in my stomach. Just looking at food made me ill, and even if it looked good, standing in line to get it was a problem. The medication, combined with the dizziness I already suffered from, caused the floor to move incessantly under my feet.

My lack of appetite didn't go unnoticed by the orderlies and interns. Soon they threatened me with intravenous feeding. Not wanting to deal with that, I began gagging down a few forkfuls of anything at each meal. At five feet eight inches tall, weighing ninety-two pounds was not ideal, and physical weakness didn't help my emotional state.

At last a staff member told me I was scheduled for assignment to a doctor, and then the *real* psychiatric treatment would begin. New hope! One whole precious week had passed with nothing accomplished. Before I could begin treatment with a psychiatrist, though, I had to go through psychiatric screening and testing.

CHAPTER TWELVE

If the only tool you have is a hammer, you tend to see every
problem as a nail.

—Abraham Maslow

"All right, Barbara," the technician said in a brisk tone. "Take a look at these, and tell me what they bring to mind."

He placed a short stack of papers on the table in front of me. Initially, I merely glanced casually at the darkly smudged sheet on top and quipped, "Looks like someone needs a new ink pen." Then a horrifying realization nearly knocked me to the floor.

"You all think I'm crazy! I've read about inkblot tests, and it usually means the person being tested is of questionable mental health."

A new terror locked my eyes to his as he assured me, "No, it doesn't mean that at all. This is standard procedure for all our patients."

I trembled and wondered who had sucked all the air from the room. My skin tingled, and my face grew numb. A scream of protest worked its way up from my very toes. It threatened to turn itself loose in the little air left.

My mind reprimanded the scream. *Oh, no, you don't. I'm beginning to catch on now. You just make your way back down to wherever you came from. If I turn you loose, I'll never get out of here.* A strong pressure filled my chest as I pushed the scream back down.

Convinced I had made a monumental mistake by coming to this hospital, I was also convinced that signing myself in had been much easier than signing myself out would be.

One day, feeling perfectly confident that it was the only logical thing to do, given my dislike of the place and my experience there so far, I told a nurse I wanted to sign myself out. I fully believed I had that freedom of choice. The staff called my brother, who sent Sally with a message: if I tried to sign myself out, he would go to court to have me committed due to mental incompetency. Sally seemed to take pleasure in watching me crumple in despair over Donnie's threat. If I'd had the energy, I would have slapped her.

My already-low self-esteem dived deeper. Feeling depressed and without hope, I checked with a few other patients who seemed to be emotionally troubled but mentally OK. They reported that a husband or family member had indeed taken them to court for a sanity hearing, whereupon a judge had sentenced them to this hospital. When I heard their stories, I didn't even inquire about my rights. Donnie and Sally had me convinced that they weren't just making idle threats.

So, I thought to myself as I sat across the table from the technician, *this is a competitive sport: me on one team and the world on the other. I've played this game before, but the arena and rules are different this time. I've got to learn the rules, and the sooner the better.*

The technician cleared his throat, "You can start anytime, Barbara."

Proceeding through the inkblots quickly, I blurted out my impressions of what they depicted as he made hasty notes. His frantic scribbling came to a halt when one particular inkblot shot me in the heart and I burst into tears. I sobbed that it looked like a woman giving birth to two dead babies. After a long, expressionless look at me, he removed the inkblots and replaced them with several sheets of blank paper and handed me a pencil.

"I want you to draw a picture of a person," he explained.

"Man or woman?"

"Which one would you *like* to draw?" he countered.

Aha, I thought. *Let the games begin. Is he trying to manipulate me? Will the sex of the figure be significant to him? Drawing a man might define me as being oversexed.* I decided on a woman.

Picking up the pencil, I started to draw when suddenly I realized there was another issue to deal with.

"With or without clothes?"

"It's entirely your choice," he replied.

She was drawn with clothes.

"Now," he said, "I'd like you to draw her without clothes."

"Front or side view?" I quipped, shooting for sarcasm since I believed he was making fun of me.

"Again," he replied without expression, "your choice."

A headache gnawed its way up from the base of my neck as I tried to figure out what he was maneuvering me toward; I felt a rise of anger at this game. He had nothing to lose, while I could lose everything. Win or lose, however, he'd go home tonight. I wouldn't.

Tears of frustration clogged my throat. "Tell you what; I'll draw her front and back. Then I'll draw a man, with and without clothes, front and back. That *is* what you'll want, isn't it?"

I set about my task poorly, rapidly, and angrily, and when finished, I spitefully tossed the pencil over my shoulder and locked my eyes on his.

"So far you haven't contributed a whole lot to this session, so will you at least give me a tissue so I can blow my nose? I realize the comfort of the mice in this laboratory is of little or no importance to you, but I can assure you I've been sufficiently humbled. Surely letting my nose run to my chin while you sit watching will add little to your understanding of me or my problem."

To my amazement, he laughed. He actually laughed! He then stepped into another room and returned not only with one tissue but also with five other men dressed in the proverbial white coats. I didn't know who or what they were and looked at them sullenly.

"Gentlemen," he said with an amused expression, "I'd like to introduce you to Barbara. Although she doesn't feel well today, she remains spunky all the same."

He turned to me. "Barbara, these gentlemen are interns here and have been observing our session from the other side of that mirror."

My humiliation grew; I hadn't even noticed the mirror that took up a fair-sized space on the wall.

"It was nice meeting you," he concluded. "A nurse will walk you back to the dayroom. Good luck."

From playing the game—their game—that I'd been forced to play, I returned to the dayroom, exhausted.

At the end of the second week, I received a letter from Aunt Billie.

CHAPTER THIRTEEN

Seize the day, and put the least possible trust in tomorrow.

—Horace

Dearest Bobbie,

    I thought I'd better write to let you know the latest news. I just got back from the doctor's office. I have some female problems and have to have surgery. I'm so sorry, but I won't be able to keep Joanie for you. It's just as well since I can't get her to eat or anything. She cries almost all the time. Bud and Mary were here last week, and she was better with Mary. You and Mary do have the same red hair, and that might be why. I didn't know what else to do, so I sent her home with them. I hope this is OK.

    Love,

    Aunt Billie

There had been more than a few times in my life when I had thought desperation would drive my mind completely away, but this topped them all. The scream that had spiraled up before threatened to do so again. The battle to suppress it was brutal. My whole body vibrated with utter helplessness.

Trying to maintain some semblance of composure, I rushed to the nurses station as quickly as the medicated fog allowed. Waving the letter at them, I begged them to let me make some phone calls.

"Now, Barbara," the nurse on duty chided as if speaking to a child, "you know you only get to make phone calls on Friday evenings and Sunday afternoons. You'll just have to wait."

"Please, just read this, and you'll understand," I implored, thrusting the letter toward her. "It's about my baby! It can't wait."

"I'm sorry, dear, but rules are rules."

Composure be damned! Both hands became fists pounding the wooden platform of the pass-through window for emphasis. "I don't care about your rules! I need to know about my baby."

Her eyes darted around. "Barbara, you need to calm down." She reached for the desk bell and rang it.

My fists moved to bang on the window. "You don't understand. My aunt has to have surgery, and she gave away my baby."

She sharply gave the bell three slaps. "You've got to get control of yourself." Three additional hits on the bell brought the sound of heavy, hurried footsteps clomping on the linoleum.

"If I calm down, will you let me use the phone?" I pleaded. "Please, I'm begging you. Just let me find out about my baby?"

Two orderlies grabbed me as rib-cracking sobs shook me. The prick of a needle quelled any energy I had for further persistence. The prescribed treatment for my "extreme upset" was new, stronger medication. It had slipped my remaining mind that I was no longer valid as a person; I was just one of the herd, requiring strict management. Their reminder was swift and thorough.

After three days on that medication, I was unable to walk without leaning on a wall, so I was placed in a barren room with other heavily medicated people. In the event any of us fell, there was no danger of hitting our heads on furniture, since there was none. We all lay on cots, mere inches from the floor.

One day a priest swished his way through our maze of cots. Turning onto my back, I stared up at him. He looked benevolent enough but distant. A Bible story I'd learned as a child about a woman being healed by touching Jesus's garment came to mind, and I became obsessed with the notion that touching this priest's robe would heal me. When he was near enough, I reached out and grabbed the hem of his robe. He looked at me with disdain and snatched it away.

"Please help me," I groveled. "Just listen to me."

He simply turned and left. Apparently listening wasn't a part of his job description. Another rule of the game.

During one of my short periods of wakefulness, a nurse I hadn't seen before entered the room. Her eyes scanned the room, and satisfied that no one there was in any great need, she turned to leave.

"Excuse me," I said weakly. "Could you please arrange for me to go to the room behind the nurses' station to sleep on a bed?"

"Well, hi," she answered. Her bright voice contrasted sharply with the darkness of the room. "I haven't seen you before. What's your name?"

"They call me Barbara in here, but I prefer Bobbie."

"How long have you been here, Bobbie?" she asked.

"Two weeks too long." My mouth attempted a smile.

"Don't like it here much, huh?"

Hmm, that's an understatement. "No, signing myself into this place is the worst mistake I've ever made."

"It's a beautiful day outside," she said. "If I can arrange it, would you like to get some fresh air? It might make you feel better."

"Outside? I haven't been outside since I came here. Going out would be great."

"You're kidding, aren't you?" She frowned. "Surely you've been taken out."

"No, honestly, I haven't. They're giving me Thorazine, and said I'd sunburn if I went out. I gave up asking."

She must have pleaded a good case to someone, because shortly she and I were outside, basking in the July warmth. Once outside, I saw that her voice wasn't the only bright thing about her. Her hair was sun blond, and her blue eyes shone with warm friendliness. She couldn't have been much older than me, and I wondered how she had kept her cheerful manner while working there.

As we made our way through the door and down a winding sidewalk, bricks from the side of the building flew at me. Startled, I ducked. The quizzical look on her face told me she didn't see them. *So this is what a hallucination is. Scary!*

"How ya doin'?" Her voice was tinged with concern. "OK?"

Telling her the truth would have assured me permanent residency in that place. "Uh, yeah, I'm OK. Just not used to the sunlight."

We sat on the lush grass because I couldn't manage to stay upright in a chair. The world spun around so crazily that she encouraged me to lie down.

"I remember as a kid," I mused, "how I loved spinning round and round and then sitting down, laughing as the world spun around me. It was fun then but not now. Now it's terrifying because I'm not doing anything to cause it."

She talked to me like a regular human being. I found myself telling her things I'd been afraid to tell anyone else on staff.

"It's going to be OK, Bobbie," she encouraged. "You'll be assigned to a doctor soon. Just tell him, or her, what you've told me. I know it's taking longer than you'd like, but just be patient. The medical-protocol wheels are in motion."

The third week began. Aside from Aunt Billie's letter, I hadn't heard from or seen anyone except Sally, the day she came to threaten that I'd better stay in there if I knew what was good for me.

At long last I *was* assigned to a doctor and went in for my first appointment. That same day I was moved to a different floor. The results of the testing and initial evaluation determined that I was not a danger to anyone or to myself and that I could room with people who were more functional. These people became my real therapy.

"The thing is, Bobbie," shared one of my new roomies, "you have to constantly pretend everything is fine and that no matter what happens or how you're feeling, you're OK. I've been in here lots of times. In fact, every time my husband gets angry with me, he signs me back in. He's convinced the court that I have a severe drinking problem, and I get hauled back here whenever he feels he has the goods on me. My situation is different than yours, though. I look at this like a vacation. Let the ol' man look after things. I get a good rest; the shrinks figure I'm dried out and send me home until next time. This place doesn't scare me the way it scares you."

Her advice about pretending made some sense, even though I wasn't convinced she was telling the whole truth. There weren't many people I trusted, and so far, she seemed more normal than anyone else. My previous roommates had been a suicidal woman suffering from a sexual-identity crisis, a compulsive swallower, and a woman who insisted she was Eve and dressed, or undressed, accordingly.

Heeding my roommate's advice, I put on an act I hoped would fool everyone in charge. This was made easier by having a doctor and new surroundings, along with a change in medication from Thorazine to Mellaril, a milder, less debilitating drug. The going was still rough, but I managed. When I noticed that patients who did arts and crafts received positive reactions, I signed up. Apparently the old basket-weaving joke was no joke! The staff interpreted involvement in that kind of activity to mean I wasn't totally withdrawn and was reaching out to good mental health. And previously I'd made a fuss about getting booster vaccinations, but my new pretense required I agree to them.

Daily baths, another issue my brain had previously rejected, were taken in the hated tub. It was a claw-footed affair absent of faucets. The drain was centered on the bottom of the tub and was opened and closed by a lever operated by an attending staff person. When the drain was opened, the water ran through a secondary pipe recessed into the cement floor. Privacy wasn't possible, since the tub sat smack-dab in the middle of the bone-chilling room. Other patients, waiting their turn to undergo this stripping of modesty, were attended by staff members. In a further effort to show I cared, I made sure that my hair sported a slightly different style every day.

The staff looked upon my behavior as real progress. I knew it was primarily because being less drugged allowed me to function better.

My appointment with the doctor I'd been assigned finally came, and acting nonchalant while fighting to keep my anxiety under control, I told her all the events that had led up to signing myself into the hospital. She, in turn, went over the results of the psychiatric testing with me. Her opinion regarding those tests was life changing.

"Barbara," she said, "I've gone over and over your case file, and I keep coming back to the inkblot that you said made you think of two dead babies. Could that possibly indicate you carry a lot of guilt about Butch and Joanie?"

Here we go again. Don't roll your eyes. "Um, it might. I don't really know." I went on to say, "By the way, I heard that your little boy has a cold. How is he?"

It seemed that question about her son's health was my ticket out of Stockton State Mental Hospital, because she signed my release the next day. My elation was intoxicating. Keeping the anxiety and dizziness under control until I was safely on the other side of that electronically locking door was still a concern. My wall of pretense couldn't become transparent.

At lunchtime, I smiled my way through the line and made cheery conversation with the cafeteria workers. As I turned to my designated dining table, a technician approached me to ask, "Anyone here interested in a ride to Concord?"

A heavy mock sigh loosed itself and a good deal of tension into the air. "Well, if you can't get any other volunteers, I'll make the sacrifice and go."

Sally brought Ricky and Binky with her to pick me up. Looking uncertain and shy, Ricky inched toward me at first. Binky, however, ran full force into my arms for a bone-crushing hug. Love, intense to the point of pain, surged through me as we hugged and kissed. My eyes couldn't take in enough of them.

Even though the kids were glad to see me, they soon became drowsy from the long car ride and fell silent. Sally, for once, had little to say. The silence gave me a chance to consider what to do with the things I'd learned from my hospital stay.

The psychiatrist's opinion that guilt over the births of Butch and Joanie may have contributed to the nervous breakdown disturbed me. Reason dictated that if guilt was the cause, then getting rid of it would rid me of my nervous condition. But how could I get rid of the guilt without getting rid of the children who were presumably causing it? Could I do that, I wondered? Did I *want* to do that? No, the guilt was worth it. But how would I keep it from making me ill?

The other thing I pondered was the doctor's response to my question, "What exactly is a nervous breakdown?" She had said we all have the same basic emotions—love, hate, fear, and so on. When one, or more, of these emotions goes beyond normal bounds and we feel too much of one of these or too little, this points to an emotional breakdown. In my case, fear had skyrocketed out of control.

It seemed only logical that if fear was the enemy causing the anxiety and dizziness, it had to be eliminated. A strong, and probably unattractive, self-centeredness claimed my belief about how to survive.

Again, as we had been many times before, we were homeless... homeless but oh so happy. Nothing compared to being with my children again—at least two of them. The game plan for the kids and me had changed, and so must the rules.

CHAPTER FOURTEEN

There is no shame in strategic retreat if it lets you remain
strong enough to go after the enemy later.

—*Jane Lindskold*

Once I was out of the hospital, there was so much to do and do quickly. My welfare grant had to be reinstated, and I needed to find a place to live. Donnie and Sally grudgingly offered to let us stay with them until we found a place of our own. The rules at my brother's were numerous and strict. According to reports from Ricky and Binky, he had been quick to use a belt on them for the most minor of offenses in my absence. The kids were eager to go home to our house, and it saddened me to tell them we didn't have it anymore.

I'd left the hospital with a prescription for Valium but didn't get it filled. The medications doled out at the hospital had made my brain too fuzzy, and I needed a clear head to take care of the business at hand. Bouts of dizziness and fear continued to plague me, but I was fueled by anger and defiance. That hospital fiasco had gained us nothing, proved to be a waste of time, and cost us everything. My little family had been dealt a harsh blow, but we weren't going down.

I called Gloria to tell her I was out of the hospital and all that needed to happen before I could get Butch. She said he asked for me every day but was fine and seemed satisfied when she told him I'd be coming to get him soon. Her kids kept him entertained and went out of their way to make him happy. Being unsure that I *would* be getting him back, I didn't dare talk to him on the phone. My heart couldn't have borne the sound of his little voice just yet. When I'd been pregnant with him, several people had urged me to put him up for adoption. Had they been right? If he had been adopted, he would have had everything a child should have that I hadn't been able to provide. The same was true of Joanie. My love for them was plentiful, but was that enough?

Based on the opinion of the doctor at the hospital, I vowed to avoid anything that caused anxiety. The best decision seemed to be for Butch and Joanie to stay where they were until things were more settled.

Mary agreed with my reasoning and encouraged me to leave Joanie with them until things were sorted out.

Within a week, I found a one-bedroom apartment, and we moved. It was a bit on the tacky side, but I was free of the hospital and of my brother's bad temper.

There were several single people living in the apartment complex, so our little single-mom family was readily accepted and even appreciated, since we moms took turns providing child care for one another. Misery loving company the way it does, we were warmly welcomed. My new life without fear or tension began each day with me enjoying coffee and sweet rolls with the other single moms in one or the other of our respective apartments. We would sit and yak about who had a new boyfriend, who was pregnant, and what we would do that night or weekend.

It wasn't really much of a life, but it was all we had. None of us, for various reasons, were motivated to change the circumstances;

we were comfortably closeted. Sometime later in the day, our group would disperse to do some semblance of housework or laundry and to fix lunch for the kids. Midafternoon, we'd drift back together for an afternoon break for more talk and gossip and then back to our own apartments to throw together some sort of evening meal.

During the day, Ricky and Binky played outside with all the other children. Life was good for them there. All of us claimed an undying devotion to our children, and for the most part, that was true. The rest of the story was that we were lonely, unhappy, and dissatisfied children with children. We had married and become mothers too early in our lives and, as a result, had become self-centered women with stunted personal growth and maturity.

Oh, we did *love* our children, but love had previously cost us so much emotionally that our love was handicapped. Now we chased fun to make up for childhoods cut short. Usually that fun turned out to be destructive.

I went to see Butch and Joanie often, but those visits invited a lot of questions from Ricky and Binky.

"Butchie come home?" Binky questioned while looking at me in confusion. "He sit in back with me."

"We better get Joanie's bottles, Momma," Ricky would tell me authoritatively. "It's time for her to come home."

Gripped by fear and apprehension, I'd freeze up inside, as I wouldn't know what to tell them. I still wasn't sure about what I should do. So while I loved seeing them, the visits got harder and harder.

Gloria urged me to reach a decision about when I would be ready to take Butch home. She said the mere visits were hard on him, too. I was already keenly aware of that, because of the broad grin on his face when I'd arrive and the tearful, sad face when I'd leave. But the theory of the hospital psychiatrist heavily influenced me. What if I brought him home and guilt over the circumstances of his birth made me sick again? Would I end up going back to

Stockton? Never. As for Joanie, Bud and Mary persuaded me to leave her with them, saying they didn't feel I was ready.

Finally I called my social worker and told her that I had decided to place Butch for adoption by Gloria's family. She said she would make the arrangements but steadfastly maintained that it was a terrible idea, one I'd regret the rest of my life.

When the adoption-hearing date was set, a grief like I'd never known before settled on me. The ache in my heart was so unbearable that the day before the hearing, I caved in, called Gloria, and begged her to bring Butch home. She cried and said she was glad I had changed my mind. There was pain in her voice, though, and a tremendous shame filled my heart for bringing such sorrow into her life. She truly loved my little son. Gloria couldn't bring herself to bring Butch to me, so she sent him with a social-services caseworker.

When his little body emerged from the car and he walked toward me, I fell to my knees, with my arms stretched out to him. He was dressed in a full-blown cowboy outfit, complete with guns and holsters on each small hip. Both hands gripped the pearl handles of his guns while he peered at me from under the brim of his hat.

Then, with a shy smile, he let his hands drop to his sides. "No be scared. Me no shoot my mommy." He leaned into me then and molded his little body to mine. Nothing else in the world could have felt as right as holding him against me did. Any guilt about his birth would just have to be reconciled somehow. That hug would have lasted for hours, but he had a big brother and sister eager to show him his new home and drag him around to show off to all their friends.

Joanie was a different story altogether. I still feared having a panic attack somewhere with her in my arms and dropping her or having her crawl away from my protection if I fell. I needed more time.

So far I had succeeded at staying away from fear by simply not doing anything of any value beyond caring for the kids. The apartment was kept clean, the children were fed, and their physical needs were met. But that was it. No more goals, no more "fancy notions," as my grandmother called them, about working or getting ahead. We lived each day as it came, and I just tried to survive it without dizziness. Dismal!

Shopping at the little corner grocery store was safe but expensive and limited in food choices. Even there, only a few things at a time were purchased so that I wouldn't have a long wait to check out. Waiting built apprehension. The checkout stand was near the door, so I could make a quick exit if necessary, and it often was. The clerks must have thought me strange, but I didn't care. Parent-teacher conferences with Ricky's teachers were attended through notes, never at school in the classroom. I would have offered them an explanation but had none I was willing to share. Only under select circumstances, ones I knew were in my control, was I willing or able to leave the safety of home.

One of these circumstances was going to nightclubs. The other women in the apartment complex and I frequented any singles bar that had live bands. We all loved to dance. Alcohol had never particularly appealed to me, and my dislike for it had been intensified by the hospital experience. At the hospital, I used to look around at other patients and think, *Look at all these people out of control of their emotions through no fault of their own, while others drink or take drugs to the point of losing control and call it fun.* To deliberately put oneself out of touch with reality simply didn't make sense to me. Casual sex was the in thing, and, after all, we reasoned, who would ever want us for wives now? We were all rather young to feel so used up, but that was the prevailing sense we had of ourselves.

At this point, I only felt safe going places where there were no expectations of me. Respectful dating wasn't an option. The fear of having an anxiety attack raised too many questions in my mind. Where might a date want to go? What if I needed to get away and couldn't? Being on a date would mean turning control over to another person, and I just wasn't ready to do that. But I could meet up with men at a club and go home with them if they interested me or if I just needed to be held.

There was no challenge in living that way. But, little by little, dissatisfaction knocked at the door of my brain, and I began to wonder if life outside that comfort zone could be handled. It was time to find out.

CHAPTER FIFTEEN

I stumbled, slipped... and all was gone that I had gained.

—*Stephen Vincent Benet*

Little by little, I began stepping out of the daily routine with the other gals in the apartments. One of those steps was to see Dr. Fisher and agree to take Valium. And another huge step was taken when the kids and I went to church for Easter services with Joanne and her brother. Joanne was one of the newer single moms in the complex. Her brother was visiting from Fairfield, where he was stationed at Travis Air Force Base. Sitting in a large, filled-to-capacity room was quite a challenge. Joanne had been forewarned about my sudden flight impulses and took great pains to make me feel comfortable and accepted, so I did all right. She made sure I had an aisle seat and promised that no one would put up a fuss if I had to leave the building. Knowing she would watch out for the kids in the event of a hasty exit helped immeasurably.

Soon I decided to see if I could withstand some pressure and expectation by applying for a job as a cocktail waitress where

Joanne worked. I was hired to work two nights a week, and I did so well with that and the pressures involved that I found an additional part-time job at another bar. Bars were very familiar to me by that time; therefore, they weren't threatening. This work schedule worked well for the kids, too, since I was home with them during the day and worked while they were down for the night.

Don Clar and I saw each other a few times after my release from the hospital. But he wasn't a likely candidate for anything beyond friendship, so I shopped for someone else. I didn't think anyone would want to *marry* me, what with all my problems, but I hoped to meet someone with whom I could have a steady, romantic relationship. One of the problems of being a single parent was that I felt empty, pouring love out to my children while needing someone to pour love back into me.

One night at work, I thought I'd met that someone.

"Oh, man!" a guy exclaimed to his friend seated across from him at a table. "Would ya just look at her? Isn't she something!"

My retort was ready for him. "Yeah, I'm something all right—something tired. What can I get for you?"

Both men laughed as the one who had commented followed up with, "Hey, a sassy one. You're funny! Bring us two longnecks."

A generous tip was proffered and gladly accepted. They hung around quite a while before the friend left, leaving the flirty one behind. He motioned me over.

"You're really cute and funny, and I was wondering if I could take you out for a drink sometime? My name is Phil, by the way, and you're...?"

"Still tired, and I don't drink." He was kind of cute, with his slightly mussed brown hair and hazel eyes, not exactly handsome but not hard to look at, either. "Sorry, it's probably time to let that joke go. My name is Bobbie."

"You don't drink?" His eyebrows shot up to his hairline with surprise, as though that concept was inconceivable. "Wow, that'll be a cheap date! How 'bout coffee? You drink that?"

"Yep, and, no, I'm not a cheap date. I'll want pie with that coffee."

"I can afford pie," he laughed. "So where should we go?"

"At this time of night, I think the only place to get pie and coffee would be the bowling alley. I'd rather take my own car, though, so I'll meet you there."

He agreed to that, so after I finished clearing tables and washing glasses, I headed to the bowling alley. We joked and laughed and poked fun at the bowlers and exchanged a few bits of information but kept it very light. Keeping the conversation focused on him by asking questions about his job, family, and background helped me to steer clear of any questions he might ask about me. Having pie and coffee and joking and laughing about some of life's absurdities after I got off work became our routine date. We had enjoyed several of these, when one night he pressed against the back of his seat, thrust himself forward, with elbows on the table, and reached for my hands.

"Well, little Miss Bobbie, we've been having a good time together, but I'd like more than pie and coffee after you get off work. I love being with you and would like to branch out a little bit, go somewhere other than here. All we do is joke around, and you know a lot about me. I'd like to get to know you—the real you, not just the sassy, wisecracking cocktail waitress."

"The real me?" *Well, this is it! This has been fun, but it's about to reach its conclusion.*

"Well." I sighed and smiled sadly. "OK, the real me." He didn't get all the minor details, but he heard the full outline of the real me and my life thus far.

Sure enough, as I talked, he started pulling away. By the time I finished, he was again leaning back into his seat. After a few moments, he sharply exhaled. "Damn."

"Yeah," I agreed. "Damn."

"I don't know, I mean, uh…" He floundered, unable to meet my eyes.

Gathering up my purse and jacket, I slid from the booth. "It's OK. Really, I understand. Thanks for the pie."

The keen disappointment couldn't be denied. He was fun and intelligent and decent…and now gone. It wasn't just him, though; it was what he represented—rejection.

Sleep ducked and dodged me all night. By early afternoon the next day, my brain was so fuzzy and tired that I went to my neighbor Jackie.

"Can I send Ricky and Binky up here to your place while Butch and I take a nap? I didn't get off work until two this morning; then I met up with Phil afterward, and we broke up. I'm just worn out."

"Sure," Jackie said sympathetically. "I'll keep an eye on them for you. You go take your nap."

After sending Ricky and Binky to Jackie's to play, I laid Butch on my bed for *his* nap and went into the kitchen. While waiting for him to fall asleep, I poured a glass of soda and sat sipping it at the kitchen table. There was no point in lying down with him, because the little twerp would want to play, and neither of us would get to sleep.

A tired depression hovered over my head like a thick fog. To kill more time while waiting, I grabbed a junk-mail envelope, and on the back, I wrote out a to-do list of things that needed to be done when I woke up.

Let's see. First I'll clean this place from top to bottom. I'll get all the laundry and ironing done. Then we're all taking baths and getting our hair washed. I'll feel better if everything around me is in order. And, my list continued, *I'm going to get Joanie this weekend. We all miss her, and I've let this go on long enough.*

With the list finished, I continued to sit and muse about positive changes in my life that needed to be made. There had to be a better but still nonthreatening way to live. Hiding out in the apartment by day and then catering to drunks by night couldn't be healthy. That was bratty, childlike behavior, but I wasn't a child—I was a parent!

Someone trustworthy, with good advice, and some guidance to help me figure out what a woman like me could do with herself were what I needed. Things had to get better. The bottom of the proverbial barrel had been thoroughly scraped and hadn't produced a whole lot.

Reaching into my purse, I took out my bottle of Valium. I wanted to make sure I took enough to get a good rest, because when I woke up, I was going to start all over again—again. It was time for the rubber-band lady to snap back into place. I reasoned that things probably wouldn't change instantly, because of the stupid dizziness and subsequent panic, but hiding from life had to stop.

When I hadn't come for Ricky and Binky by dinnertime, Jackie brought them home. She found me unconscious, alone, on the bed. Butch, having napped and awakened, contentedly played on the floor with his toy cowboys. Spotting the empty Valium bottle on the counter in the kitchen, Jackie frantically ran back to her apartment with the kids to call an ambulance.

CHAPTER SIXTEEN

If this is coffee, please bring me some tea; but if this is tea,
please bring me some coffee.

—*Abraham Lincoln*

The screams of protest could be heard throughout the entire complex. "Get out! Get out, and leave me alone. I'm resting... just resting; leave me alone."

Groggy, I couldn't figure out who was making such a fuss.

"Mrs. Elling," a voice commanded through the fog. "Mrs. Elling, quit fighting. You can't go back to sleep. Wake up, Mrs. Elling."

Hands pulled at me, and bodies pushed against me. Drowsiness and confusion held my brain hostage.

"Stop it, ouch. Stop it. You're hurting me; let me go."

It was a struggle, but my eyes finally opened, though they refused to focus. Blurry faces danced around me. My spongy legs refused to stand.

Why are all these people in my bedroom? I wondered. Then my eyes settled on Sally standing in the doorway and holding a baby.

"Joanie, my little Joanie," I muttered, reaching for her. "Oh, God, I'm so glad you're back. Momma won't ever leave you again."

But it wasn't Joanie; it was Sally's baby. I vaguely wondered why she was there as I began to fade out again.

"OK," a male voice barked. "I'll get her head; do you have her legs? Let's get her on the gurney."

The fog cleared again as the ambulance door came into view. "Please don't put me in there," I begged, still unclear as to what exactly the problem was. "It looks like a hearse. Please, I'll be good. Let me ride in front."

They belted me into the front seat of the ambulance as I slipped back into darkness.

"Barbara." This time it was a gentle female voice. "Barbara, drink some more of this, and then I'll stop bothering you for a while."

Horribly nauseated, I became aware that I was strapped to a hard table.

"Please." My voice was weak, and my throat was sore. "Please untie my hands and feet. Why am I tied down?"

"Well," the voice answered cheerily, "she speaks! Glad you've finally decided to rejoin us! As soon as your blood pressure goes up to normal, I'll be happy to unstrap you. Now be a good girl, and drink this for me. You only have to stay on this table a little bit longer."

She put coffee to my lips, and I tried to swallow it but wound up wearing more than I got into my stomach.

"I'm not sure how much good that coffee will do for you on your blouse, but nice try anyway," she said. Satisfied with my efforts, she let my head relax again on the table. Suddenly the table moved! It rocked in a seesaw motion, raising first my head and then my feet.

"Don't be alarmed, sugar," she said. "This contraption is to help raise your blood pressure. It keeps the blood flowing and circulating around."

With that assurance, I slipped back into sleep.

It was only after I'd been moved from intensive care to an area called *M* Ward that I became fully aware of where I was. Lying in a bed, I felt a weight on my feet and opened my eyes to see a little girl. Her skin was the color of dark chocolate; her wiry and bushy hair shot out at varying angles all over her head. She looked to be around eight years old.

"Hi," she said. "Duz you know why I's black?"

"Uh, no," I responded, trying not to laugh. She had posed her question so seriously for a child. "Why are you black?"

"My mama sez we's black 'cause we wuz born too close to the equator," came her reply. With that important tidbit of information shared, she scooted off my bed and ran out of the room, leaving me to laugh aloud.

M Ward was a section of Contra Costa County Hospital that was referred to as a therapeutic community. Emotionally disturbed people were placed there for evaluation to see if they required further and more intense hospitalization or if they just needed professional guidance and counseling before being released.

Oddly enough, I loved it there. It was what I imagined college dorm life to be. The patients were free to come and go around the campus as long as we had a staff escort to accompany us. We wore our own clothes, did laundry, helped in the kitchen, and were assigned other household-type chores. I shared a homey, spacious room with three other young and personable women.

My only responsibility was my own behavior. Group and individual therapy was an understandable requirement, but the doctor on staff was a wonderfully caring, responsive man. Unlike Stockton State Mental Hospital, all the scary things were locked outside instead of in, which made me feel protected and cared for. Living the rest of my life in that environment would have suited me just fine. Fear didn't live there, and fearful situations weren't even allowed to visit. The obvious drawback, of course, was that my children couldn't visit, either. I missed them dreadfully and agonized over what must be going through their little minds.

The doctor sympathetically listened to my lamenting.

"My poor kids," I said. "I guess I've really done it this time. And you know, I don't even know how all this happened. You may not believe this, but I really used to be OK. I had a job once. Yeah, really. But I don't know what happened. Am I crazy? I wish someone would just answer that, once and for all. If I am, fine. Just put my kids in a good place, and take care of me. Just don't place them with my family." Hot tears flowed. "I'm so lost! I've tried, honest; I've really tried. But since this nervous-breakdown thing almost a year ago, every decision I make is wrong. I keep going from bad to worse. What's going to happen to me now?"

"Barbara," he said, "I've reviewed your case history, and I personally feel that hospitalization is the worst thing for you. My recommendation to the judge will be that you're discharged...with conditions, of course."

"Judge!" Shocked protest yanked me out of the chair. "What judge? What are you talking about? And what conditions? I *liked* you! I thought you liked me and were on my side."

"Barbara." He sighed. "I do like you. As far as sides in these matters, I can only take the side of my professional opinion. It's clear to me that you didn't intend to commit suicide. But since you did overdose on Valium, there will be a court hearing to determine if you're stable enough to properly care for your children. Charges of being an unfit mother have been brought against you by certain members of your family. When these charges are heard, I'll present your side to the judge. At that time he'll decide whether your children should be returned to you or not. I'm sorry, but this is state-mandated procedure."

This unexpected news sent me back to my room on trembling legs. My greatest concern was how I'd handle myself in the courtroom. What if I had an anxiety attack in front of the judge? If so, my fearful prediction was that it would influence his decision. He might decide I was too sick to care for the children and never let me have them back. Given my recent history, I wasn't altogether sure I'd blame him.

CHAPTER SEVENTEEN

*They who have put out the people's eyes reproach them
of their blindness.*

—*John Milton, Apology for Smectymnuus*

When the ambulance had taken me away, the welfare department took my children and placed them in juvenile hall to await my hearing. My mother, thinking it would only be for a few days, picked them up and took them home with her. When it became apparent that I would be detained more than a few days, she took them to Grandma's, because she worked and had no one to watch them. They were to stay there until my fate was decided.

By the time the hearing rolled around, my nerves were shot. The rest of the patients tried hard to keep my morale up and did their best to encourage me. The women in my dorm even went so far as to do my hair and pick out the clothes I should wear to court. By the time I was due to go into the courtroom, I was numb with weariness and worry. Feeling detached and numb was actually the best I had felt in a long time; at least I didn't hurt and, amazingly, was no longer particularly scared. In my mind, there were two possible outcomes, and with either of them, the children would be OK.

As the doctor escorted me into the courtroom, I stopped so abruptly he collided into me. It wasn't the room itself that so suddenly immobilized me; it was the people *in* it. The room looked almost familiar, since it was similar to those depicted in television programs: dark, wood-paneled walls and multiple rows of chairs divided by an aisle, which led to a banister, complete with swinging gate. Through the gate were two long, broad tables, one on each side. Two large metal ashtrays, one red and one green, were placed on the gleaming tabletops. On a podium, standing impressively in front of a bench, a brass nameplate declared that Judge Walker would be presiding over the festivities. What startled me was the sight of my grandmother, mother, brother, and sister-in-law sitting at one of the tables. With them also sat Aunt Nina, Aunt Dot, and Aunt Hilma. These aunts lived in Oklahoma, and I hadn't seen them in years!

The doctor motioned me to sit at the other table with him.

"Relax, Barbara. That your family is sharing the same table doesn't mean they share the same opinion about you and your children." He chuckled and then sighed, passing a hand over his face. "There's nothing like a custody hearing to shake normally disinterested people out of their ho-hum lives."

My own thought was that in order for all of them to be there, bloodshed must be expected.

It seemed like hours passed while the judge shuffled and read through a thick stack of documents in front of him. While he read, I stared in shock at my family. Not one of them looked in my direction. They fidgeted in their seats, looking stern. Sadness nearly smothered me. My eyes shifted to the bear on the state flag. As I forced myself to breathe evenly, my thoughts wandered down sorrowful family history trails.

All I'd ever wanted was to feel like I belonged to them, but I never did and probably never would. The very word "belong" had a warm, secure sound to it. Presumably a court hearing was to judge between right and wrong. The question that slogged through my mind was, did all the people sitting at that table together as a family think they represented right and I, sitting alone, wrong? Whatever the case, I didn't want my children to be raised by these people. If I couldn't raise them, so be it, but they needed to be where they felt they belonged. I had always judged my mother so harshly, and now, here I was—in a child-custody hearing to determine my parental fitness. I'd turned out worse than her!

"Ahem." The judge cleared his throat, getting our attention. "Which one of you is Mrs. Elling's grandmother?"

Grandma raised her hand. "That's me, sir."

"Let's see," he continued. "That's Mrs. Roxie Dickerson; is that correct?"

"Yessir," she replied.

"Mrs. Dickerson, I understand you presently have your grand-daughter's children staying with you?"

"Yessir," Grandma replied, "and I'll keep 'em, too, until Bobbie Jo kin have 'em back. I know I'm jes' a dumb ol' farm woman, but I know a good mother when I see one. Bobbie Jo loves her young 'uns more than anyone I ever heard tell of. It'd be a cryin' shame to keep them babies away from their mama. Why, lil Butch won't hardly eat a thang, jes' wantin' his mama. Bobbie Jo had some high-falutin' notions 'bout goin' to school and workin' in an office, but she's over that. She'll be jes' fine now."

"So, Mrs. Dickerson," the judge probed. "In your opinion, Mrs. Elling should resume the care of her children. What about her current problems with the dizziness she complains of? Don't you think that might get in the way of taking adequate care of her children?"

"Why, shoot, Yer Honor," Grandma replied sassily, assuming her sly Foxy Roxie expression. "All that girl needs in this world is a good man to take care of her and them young 'uns. Why, she'd be jes' fine then. Ever'body gits to ailin' sometime, and Bobbie Jo

85

always was a sickly child and, well, you know, uh, differ'nt from the rest of us."

She turned to my mother. "Why, Christine, don't you recollect how when Bobbie Jo was a child, she'd git her feelin's hurt and hightail it to that tree she called a buffalo? She jes' needs to git all them foolish notions 'bout workin' and all out of 'er head and go on."

She turned to the judge again. "She needs help, though. She's jes' got too much to carry alone. That's all they is to it."

"Just a good man, huh?" Judge Walker smiled and looked down at the papers in front of him. Then he looked at my brother. "Since you're the only man in the room," he said, "I assume you are Mrs. Elling's brother, Mr. Everett."

"Yes," Donnie responded. "I'm Mr. Everett, and if I were you, I wouldn't pay any attention to what Mrs. Dickerson just said. She doesn't really understand what's going on here. She'd never believe my sister would do anything wrong. A good man," he sneered. "What decent man is going to want her?"

"Well, Mr. Everett," the judge replied. "You're not me, and from what this court has been told about Mrs. Elling's history by her doctor and social worker, your grandmother has a fine comprehension of what's going on here. You might show a little more respect."

My brother flushed with anger.

The judge went on. "I understand you have very strong feelings about the custody of the minor children concerned. Why is that? Do you want custody of them yourself?"

"No," Donnie tersely answered. "But I sure don't think Bobbie should have them. She's unfit to be their mother. You should see them. She doesn't even take them for haircuts. She's more than half crazy, claiming she has dizzy spells. She's not too dizzy to leave them with a babysitter while she goes tramping around to bars all the time."

"I see," the judge said in response. "And you, Mr. Everett? Do you, out of love and concern for your nieces and nephews, take them places? Have you ever taken them for haircuts? Have you ever taken them to church? How many times would you say you and your wife just paid a visit to your sister and the children?"

"It's not my responsibility to do those things," Donnie shot back. "No one told her to go out and give birth to two illegitimate brats. She made her bed; now let's see her lie in it."

At that point, Sally piped up. "Yeah, and if you leave those kids with her, Binky will be a whore by the time she's twelve."

Up until then, I had sat quietly, but her statement penetrated my fog. Fury yanked me to my feet, and tears of rage nearly blinded me. My hand grabbed one of the ashtrays and, without taking careful aim, hurled it at her. Fortunately I missed her targeted head and everyone else's. It clanged off the gate railing and hit the floor. My doctor grabbed me and pressed me back into my chair, while Judge Walker shot me a disapproving look.

"See! See!" my brother exclaimed triumphantly. "She's nuttier than a fruitcake!"

"Mr. Everett," the judge said, "I dare say that if you were to say that to my wife, you would get the same reaction, and she is not, as you so delicately put it, nuttier than a fruitcake. Now let's all calm down and finish up the business at hand."

He referred to his notes again and then asked, "Which of you is the mother of the fruitcake?" As he said this, he looked my way and winked.

My mother stood. "I am, Your Honor."

"So what is your reaction to all this?"

Mother was visibly agitated. "I don't know what to think. Donnie and Bobbie Jo have never got along. I don't know what's wrong with them. It's a shame."

"Yes, well, how about you?" the judge pressed. "How often are you able to relieve your daughter of some of her burden? Are you able to visit her frequently for mother-daughter chats? Are you able to take your grandchildren for visits? What exactly is your relationship with your daughter currently?"

"Your Honor," she began, "I don't have time for any of that. I work hard all day as a meat wrapper, and when I get home, I'm pooped. I have another daughter at home with me, fourteen years younger than Bobbie Jo, who takes up my evenings. My days off go to doing housework and laundry. When I do go visit Bobbie Jo, I get so disgusted with her and the way she lives that I don't do it very often. Why, do you know that when I do go over there, dishes can be piled sky-high in the sink, and she'll just be sitting on the floor, playing cars with Ricky and Butch? Or she'll be coloring or reading to Binky."

"Yes, I see your point, Mrs. Remel." The judge's reply oozed sarcasm. "Clean dishes are just about the most important thing in the world to a child." Massaging his temples, he looked at the remaining women in the courtroom. "I'm sorry; I don't know who the rest of you ladies are. Would you please identify yourselves?"

"Oh, you might as well not involve them," my brother interrupted. "They don't have anything to do with all this. They're just in California visiting Grandma."

"Mr. Everett," the judge said, "if you don't mind, this is my courtroom, and I'll involve anyone in this hearing I see fit. Ladies?"

"Hello, Yer Honor. I'm Skeeter's aunt Dot from Oklahoma."

"Skeeter?" inquired the judge.

Aunt Dot chuckled. "Oh, that's just the nickname my husband, Pokey, give Bobbie Jo when she was just a little-bitty thang. He ust'a call her his little Skeeter 'cause she wasn't no bigger than a mosquito. He always loved this child."

"Thank you, Dot," the judge said. "Do you have anything you would like to say on behalf of Skeeter or about the custody of her children?"

"I don't reckin so, Yer Honor," Dot said tentatively. "I cain't really say as how I know too much 'bout what's going on. I will say I was surprised when I got to my mother's house and found Skeeter's kids there. Last time I was out here, Skeeter was jes fixin' to leave her husband. She said she couldn't take him hittin' on her anymore. I told her she should stick it out with him. Good men are hard to find, you know.

"Then I started hearing thangs about her from the family. She always was an unhappy child, and I hoped thangs would get better for her when she growed up. My mother says she's never seen a momma love on her kids the way Skeeter loves on hers, though, so I don't know why you don't just let them be."

At her last remark, the judge smiled at me as Dot took her seat and another aunt introduced herself.

"I'm Nina. Like Dot here, I'm jes' visitin'. And this hearin' happened to come up, so we came to be with our mother. I don't know anything either 'cept what I'm told. I hate to see Bobbie Jo hurt like she does, and I agree she should get her children back—uh, well, 'cept for Paula."

The judge scanned the paperwork in front of him and then looked at my doctor over the top of his glasses with a frown. "Doctor," he asked, "who, may I ask, is Paula? That's a new name in the mix."

"Paula is actually Joanie, my patient's youngest child," my doctor explained. "It gets a little confusing at this point, Your Honor."

"Yes." The judge went back to rubbing his temples. "You could say that."

My doctor went on. "Upon entering Stockton State Mental Hospital, Mrs. Elling placed Joanie in the care of another aunt, a Billie Thomas. Mrs. Thomas then placed Joanie with an uncle, Bud Dickerson, and his wife, Mary, who, for whatever reason, call her Paula. It has been Mrs. Elling's desire to have Joanie returned, but the aunt and uncle have worked hard to convince her that this would not be in the child's best interest. Mrs. Elling has been torn between wanting to maintain a family relationship with the grandmother and other relatives and wanting Joanie home with her. She fears that reclaiming Joanie will mean certain alienation from the family. Mrs. Elling has finally decided that, depending on your decision here today, she would like to be reunited with all four of her children and make a fresh start."

"Your Honor," Nina interjected, "that would be a terrible mistake. Bud and Mary are so attached to Paula, and she is to them. Why, it would break their hearts to lose that little girl now."

Judge Walker turned his frown on her. "My dear lady, what about Mrs. Elling's heart?"

Nina squirmed in her seat and made no reply, but everyone looked even tenser than before.

The judge gave a deep sigh and leaned back in his chair. He remained sitting quietly for an eternity and then turned to me.

"Well, Mrs. Elling," he began, "it's been quite a day for you, hasn't it?"

The tears I'd been holding back began silently streaming down my face. I didn't trust myself to speak for fear that I would break down entirely and become totally incoherent. I only nodded my agreement that, yes, it had been quite a day.

Turning back to my family, he said, "I have a strong suspicion that Mrs. Elling has been battling hard for so long to please the family that she's allowed herself to be put in a weakened position. I don't know what it is she feels she owes you, but I'm afraid I just don't see the debt here." He briefly looked through the stack of papers again before going on. "While I'm not required to give you an explanation, I want to share my decision with you so that there will be no question about how things are to be.

"Barbara, Bobbie Jo, Skeeter, Mrs. Elling, or whichever name you think of yourself as," he said, and I couldn't suppress a chuckle despite the seriousness of his tone. "It is my recommendation that you be reunited with your children. I have come to this conclusion with no doubt in my mind that this is the best decision for you and them. This recommendation, however, comes with two conditions. One, you are to move. You are to find a place as far away from your family as you possibly and comfortably can manage. I can assure you, my dear, that you don't belong with people such as these, so stop trying."

Gasps of shock, my own included, echoed through the room.

"Two, you will, and this is mandatory, obtain and continue suitable therapeutic counseling through the county mental-health department wherever you set up your new residence. You will be detained here at *M* Ward until this court receives proof of that residence out of town. After moving, I will request knowledge of your whereabouts and confirmation of therapy attendance from the welfare department within ninety days. If at the end of ninety days, you have not complied, you will be served a warrant for your return here and your children will be placed in foster care."

He removed his glasses and leaned forward, looking at me earnestly. "Barbara, you got off to a good start with your children. Now finish what you've started, and find the right battles to fight."

Turning back to the family, he said, "It's unfortunate that Mrs. Elling carries the symptoms of this sick family. I see this happen often in these hearings, and it saddens me each time. Good day to you all."

He stood and faced me. "Good luck, and hopefully I won't ever see you here again."

CHAPTER EIGHTEEN

Forgive your enemies, but never forget their names.

—*John F. Kennedy*

My doctor stood and thanked the judge, while I could only remain in my seat, dumbfounded. The way he had spoken to my family was unbelievable. After all, I was the odd one, the one who didn't fit in.

Everyone looked around uncertainly as my doctor took my arm and led me to the exit. Feeling like the biblical woman at the well, I turned to look back at my accusers. They huddled together, buzzing in hushed but excited tones. Too dazed to care, I only wanted to lie down and be left alone. As we walked toward the dayroom, confident the worst of this day was over, I thanked the doctor for his part in the judge's decision.

The sudden sight of Nina, Sally, and, of all people, Mary walking toward me froze me in my tracks. Flabbergasted, I didn't want another confrontation with them but didn't know how to avoid it.

Seeing Mary completely surprised me, since she hadn't been in the courtroom.

Nina was apparently the appointed spokesperson. "Bobbie Jo, can we talk to you for a minute?"

Don't they see or care about my bone-penetrating weariness?

"Nina, there really isn't anything to talk about. Please, just leave me alone. I'm not mad at anyone, and I just want to get out of here to get on with my life. If that's rude, I'm sorry, but this day has been more than enough for me to handle."

Looking at Mary, I asked, "Hi, where were you hiding out? I didn't see you at the hearing, so I didn't know you were here."

"I waited outside ta hear what the judge had ta say," she replied. "I wanted ta know what wuz gonna happen to Paula."

"You mean Joanie," I corrected.

She flushed. "Well, yew know, we thought it wuz cute. Since our boy's name is Paul, we jest natchurly started callin' er by her real first name." She studied the ground for a minute. "Nina tol' me the judge sez yew kin keep custody of yore kids, and I'm glad fer ya. But what with havin' ta move and all, I wuz wonder'n' if we could keep Joanie with us until yew get settled? I know yew been under a strain, and we shore wouldn't mind." Her face took on a strained, almost-pleading expression.

Feeling torn, I studied her face. "Mary, I'm grateful for all you've done, but right now I don't trust anyone, not even you."

Mary turned to Nina and Sally. "Why don't yew let me and Bobbie Jo talk alone fer a minute."

Nina quickly nodded her agreement and turned to go. Sally glared but went with her.

Mary and I strolled along the sidewalk between the courtroom and hospital dayroom. "Ever since I married inta this crazy family," she began, "I've watched yew ahurtin'. No one should be hurtin' like yew have. I'm not the kinda person to kick a body when they's down. Why, I've knowed yew since yew wuz knee-high to a grasshopper, and as yew growed up, I felt closer ta yew than any of this bunch. I know Joanie's goin' home with yew; we jes' wanna help."

Reflecting back over the years, I thought that, yes, we had been sort of close. Maybe I was being silly. After all, she was right. It was going to be difficult to find a place out of Concord and get moved. Mary did have a gentle way with babies, and I knew she treated Joanie well.

"I'm sorry; I should be ashamed of myself," I said. "Here you are, taking care of my daughter, and I'm treating you like you've done something wrong. I guess I'm not thinking too clearly. It hurts to know I've let my family down and shamed them so much. You're right, I guess. And since you and Grandma live next door to each other, Ricky and Binky and Butch can see their baby sister."

"Why, shore." Mary beamed. "That'll work out jes' fine. Yew'll see."

Wariness still nagged at me as I agreed to let Joanie stay with Mary and Bud, but it was understood that I would get the other kids as soon as I was released from the hospital and settled in somewhere. A lot had to happen before then.

We said good-bye, and with people yelling out their congratulations, I passed through the dayroom on into the women's dorm to lie down. Weary and bewildered, I wondered, *Now what? Does that judge realize how tough his order will be? Haven't we just been through this? But this time...out of town? Where? How?*

CHAPTER NINETEEN

A whole stack of memories never equal one little hope.

—Charles M. Schulz

"Barbara." One of my roomies shook my shoulder. "There's a good-looking blond guy out in the dayroom to see you. Get up!"

"I only go for guys with dark hair. You know that." My attempt at humor was halfhearted. "Tell him to go away."

"Up to you," she shot back, "but if he was here to see me, I'd snatch him up in a heartbeat."

Slowly I sat up and tried to clear the cobwebs from my brain.

"Hmm, a cute blond guy," I mused. "I wonder who in the world it can be?"

Walking into the dayroom, I looked around. Spotting a blond guy I knew wasn't a patient, I headed toward him. My roommate was right; he *was* nice to look at. His face reflected terminal cheeriness, with bright-blue eyes full of humor.

My approach was a bit tentative. "Hi, I'm Bobbie, uh, or Barbara. Did you want to see me?"

"Hi. Don't you remember me?" he asked. "I used to drive you to school. You were friends with my sister. Remember? I'm Pat—well, actually, Gary—Atwood."

"This is embarrassing," I confessed. "I'm not really sure."

"Remember a guy by the name of Bob Guyan?" he asked. "You may have forgotten me, but all women remember Bob."

"Oh, that's right," I exclaimed. "Yeah, I remember you and Bob. You *did* used to drive us lowly freshmen to school. You'd let us out way before the driveway to the school so your friends wouldn't see you with us."

We laughed at the memory of how his dignity had been injured by having to chauffeur his little sister and her friend.

"Well, if you can forgive me for forgetting your unforgettable self," I teased, "come on; I'll fix you a cup of coffee."

"Seeing where you currently reside, I can forgive you out of sheer pity, but I'll still take the coffee."

"I know. I know," I retorted. "What's a nice girl like you…?"

We got coffee from the refreshment cart, found a table, and sat down.

"So," I pressed, "what brings you here? You don't *look* emotionally disturbed."

He laughed. "You don't look it, either, but here you are! I ran into Bob last night, and he told me he's dating a neighbor of yours. She told him about your accident. Uh, it *was* an accident, wasn't it? Anyway she told him where you were, and I decided I'd like to see you. It's been so many years! I always thought you were a neat kid and wondered if I could help—that is, if you need it."

"Boy, do I ever! But you mean to tell me that you'd take time out of your life to help someone you haven't seen for eight years? You're sure different from other guys I've met lately. And to answer your question, yes, it was an accident. I only meant to take a nap, but I was so upset and preoccupied that I lost track of how many pills I took. I feel pretty stupid."

"What could get you that upset?" he asked. "You were always so funny and easygoing back when I knew you."

"Oh, it all started a year ago," I answered, shrugging. "I started having dizzy spells, and when I went to the doctor to find out what caused them, he said there was nothing physically wrong with me and that it was probably something emotionally induced. So I went for psychotherapy, because he thought I was having a nervous breakdown. I wound up in a mental institution, but once they decided I wasn't a total looney tune, they released me. I still have the dizziness, but every medical professional says the same thing: there's nothing physically wrong with me. I've tried to live in a way that won't cause a lot of tension or upset, but the spells continue on. I'm afraid to go almost anywhere.

"Once I went to a dentist, and panic hit so hard I couldn't get calm enough to let him near me. I almost ran out of his office. Boy, he was mad. He told me he was glad he didn't have any other patients like me. I was so embarrassed. After I left his office, I thought about the steps a dentist takes to fill a tooth; you know I couldn't think of one thing about the whole process that scared me.

"Then I started thinking about stores and other places where I've had these panic attacks, and nothing about the places themselves scares me. The only thing I've come up with is that I'm just afraid of fear. I'm convinced that fear put me in the hospital and fear will put me back. It's as though it lives at certain places, so I avoid going there."

Pat sat looking puzzled throughout my explanation. "I can't pretend to understand what's going on with you, but I'd still like to help in any way I can."

I snorted. "Well, help is sure something I need a lot of, but I don't know if anyone has the kind I need."

As I related what Judge Walker had said, a smile spread over his face.

"I can't believe this!" he exclaimed, smacking his forehead with the palm of his hand. "Listen, I'm in the air force, stationed at Travis Air Force Base, just outside of Fairfield. Ever hear of it?"

"As a matter of fact, I have." *Where is he going with this?* "A friend of mine has a brother stationed there."

"Tell you what I'm gonna do," he said excitedly. "When I get back to the base, I'll call around to see if there's a mental-health clinic in town. Then all you need is a place to live and a couple of strong backs to move you." He flexed his muscles jokingly. "The base housing office usually has leads on places off base, so I'll see what it can recommend. Hey, the way I see it, your troubles are over."

He sat there, looking pleased with himself. For the second time that day, I felt dumbfounded but for a much happier reason.

His positive attitude put me in jaw-dropping awe. "Pat, I don't know what to say. Would you really do all that for me?"

"Yep, that's me: a real knight in shining armor," he boasted with a grin. "One of the air force's finest grunts to the rescue. You just kick back and relax. I'll be back in a few days to let you know what I find out. Then we'll ask your doctor if you can be released to me, OK? We can make this work."

My mind fixed itself on the word "we." It sounded so good to me.

"I can't begin to tell you how much I appreciate this. You're like a miracle. I didn't know what I was going to do. Even if things don't work out the way you've planned, I want you to know that I'm grateful to you for offering to help."

At the door, when he left, he kissed my cheek and promised he'd see me soon. In wonder, I watched him walk away. I was hesitantly hopeful that things just might turn out OK after all.

CHAPTER TWENTY

I like nonsense; it wakes up the brain cells.

—Dr. Seuss

My heart felt lighter than it had in a long time as I talked to my doctor about my plans. He was very enthusiastic about the move to Fairfield and Pat's offer of help.

"In view of the rough start you've had, you've ultimately wound up in a good place in life, with good goals, four children whom you love, and a remarkable resiliency. My hope is that you will be able to go back and grab those dreams you had a year ago and take them into the future with you and make them come true. You can do it! Try to think of all this as a temporary setback, and press on."

That was his parting pep talk. It was nice to hear someone believe so strongly in me. His confidence was enviable. I wished it would rub off on me.

Pat either called or came to see me every day during the time it took to make all the counseling arrangements and find a place to live. He was my life preserver in a rough sea. There was little I could do to help from the hospital. So I depended on him for everything, but he didn't seem to mind. He made me laugh and feel positive about things. He treated me so well and didn't fall over in a dead faint when I told him I had four children; he and his ex-wife had five. He also didn't treat me as an emotionally handicapped or sick person but rather as the girl he had known in high school. Was I falling in love with him? In like, most certainly. Falling in love or falling in gratitude? It was difficult for me to differentiate.

Pat had been my only visitor until one day, much to my surprise, my mother walked into the dayroom, where I was playing cards with a new patient. A very nice-looking man accompanied her.

"Hi, honey," she said. "This is Ray Williams."

"Hi, Ray." I stood and offered my hand. "Nice to meet you, although this is a strange place to meet a friend's daughter for the first time, a little embarrassing. I'm surprised Mother brought you here."

He was terrific! He merely smiled and said, "Well, let's not hold it against her, OK? I've wanted to meet you for weeks and just today convinced her to bring me."

We found a fairly private place to sit and talk. I looked back and forth between the two of them and thought, *Well, well. I bet I'm going to have a new stepfather.* As I took in his pleasant face and easygoing manner, the thought pleased me.

We were still talking when Pat came in. It was my mother's turn to raise surprised eyebrows as I introduced everyone, a most enjoyable moment for me. She hadn't met many of my previous boyfriends, and those she had met, she hadn't liked very much. It was obvious she liked Pat, but then who wouldn't? He was cheerful and friendly, and his being in the air force meant to my mother that at least he wasn't a bum.

Pat brought me the good news that he had located an apartment for me and the kids in Suisun City, a little town just next to Fairfield. He had already paid the first and last months' rent and deposit and was all set to move the kids and me that weekend.

"Wow, you've been a busy boy!" my mother said.

"Purely selfish," Pat told her. "I'm tired of the long drive to see her."

After a little more small talk and a report on the kids, Mother and Ray said their good-byes. As soon as they left, Pat and I talked to the hospital staff, who agreed to release me the next Friday night.

So good-bye to another hospital, as I rushed with Pat to reunite with my children. As previously agreed upon, I only picked up Ricky, Binky, and Butch, but I longed to at least see Joanie and just hold her for a while; however, Mary wasn't even home with Joanie when I arrived.

"Grandma, didn't Mary know I was coming tonight?"

"Well, I reckin she did," was her answer.

"Then why isn't she here with Joanie?"

"I don't know." She shrugged. "I reckin she jes' had somewhere she had ta go."

I was more than a little dismayed and disappointed beyond belief. The other kids were tired and needed to go to bed. So after a short wait, I thanked Grandma for taking such good care of the kids, and we left.

Pat and I said our good nights, and he went on to Bob's to spend the night and get a truck for the move. The kids and I were all excited to be together, but I refused their requests to stay up a little longer. After they had been bathed and cuddled, I put them to bed and started packing. Once I finally went to bed, excitement chased sleep away, even though I was exhausted and so sad about not seeing Joanie.

Bright and early the next morning, Pat pulled up with the moving truck. When we finished loading, I said my good-byes to the friends we had made there, and we were off to Fairfield. The kids were dubious about this move we were making. So I painted a happily ever after picture for them, and they quickly bought into it.

Since Pat had five children of his own, getting along with my three was no problem for him. For their part, the kids acted like they'd known him all their lives. It was great having someone around who didn't look at my children as nuisances merely to be tolerated, as had most men I'd met.

"It's going to be great living in this new place," I promised, "and the best part is we won't be separated ever again."

"Good," Ricky put in. "I love Grandma, but she don't sing and dance with us."

"Yeah, Mommy," chimed Binky. "I loves Grandma, too, but I loves you best."

A stab went through my heart as I thought of all the upheaval the kids had gone through in the past year and a half. I vowed to do everything in my limited power to see that we really *wouldn't* be parted again.

The apartment Pat rented was the nicest place we had ever lived. Several air-force families lived in the complex while they waited for base housing; consequently, there were hordes of children living there, which really lit up the eyes of the kids. The grammar school was just down the street, so the kids could walk. Binky would be starting kindergarten, so this was important. It was perfect. The apartment had two bedrooms, so Ricky and Butch claimed theirs and left the other smaller one for Binky and me.

"Our room's bigger than your room," Ricky taunted his sister in a singsong voice while dancing around the room.

"I doesn't care; I gets to sleep with Mommy," Binky replied.

That brought Ricky to a halt. His five freckles nearly disappeared as he crinkled his nose. He looked like he was trying to decide whether or not this merited a protest on his part.

Time for parental interjection. "Oh, my gosh, kids. Just look at this carpet! And check out this kitchen; what a nice floor. I bet there're no cockroaches here like our house in Pittsburg. This is great!"

They all looked around appreciatively; they didn't see the bars on the windows and the barricade on the front door that I saw.

Fear created and installed them to prevent me from leaving the apartment. It was a good thing I liked the inside of my new home, because unless Pat came over and took the kids and me somewhere, I had no desire to leave it, so I didn't.

Once again I became a child playing house. The kids were my dolls, and Pat was the daddy, even though he didn't live there. He came to see us after work each day, and by the time he left at night, the kids were in bed; so the game was over for the day, and I went to bed as well.

This game served a good purpose; I kept the place absolutely spotless and began cutting recipes out of magazines, thus becoming a pretty-good cook. With menus planned for each month in advance, Pat would take my grocery list for whatever ingredients were required and buy everything at the commissary on base. That solved the problem of dealing with anxiety while waiting in line at the store. The kids got my undivided attention. We played cars on the floor together, worked puzzles, did Ricky's homework, and generally caught up on the time and sense of security lost due to the events of the previous year.

Seeing me so perfectly content to go on like that, Pat reminded me that I needed to get into therapy sessions soon, or I would be in violation of the court order. Promises that I would make the necessary arrangements were broken as one day passed into the next. There was no shortage of excuses as to why I couldn't make the walk across the street to the pay phone to call the mental-health clinic. Fear and anxiety were locked out as long as I was locked in. Even doing the laundry waited until Pat was there, because in order to get to the laundry room, I had to leave my sanctuary to walk around the corner of the building, something I felt unable to do alone. Pat also took the boys for haircuts and handled anything else that had to be done outside that front door. If my neighbors thought me weird or unfriendly, that was OK with me. They wouldn't have understood anyway.

A month passed, and Pat, fed up with the game, firmly informed me, "I've lined up a babysitter, and you're going dancing with me tonight."

I gave him a stricken look. "I can't. I don't want to. I want to stay home with the kids."

"Look," he persisted, "the kids will be fine. The sitter I hired is reliable, and they'll be OK. You haven't gone anywhere for a month, and you need to get out. This isn't healthy for you."

We argued back and forth until finally he convinced me. *After all*, I reasoned, *I'll be with Pat. He'll take care of me.*

We had fun at the club, dancing to a live band, and while it felt strange at first, it wasn't bad at all. After that ice-breaking night, we began going out more often, not only to nightclubs. We went to Grandma's every Sunday to visit her and Joanie, but more often than not, Bud and Mary weren't home.

Each week I'd tell Grandma, "Please tell Bud and Mary that I want to see Joanie. If they have to go somewhere, maybe they could leave her here with you until I come."

"Well, we'll see," would be her noncommittal response.

We also visited Pat's ex-wife and children and often took all eight kids to the park for picnics. These outings were fine, but I drew the line at going to the movies or having anyone visit me at home. Whenever Pat pressed as to why I didn't want to go more places, I would tell him I didn't belong. I couldn't explain *why*, but I was convinced I didn't. It was a bittersweet but bearable fact for me.

CHAPTER TWENTY-ONE

*What other dungeon is so dark as one's own heart! What
jailer so inexorable as one's self!*

—*Nathaniel Hawthorne*

The ninety days the judge had given me were nearly up. No
more putting it off. Time to make that call.

Fairfield and Suisun City were so windy they were often referred
to as little Chicagos. The wind that blew off the nearby sloughs
made the air bitterly cold. It was particularly windy and cold the
day I finally used the phone booth around the corner and across
the street. What should have been a five-minute, or less, walk to
and from it, including the call itself, turned into a two-hour ordeal. First I had to get my front door open. Trembling, I stood
looking at it for several minutes and then backed away. I drank a
glass of soda and smoked a cigarette and then tried again. It took
several tries before I was able to open the door.

*Well, how 'bout that? Now all I have to do is just step out. I have the
dime and the number. All I have to do is just walk over there.*

After I stared out the door for several more minutes, my stomach felt queasy. *What if I get sick out on the street?* Along with that worry came another. *Come to think of it, my muscles ache, too. Maybe I'm getting the flu and shouldn't go out into this cold air.*

Retreating back inside, I passed the calendar on my way to the kitchen table. As I looked at it, the date jumped out at me, and I realized that I was out of time. Feelings of anger and resentment toward the judge and the world at large shot through my body. Intellectually, I knew these feelings were unreasonable, but emotionally they were very real.

My face felt hot and flushed. The anger and resentment buzzed in my brain. *Why do I have to do this anyway? I'm OK...limited but OK. I don't have to leave here. They can't make me.*

But the little voice I'd picked up along with the anxiety a year ago taunted me. "Look, dummy," it growled harshly. "What's the big deal? Just go make your phone call, and get it over with. What's the fuss? Just get your tail over there, and do what you were told to do." The voice sounded like my mother.

Tears burned my eyes as shame and defeat washed over me. My arms and legs and the back of my neck were sickeningly weak. It didn't seem I could make it. A nice, deep, cleansing breath might have fortified me, but I couldn't get enough air to venture that deeply into my lungs. Armed with another cigarette and a glass of water, I forced myself back to the door. Opening it again, I stepped out to take a look around. People, wearing heavy sweaters and jackets, were going to and from their respective apartments.

Mildly unkind thoughts ran through my mind. *These people are nuts. It's hot out here. A person could pass out from this heat and hot wind.*

Finally managing to walk to the end of the building, I cautiously peered around the corner and scrutinized the phone booth.

Gauging the distance brought on an inner wail. *It's too far! I can't make it that far by myself. This is ridiculous.*

"*You're* what's ridiculous," the harsh voice chided. "Stop this nonsense, and get on over there."

Intense pressure pummeled the top of my head and gave me a lopsided feel as I walked toward the phone booth. Finally I stopped focusing on it and concentrated on placing my feet one in front of the other. I looked up just in time to not pass it and then stood rooted to the ground.

Whimpering noises squeaked from my mouth. *Here it is. I made it!*

A different, more encouraging voice spoke. "Yes, there it is. You can do it. Come on; it won't take long. Just make the call to set up an appointment, and then you're free to hurry back home, where you'll feel safe."

This voice was more to my liking. Skin burning and gasping for air, I entered the booth. My hands shook so hard I could hardly get the dime in the slot and dial, but at last I managed.

"Solano Mental Health Clinic," a crisp voice answered. "May I help you?"

My hands were so slippery with perspiration they could barely hang on to the receiver. Clutching the little shelf with my other sweat-soaked hand helped me stay upright. My whole body quaked, causing my legs to weaken even more.

"Yes, please," I rapidly choked out. My mouth was so dry. "I have to hurry! I need to—uh, I mean, I *have* to come in to see someone. My name is Barbara Elling, and a judge told me I had to see someone."

"Hold one moment, please," she said. "I'll get right back to you. Now stay right there; I won't be long."

"No, no, oh, please! I can't stay here. I need to get home." My desperate plea was too late; she had put me on hold.

Raising my head a little enabled me to see my apartment. Staring at it might prevent my safety from being stolen. After all, safety had been stolen from me before.

"OK, Barbara," the woman's voice returned. "When did you want to come in?"

In a barely audible voice, I answered, "I don't care. I don't *really* even want to go there. Can you come to my home? I don't know where you are."

She gave me the address and directions and then informed me, "I'm very sorry, but our staff doesn't make house calls. You will need to come here. Barbara? Are you still there?" Her voice took on a gentler tone as she encouraged me. "Trust me; it will be all right. You come in whenever you feel you can make it, and I'll make sure someone can see you."

"All right. OK." Increasingly thickening air had me gasping. "I'll try to come tomorrow. I'll really try; I promise. Thank you. I can't stay here any longer. Good-bye."

Crashing the receiver into its little metal cradle, I tried to return back home hurriedly but could only move as if in a nightmare and slog along in slow motion. The air had become too dense to breathe in.

Oh, God! I'm going to die of suffocation. My kids will come looking for me and find me dead right here in the street. My thoughts were jumbled and erratic; they mimicked the way the world looked to me at that moment.

But of course I didn't die. I made it through the front door, and when I turned to close it, I decided to lock it as well.

There, you just stay out there, you old...whatever you are. Just stay out!

Little by little, I didn't feel so bad. My skin cooled down, and my stomach was less upset. After a bit, I actually felt a little victorious.

Congratulations were in order. *Not bad for a chicken. I did it!* But I wasn't eager to do it again any time soon.

The next morning, I had to face when I would actually go to this mental-health place. As I thought about it, all those ugly, sick feelings returned.

Waiting for Pat to come over to take me seemed the best decision, albeit a cowardly one. That way, I reasoned, he could watch the kids, too. To tell myself that having him take me wasn't because I was scared was a lie. After all, I reasoned further, I don't know my way around this town and would probably get lost. Yep, I would just wait.

The day Pat did come over to take me, the ride there was fine, and so was waiting in the reception area. But then I had to leave the safety of Pat and the kids and pass through a door alone. As I tried to walk through the doorway where a tall, brown-haired woman stood calling my name, the carpet grew up around my feet and almost tripped me.

"Are you Barbara Elling?" she inquired. "My name is Barbara, too, Barbara Callahan; nice to meet you."

She extended a hand to greet me and then, sensing the difficulty I was having, tucked a folder under her arm and extended the other hand as well, gently urging me forward. She seemed to share my doubts about whether I could make it or not.

I could only nod in acknowledgment to her question about my identity and allow her to lead me into her office. Just inside the room, a man sat in an armless, chrome-and-maroon upholstered chair next to a typewriter table sans the typewriter. Judging by the long white coat he wore, I assumed he was a doctor. The sight of that coat frightened me, but then so did almost everything outside my own front door.

"You can call me Miss Callahan," she offered, "and this is Dr. Wright. Doctor, this is Barbara Elling."

He stood, and I shook the hand he proffered but was so embarrassed by the moisture on my palm that I cut the handshake short. If he noticed, he made no mention of it.

Miss Callahan motioned me to sit in the chair next to her cluttered desk. She sat in a brown tweed swivel chair. The spiral notebook in her lap was a twin to the one the doctor held.

With her pen poised above the pad, Miss Callahan began the session. "So, Barbara, how can we help you?"

My face numbed, and I rubbed it to reassure myself I wasn't fading away. Nervously, I licked at my suddenly parched lips. "Could I have a drink of water, please? And I hate to be a bother, but would a wet paper towel be possible?"

A glass of water was poured for me, and I sipped it gratefully while pressing the cool, moist towel against my hot cheeks and forehead.

"This is really embarrassing," I started. "I, uh, recently accidentally overdosed on some pills. At the court hearing in the hospital, the judge said that I had to move out of town and get help."

Furtive glances were exchanged, and Miss Callahan asked, "Do you know why you overdosed?"

"I was tired. I wanted to take a nap." Needing to stress the sincerity of my words, I leaned forward a bit. "I didn't mean to hurt myself; I was just so tired and didn't realize how many pills I took."

"What could make you *that* tired, my dear?" the doctor asked.

"Well," I sighed, "for the past year, since I've got out of the hospital, I seem to fight with myself a lot. It's like there's a lot of people inside my head who don't like each other. They especially don't like me, and they fight a lot. It makes me tired."

Again the furtive glances. Dr. Wright then asked, "Do you know who these people are? Do you actually hear the voices speaking aloud?"

"No, I don't actually hear their voices like I hear yours. It's more like thoughts with attitudes. I think one of them is my mother saying she is fed up with me for being so stupid and worthless. Then there's another person who encourages me when I'm feeling scared and dumb. Then there's the baby! *That* one drives me up a wall."

"What does the baby say?" asked the doctor.

"It says, 'Hold me,' or, 'I'm scared,' or, 'Don't make me do that.' Mostly it cries a lot."

Upon hearing that, both the doctor and Miss Callahan scribbled notes furiously.

"You mentioned being in a hospital," Miss Callahan said. "Tell us about that."

"No." My back stiffened. "I don't want to talk about that—ever. Wait a minute; you aren't thinking I should go back, are you? I can't! I won't! The judge didn't say anything about going back there. He told me to go out and fight, and that's what I want to do."

My tone changed from defiant to plaintive; my shoulders dropped. "I just don't know how."

Miss Callahan reached over and touched my arm. "You can believe us. We have no intention of sending you back to any hospital. That's not what we're about. We don't believe you should be there, either. We just wanted you to share that experience with us."

Stalling, I lowered my eyes to my lap and studied my wringing hands with fingers weaving themselves in and out of tangles. *Could I share that with them?* Annoyance set in.

Firmly, I said, "Look, I just need help finding out why the ground moves around under me. I don't want to relive that hospital experience again. I'm not here by choice, but I'll lose my children if I don't do what the judge said. I realize I'm in a tight spot, but I only want to do what I have to do to get well and have some questions answered."

Miss Callahan leaned back in her chair and conceded. "OK, Barbara, we don't have to discuss that now. What we *do* need now is for you to try to relax. We won't press you to say or do anything that makes you uncomfortable. We have lots of time, and it's yours to do with as you want."

She seemed sincere enough. Maybe I had been too harsh. I fumbled through my Rolodex of feelings and came up with a starter offering. "I don't feel safe."

I wondered how they would react to that.

"So," Dr. Wright questioned, "you don't feel safe. Do you feel unsafe all the time or just part of the time?"

His question took me a moment to consider. "I used to feel safe all the time. But then I started having these dizzy spells, and now I only feel safe at home."

"What is it that scares you when you leave home?" he probed further.

"The attacks of panic. I'm afraid to go anywhere because that panic is out there, hiding."

"Do you feel scared right this minute?" he asked.

Time to confess. "Sort of. I mean I feel kind of OK but on guard and ready to protect myself from the dizziness. I never know when or where it will strike."

"So you remain all tensed up. Is that accurate? You need to be prepared to fight at all times?"

"Yes, that's it exactly. I have to be prepared to run in case it happens. If it happened right now, I'm sorry, but I'd have to leave."

"I see," he said, adjusting his glasses. "Barbara, are you on any medication right now?"

"No, I'm not. Why do you ask? I don't want any of those drugs they gave me at the hospital. They make you crazy."

They laughed at my unintentionally ill choice of words. "Well, I'd like to see you able to relax a bit." Dr. Wright smiled. "How would you feel about a small dosage of Valium?"

I pushed my arms out and waved my hands, palms out, to emphasize my answer. "Oh, no, no, thank you. That's what I overdosed on. I don't want to chance that again."

"I understand," he said, "but was the Valium effective? Were you more relaxed?"

"Sure," I conceded. "At least I could eat without getting sick."

"Yes, you are rather thin," he chided. "Why don't we just try a low dosage of Valium on a daily basis? I'll monitor you closely and won't prescribe enough to do any harm. I'd truly like to see you more relaxed."

My reluctant agreement ended the session. They told me it would be best if I came in daily for a while. Appointments were set up around times when Pat could take me. During my sessions, he could take the kids back home or to the park or maybe for ice cream.

Even with the aid of Valium, I remained extremely tense. During one of my sessions with Miss Callahan, an ambulance siren wailed nearby, which prompted me to dive under the table. I cowered there, pleading with her for an answer.

"What's happening to me? I haven't always been like this; honest, I haven't. Mostly I'm a fairly intelligent woman. I function fine in my home, but out my front door, I'm a basket case. No wonder they locked me up. I deserve it when I act like this, but I didn't act this way before the dizziness started."

Miss Callahan merely sat on the floor under the table with me and comforted me. "No one *deserves* to be locked up for suffering. We'll get to the bottom of this. I promise you. Did you think the ambulance was coming for you?"

"Rational reasoning tells me it's not, but rationality isn't my strong point these days. Like so many other things, the sound of sirens startles me."

As I had feared, just like the first therapist and everyone else I had seen for counseling, Miss Callahan wanted to dig up my past to find causes and clues. She was certain that answers lay hidden there that needed to be revealed and examined. Cooperation was my only choice.

"One thing we know for sure," she said. "You weren't born with these fears. They developed somewhere along the way. Let's see if we can figure out why and how. You say you wonder *why* you're this way? Well, so do I. Was there a place when you were a child where you felt safe and unafraid?"

The answer to that came to mind easily. A smile formed on my lips as I thought of the visits to see Uncle Pokey and Aunt Dot.

CHAPTER TWENTY-TWO

Let us not look back in anger, nor forward in fear, but around in awareness.

—*James Thurber*

"Why, Bobbie," Miss Callahan remarked, "you're smiling. Tell me about what put such a peaceful expression on your face."

"I'm just remembering my yearly trips to Oklahoma. I got to visit an aunt and uncle there. I didn't get to spend much time with them, but the time I *did* get to be with them was the happiest of my entire childhood."

"Why couldn't you spend more time with them?" she queried. "And tell me, what made those visits so special?"

"When I was three, my parents divorced, and I came to California with my mother to live with my grandparents. Every summer, Grandma, my aunt Billie, and I would take a Greyhound bus to Oklahoma to visit Aunt Dot and Uncle Pokey. I guess the visits were so special to me because Dot and Pokey seemed to really love children…*all* children. I mean, I know parents love their *own* children, but they don't necessarily love anyone else's.

"For example, they always seemed so happy to see me. They'd hug me and fuss over me like no one else ever did. Uncle Pokey would always take me out on the front porch and let me just sit on his lap for as long as I wanted. He'd bounce me on his knee and sing the silliest songs just to hear me laugh. He called me his little Skeeter, because I was so small. Grandma would tell him, like she did everyone, that I was the ugliest grand-child she had because I was so puny. He'd tell her, 'Roxie, with this child's gold hair and dimples, she puts Shirley Temple to shame.'"

My voice broke from the tears that nearly choked me to death. The memories of what else came with those happy visits hurt.

"Skeeter, huh?" Miss Callahan smiled as she handed me a tis-sue. "I guess you loved them a lot. Didn't anyone else ever tell you that you were pretty or hold you like that?"

Shaking my head, I blurted out, "It makes me so angry!"

"It makes you so angry that no one ever held you?" Miss Callahan quizzed.

"Oh, not so much that, I guess." I sighed heavily. "The other people in my life were what they were, just like I was what I was. I can't hold it against them that they didn't love me or treat me like Pokey did. I've learned one thing, if nothing else: you can't *make* people love you. It just can't be done. That's what was so great about Pokey's love. I didn't have to earn it or force it out of him. It was just there waiting for me year after year.

"Once, I disobeyed him and went somewhere I wasn't supposed to go with my older cousins, his son and daughter, and got sucked into some quicksand. My cousins ran screaming for Pokey to come pull me out. By the time he got to me, I was up to my shoulders in the stuff. As I was being sucked in, I almost wished I'd die rather than have to face him knowing I'd disobeyed. I was terrified that when he got ahold of me, he would beat me to death. Instead he bawled out his own son and daughter for not taking better care of me. Can you imagine?

"I'm sorry for all this crying." Another tissue became a casualty of my emotional war. "It's just that I used to pray for a miracle that would let me belong to Dot and Pokey. It didn't happen, though.

"Once, a big grasshopper jumped up onto my blouse and scared me. When Pokey heard me screaming, he came running and brushed it off. Then he grabbed me and swung me high into the air and caught me in his arms. He didn't make fun of me for being scared. He just held me and comforted me. He was full of surprises…and I loved him so much."

Thoroughly choked up, I had to pause again before going on.

"So what is it that makes you so mad?" she urged.

"Well, every year followed the same routine. On the third night there, I'd go to sleep all crunched up in a double bed with my aunt Billie and cousin Theda. Sometime during that night, I'd hear voices, hushed and quiet, and a man would lift me out of bed. I'd be put in a car and driven somewhere, taken out of the car, and put into another bed. When I'd wake up in the morning, I'd be in my father's house. Poof, presto! Nothing or no one there familiar, just a man who was my father, a man I'd never heard one good thing about. On the contrary, I'd been told terrible things about him.

"At my father's house was this little boy named Donnie. They said he was my brother, which I thought was odd. After all, didn't brothers and sisters live together? We'd spend the day eyeing each other suspiciously, and then that night Donnie would disappear while I was asleep.

"I'd be stuck there for three months, and that makes me mad to this day." This confession came through gritted teeth. "What gives people the right to do that kind of thing to a child?" My hands became fists that pounded my knees. "Then after three months, I'd go to sleep at my father's house and, in the middle of the night, be taken back to Dot and Pokey's. That boy, Donnie, would be there asleep on the sofa but gone in the morning. I was always so glad to be back at Pokey's, but sadly we'd leave the next day.

"This went on for four years, and I often wonder what I would be like today if I had gotten Dot and Pokey's kind of love three hundred sixty-five days a year instead of just three. I wonder what it's like to feel that good all the time."

Miss Callahan handed me more tissues, as this session had become more than a two-tissue cry.

"Well, we sure destroyed that smile, didn't we?" she gently commented. "I'm sorry. And I agree with you. Children *should* experience that kind of love more than three days a year. About the anger, do you still feel *that* angry about things that happened when you were a child?"

Slowly blowing out a deep breath, I admitted, "Yeah, I suppose I do. But when I feel it bubbling up, I push it back down, because what good does it do?"

Our time was up for the day, so I got no answer. She merely said, "We'll talk more about what makes you angry next session."

CHAPTER TWENTY-THREE

Child abuse casts a shadow the length of a lifetime.

—Herbert Ward

Becoming angry was easily accomplished at our next session. Miss Callahan asked me about my father, a subject that never failed to get a full rage boiling inside me.

"You've told me a lot about your mother," Miss Callahan began, "and to make sure I've got the picture, let me recap what you've shared. You've painted a picture of a woman who was aloof and distant, didn't live with you, and was the black sheep of the family, beautiful, and funny. She didn't enjoy children as much as she did good times, pretty clothes, and freedom from responsibility. Is that a fairly accurate image?"

Chuckling, I said, "It'll do for a recap. That just about covers her. I'd only add that she gives the impression of being very strong, but I'm not sure she really is. That's what she'd have you believe, though."

Picking up a pen and notepad, she asked, "Ready to tell me about your father?"

"What's to tell? He's a miserable wretch who shouldn't be allowed to live. He's been sick for years, so hopefully he'll be dead soon. The world will be a better place with him gone."

"Wow! That's a strong reaction," Miss Callahan exclaimed. She was unaccustomed to me expressing such intense anger. "You *really* hated those trade-offs that took place in Oklahoma, didn't you?"

"Those trade-offs aren't the reason I hate him." A renewed anger at having to be in therapy sprang up. My body shook with old rage just thinking about him. "I can't stay here today," I announced, rising abruptly from my chair. "I'm leaving."

"Please stay, Barbara," she cajoled. "Here, I'll open the door and window. Turn your chair toward the door, and know that you can leave whenever you feel you just can't stay any longer, but please try. Just take your time and try. I firmly believe it will help me help you. I need to know what made you who you are. I need to know the people and events that brought you to the emotional place you find yourself in. Won't you stay and try?"

Stiffly returning to my chair, I perched on its edge, poised for flight. My hands clenched the arms of the chair; my every muscle was tensed.

"One summer the trade-off trip didn't happen. Instead Aunt Dot and Uncle Pokey brought my brother to Grandma's in California. I overheard them say that Donnie was supposed to go back to Oklahoma with them but that they had other plans. He was going to stay in California. All I cared about was that they didn't say *I* had to go."

The need to release some adrenaline snatched me from the edge of the chair. For relief, I paced in a small circle as I shared my story:

My mother was marrying this guy named Mel. Donnie and I were going to live with them. Well, Donnie *did* stay, and Mother *did* marry Mel; and we all lived together but not very happily ever after.

Just before I turned fourteen, Mother became pregnant with my half sister, Charmaine. Mother and Mel separated before she was born and divorced shortly after. It was awful! I'd grown to love Mel and his family and feared I'd be sent back to live with Grandma. Since it had been when Mother was single that I'd had to live apart from her before, I assumed I could only live with her if she was married. I wasn't sure what would happen to Charmaine and Donnie. I guess that was pretty stupid of me.

Anyway, not that Donnie and I were angels *before* Mother and Mel divorced, but we got a lot worse after. Mother told people I'd gone wild because I'd stay out all night. The truth was I just didn't want to be home, so I'd stay with whoever would take me in. Mother dated a lot, but nothing ever came of those dates, even though she'd have some pretty-neat boyfriends. She usually told them I was her sister when I'd meet them. She must have been lonely; she made it pretty clear that we were burdens on her.

Donnie got into some kind of trouble. I don't remember what it was, but he wound up in juvenile hall. The authorities told Mother that if she couldn't do something with him, they would send him to a permanent home for boys until he was eighteen, partially at her expense.

She was furious! She told the juvenile officer that she would just send both of us to our father in Oklahoma. She maintained she didn't stand a chance for happiness as long as she had us anyway. No man she met wanted children as old as we were and especially children who were nothing but trouble. The authorities decided to fly Donnie to Oklahoma but not me, so she said she would make other arrangements to send me there.

Hearing that, I began remembering all the horror stories she'd told us about our father and got really scared. I hadn't seen or heard from him since I was seven years old, and that had been fine with me.

We'd been told that he used to beat her and us, even though we were babies. She said he drank all the time and that once during a drunken, jealous rage, he tried to kill us all. She'd locked herself in the bathroom with us to escape his rampage. She'd told me that when I was only six months old, he would beat her *and* me if I cried too much.

Donnie never talked about him or his life in Oklahoma, so I only knew what Mother told me. She said she'd only married him to get off my grandfather's farm, where she had to work so hard, and that it had been the biggest mistake of her life. The only reason she'd had children was that there wasn't any way to prevent them.

So knowing only these things about my father, rather than be sent to live with him, I ran away. For a month, I went from house to house and stayed with whoever would take me in. The parents of my friends were sympathetic but didn't want to get too deeply involved. Then the family of a boy I had previously dated heard about my predicament and decided they would try to keep me through a foster-care program. Relieved and grateful, I was amazed that they would do this for me.

The mother, Ruth, called my father to tell him of her plans. To her shock, he told her that he was an auxiliary police officer and that if they didn't take me back to my mother's house within three days, he would have them arrested for kidnapping. His sister-in-law and her family were going to be in California and had agreed to pick me up and take me to him. It might have been a bluff, but no one wanted to call it. Ruth and I both cried buckets. She kept apologizing, and I kept assuring her that I understood; it wasn't her fault. For a time, we considered just running for it and hiding, but we didn't dare. Ruth had her own three sons to think about.

So I returned to my mother's house to wait for these people who would take me away. For the next three days, my mother didn't come home after work and stayed out late. I guess she hoped I'd be asleep when she came home. She had already hired a live-in sitter for Charmaine, so with her taken care of, I guess Mother felt she had no reason to come home.

Too quickly the day came for me to leave. But come it did, and I was on my way to Oklahoma. The woman who came to get me was my stepmother's sister, and I liked her a lot. She and her husband were almost another Dot and Pokey: gentle and kindly considerate of my despair. During the three days and nights it took to get there, I asked questions about my father and stepmother. Apparently he had found someone else desperate to get off a farm is what I thought.

They portrayed my father differently than my mother had. They reported that my father, whom they called Red, and his wife, Alberta, had four other children of their own, who were all looking forward to meeting their sister from California. Even hearing that didn't encourage me, and I continued to cry the entire trip. The only thing my stomach would tolerate and keep was milk, which kept my transporters pretty concerned.

"Barbara," Miss Callahan interrupted, reaching over to touch my hand, "you look terribly distressed. Are you OK?"

"How would I know if I'm OK or not?" I blurted out. "I must not be OK, or I wouldn't be here telling you all this." A mix of sorrow and utter frustration raised the volume of my voice to a near shout. "Actually, I've never been OK, because I've never been in control! If *I* had been in control, none of these things would have happened, I'll tell you *that*!

"Would *you* be OK if *you* got sent wherever it suited someone to send you, whether you liked it or not? Would you be OK if your father sexually molested you because you looked like your mother?"

Silence swallowed the room. I continued to tremble with the mix of emotions while Miss Callahan sat looking at me blankly.

"Did you hope to shock me?" she asked gently. "You succeeded. I'm aware that these things happen, but, yes, it still shocks me every time I hear about it. And now that you've got that out, do you want to go on, or would you rather wait until tomorrow?"

"Might as well get it over with," I said, sinking back into the chair. The words poured out of me:

I tried to like it there with Red and Alberta, but he made me uneasy. Sometimes I'd be watching TV with their daughter, Louise, and I'd catch him looking at me in a way that gave me the creeps. Once I got up the nerve to ask him if something was wrong, and he said, yeah, I looked too much like my mother for my own good.

Then one day he came home from work while I was on the phone with Don Bales, a boy I'd gone to school with in California. Don asked why I hadn't written to anyone, and I told him I'd written to *everyone* but hadn't received any answers to my letters. He said he knew a lot of people who'd gotten Red's address and had written to me. That was eerie! I told Don how unhappy and homesick I was and how I wished I could find a way back to California. He said he'd drive out to get me, and we started making plans for my great escape.

Suddenly the phone was ripped from my hands. Red tore it right out of the wall. Anger overtook any caution I usually would have had, and I confronted him—demanding to know why I never got the letters from my friends and they'd never gotten the ones I'd sent to them. He shouted that he had intercepted them for my own good. A sarcastic laugh erupted from me, and I told him if people didn't stop doing things "for my own good," I'd kill myself.

I slammed into my room and stayed there fuming until Alberta called me to help her with dinner. She asked me to forgive Red, and I promised I'd try. I figured she had enough to put up with from him and didn't need additional trouble from me. She was a nice woman, and I couldn't understand what she saw in that mean, nasty-tempered man.

After dinner, Red said he wanted me to go to a movie with him to make up for all the fuss and that if I did, he would even let me drive, something I loved to do. I said OK but was still upset and more homesick than ever after talking to Don. Red drove to a store and then toward the drive-in-movie place.

At the time, Oklahoma was a dry state, so I don't know how he bought liquor. But he did. Red drinking surprised me because he had ulcers so bad that he'd had several operations. Three-quarters of his stomach was plastic; the rest of it had been surgically removed.

He pulled into a parking slot and turned off the engine. He fished two cans of RC Cola from a sack and poured half of each out and filled the rest of the cans with vodka. I told him I didn't drink, and he said I must be lying, because Mother told him I did.

That made me so mad that I defiantly took one of the cans. After a few angry sips, I had a hard time keeping up with what went on around me. The movie screen went out of focus, and the sound was tinny. Meanwhile Red sat and talked about how happy he wanted me to be, all the while chugging down his horrible concoction.

It was true I didn't drink, but I did smoke cigarettes, something Red had previously forbidden me to do. It surprised me when he told me to go to the snack bar and buy cigarettes if I wanted. I was in a real nothing-matters depression and felt hopelessly lost. I couldn't figure out how to get out of the mess called my life.

I barely made my way to the snack bar and bought some cigarettes, but then, so woozy and disoriented from the vodka, I kept trying to get into the wrong car. Red found me wandering around crying and guided me back to his car. Once inside the car, he tossed the speaker out the window and took off down the road.

I leaned my head against the window and continued to cry while I watched the roadside pass. That was the last thing I remember.

My next memory was asking him why he had done it. I was twisted around in the front seat of the car. The passenger-side door was open, and my bared legs were dangling out of the car. Mostly I was numb, but I felt something I couldn't identify. I fought to sit up and noticed my panties on the floorboard of the car. I picked them up and stupidly asked him what I should do with them. He told me to put them in my purse. I asked him, "Why, why have you done this to me?" And he said he just wanted to see if what my mother had said about me was true. I didn't have the presence of mind, nor did I care, to ask him just what it was she'd told him.

He said he'd have to get me shaped up before getting me home and pulled into a drive-in burger place. The carhop came to my side of the car to ask what I wanted. Red leaned across me and ordered two tomato juices.

When she returned with the juice, I rolled down my window so she could hang the tray on it and begged her to help me. My voice didn't sound right, and my tongue had swelled to such a degree that I didn't make sense. With a look of concern on her face, she asked, "Why, sugar? What's the matter? You sick?"

Red gruffly told her nothing was wrong and to mind her own business. He hurriedly tried to shut the window. I kept right on trying to beg her for help when, with no warning, my stomach hurled its contents into the air; some of it landed on her blouse. Wave after wave of nausea overcame me as my body rejected the alcohol, the angry helplessness, and the horror of what he'd said and done. The carhop backed away from the car with a look of revulsion on her face. Pity for her penetrated my mind. Poor thing, what an ugly sight for her to witness, I thought.

Red drove home while I continued retching. I was a mess. The car was a mess. Everything was a mess. He left me in the car, went to the house, and sent my brother out to drag me in. Needless to say, Alberta was stunned when she saw me. Red made Donnie clean the car, and Alberta put me in a tub of hot water. Still very drunk, I couldn't talk intelligently. I barely managed to put on a nightgown before falling into bed.

The next day was Sunday. Red came in and ordered me to get up and get ready for church. I couldn't believe my ears. I was still sick and hurt all over, while he acted as though nothing had happened. Everyone else was quiet. No one mentioned or asked about the night before. I wondered what they knew or thought they knew. In church, still dazed with disbelief, I sat in the balcony alone on the pretense that I just preferred it that way. I almost fell over the railing when, right before my bloodshot eyes, Red answered an altar call to receive Jesus as his savior! I watched him walk up that aisle, and it took every bit of restraint I could muster to keep myself from screaming out what he had done the night before. I decided then and there that if Red was the kind of man Jesus wanted, he'd never be bothered by me. You'd think it couldn't have gotten worse, but it did.

I'm sure there was some conversation on the drive back to the house, but I was oblivious to it. Everyone piled out of the car, but Red asked me to go with him to his auto shop. This was it! We were going to have it out. I imagined he would say how sorry he was and beg my forgiveness. I'd promise never to tell anyone if only he'd just let me go back to California. I was rehearsed and prepared.

Imagine my surprise when he said absolutely nothing. He made small talk about other things but made no reference to what had happened. Finally I couldn't stand any more and turned on him in a fury. He denied everything, and when we returned to the house, he dragged me out of the car to the backyard. Taking a switch from a tree, he threatened to beat me to death. Totally void of fear at that point, I told him that would be fine with me.

"How did you finally get away?" Miss Callahan asked softly.

"A few days later, a couple living next door came over and asked Alberta if I could watch their kids for them while they ran some errands. She gave her permission, and while I was babysitting, I called the father of a friend who lived down the block and asked him to come over. When he got there, I told him everything and begged him to help me.

"Red had told his version of that night to the family and warned me that I could say anything I wanted, but no one would believe me. Only Donnie had asked me about that night, but I wouldn't tell him. I was so relieved when my friend's dad believed me. He suggested he stay with me until the people I was sitting for came home, and then he would take me to the police station.

"But apparently Red had called Alberta, and when she told him I was next door, he yelled at her to get me home and asked her how she'd dared to let me go in the first place. He raced home from work and flew into these people's house and ordered my friend's dad to leave. The man told Red he wanted to talk to him, and they went outside. I heard an occasional loud voice but nothing else.

"Red charged back in alone, shouting, 'You want to go back to California? Well, you're going, all right!' Then he stormed out the door. When the parents came home, I went back to Red's house; I was dragging my feet in dread, certain that my friend's dad hadn't really believed me and had abandoned me. No sooner had I cleared the front door than Red dragged me out to the backyard. This time, after grabbing another switch, he did beat me. He pulled and pushed me into the car, gave me a dime and a ticket, and then dumped me at the Greyhound bus station.

"I was finally on my way to California, with no clothes, no money, and no food for the three-day and three-night trip. The trip was miserable, but I was free of Red and Oklahoma!"

"Do you mean to tell me you had no food for three days?" Miss Callahan demanded.

She got my best attempt at a smile. "Not exactly. A young sailor got on the bus at one of the bazillion stops and sat by me. I'll never forget him. At the next stop, he offered to buy me a Coke, and I asked him if he would buy me milk instead. He must have thought I was some kind of weirdo, but I'll tell ya, that milk has gone down in my personal history as the best ever. I was so hungry.

"The bus pulled into Pleasant Hill, California, at eleven thirty-six at night, and I used my precious dime to call my mother. When she answered the phone, I said, 'Hi, it's me; can you pick me up?'

"Her maternal answer was one of her long-suffering sighs and, 'So you're back, huh? I'll be there in a minute.' That was it! Welcome home, Bobbie."

CHAPTER TWENTY-FOUR

Severe truth is expressed with some bitterness.

—*Henry David Thoreau*

At some point while telling Miss Callahan about that part of my life, I'd stopped leaning forward so tensely, and by the time I finished, my body had turned into a blob of gelatinous matter dumped into the chair. Depleted of anger, I only felt exhaustion. No words left to say and no energy to speak them anyway. She remained silent as well, so we just sat marinating a moment before she suggested we call it a day. Just barely, I gathered the strength to stand and walk out the door.

The next day, our session started out as the last one had finished...in silence. She sat, waiting for me to begin, and when I didn't, she initiated the conversation.

"I need to be clear on something," she began. "It's been nine years since the incident with your father. That's a long time to carry the memory of it around without achieving some sort of reconciliation. Surely you've talked about it with someone before now. Why *now* is it still so hard for you?"

I'd been staring out the window over her shoulder and trying to lock out all feeling as she talked. Finally I focused my eyes on hers. My voice was nearly too tired to make itself heard, but finally I managed to say, "Since I've become ill, or whatever I am, people in your field have told me that something in my past, something in my subconscious mind, is the cause. Well, don't you see? If things that happened in my crazy childhood are the cause, then there's no hope of ever being well, since I can't go back and change them. The past has made my future totally meaningless. If that's true, I have two concerns. One is the kids! I can't just give up and die! I have to live long enough to raise them! Oh, I'm aware that if I truly, unselfishly loved them, I'd give them up to good homes, where they'd have a normal life. But you know what? I have absolutely nothing else to live for. I love them and just can't do it. I only hope they'll forgive me. It makes me sad to think they'd ever look at me and be sorry they were born or hate that I'm their mother.

"The second thing is that when I was a kid, I thought all I had to do to survive was just grow up, take over control of my life, and change it. I believed I'd never let anything happen to me that hurt as much as things done while others had been in control. Well, I *did* grow up, and I failed; I just failed! Unlike the King Midas touch, everything I touch turns to rusted tin. Not only is my life ruined but also are the lives of four innocent children.

"You know what else? If I die without ever knowing normalcy again, it will be like miscarrying a baby who was on its way to a life but died before having the chance to live it."

The window recaptured my attention as I turned my eyes away from her face and stared out, seeing nothing. A deep sleep was the only thing that held any appeal for me.

"I know you're feeling bad about yourself right now," she sympathized. "And I can see that you're tired, but you're at a beginning, not an end. It's true your past has some bearing on what you are and what you feel, but it doesn't have to ruin your future. You can get that belief out of your head right now.

"As for being normal, you *are* normal!" She went on encouragingly, "Just because you're not functioning at one hundred percent doesn't mean you're not normal. True, it's going to take time, maybe *lots* of time, but it will get better."

She smiled and then grabbed her pen and notebook. "For now, let's move on. You know you've never mentioned your husband; what was marriage like for you?"

"Ha." I snorted. "I wouldn't know the first thing about marriage. I don't feel I was ever really married."

"So have I struck on yet another issue you don't want to talk about?" she prodded.

"As a matter of fact, I don't." I gave her a weak smile. "So I guess that means you especially *do* want to talk about it?"

She gave a small chuckle. "You guessed right!"

"Well, this topic will be easier anyway. There isn't much to tell. So from the top." I tried to be light and casual about this new subject. "Dick and I met in kindergarten; isn't that cute? He and I were special friends from then until third grade. In fact, he was so special to me that I used to do backbends at the school-bus stop to impress him." We both laughed.

"Ooh, a real sex symbol, huh?" she joked.

Joking back, I said, "Yep, that was me all right. This was when I still lived with Grandma. When Mother married Mel, we went to live in a different school district. I didn't see Dick again until we were both sixteen and ran into each other at a basketball game.

"He sure had changed since kindergarten. He was six feet six inches tall, slim, and gorgeous. With his brooding brown eyes and full, pouty mouth, he looked like Elvis Presley. He even wore his dark, curly hair like Elvis. I remember wishing I could still do backbends, although they probably would have been wasted on him. He recognized me easily, since I was so underdeveloped at sixteen that I was just a taller version of that little girl he'd known.

"All that summer we hung out with the same bunch of kids, but he never asked me out on a date, which crushed me, because I was nuts about him. One night after I had just about given up hope, we were at a party, and a bunch of us were sitting around, singing doo-wop music. When he heard me sing harmonies, he sat up and took an interest. We started going steady, and I joined his vocal group, the Five Shades. We sang at school dances and parties and events like that, on our way to fame and misfortune. Dick had always hung out with girls with, shall we say, loose reputations. I hadn't been that kind of girl, but I was told that if I wanted to keep him, I needed to become one. I decided if that was what he wanted, that's what he'd get. Besides, my mother had always told me that men only wanted one thing."

Miss Callahan laughed. "Don't tell me you fell for that?"

"Only like a ton of bricks.," I laughed with her.

It's ironic, really. I'm sure my mother told me things like that to turn me against men and sex, but the message I got, especially after the thing with my father, was that she was right. I felt that was all I was worth and had nothing else to offer. Over that next year, I became a scholastic slob. My junior year of high school was a disaster. What did I care, though? I was going to grow up to be a famous backup singer; who needed math and history for that? Mother told me if I couldn't do any better in school, I might as well not go at all. So she pulled me out of school to watch my baby sister, Charmaine, and thus saved her childcare money. When I dropped out, so did Dick.

Meanwhile, Mother married again and, also again, not happily. She became pregnant but aborted the baby at home. For weeks, she lay on the living room floor with a tube inserted into her uterus and made a game of Charmaine bouncing up and down on her stomach. Charmaine thought this game was a lot of fun. I was horrified because it confirmed for me her dislike of children and motherhood. The abortion didn't go the way she planned. I got home from a date with Dick to find bloody towels on the living room floor and a note from Aunt Billie telling me Mother was in the hospital. The note said I should call her and she would come get me if I wanted to stay with her awhile. After Aunt Billie told me what had happened, I asked if I could just go live with her permanently. She said yes, so away I went.

Life at Billie's was so happy. She had two little boys, Denny and Johnny, whom I dearly loved, and I had always adored her. She taught me how to cook and sew and all those other home-maker-type things. We had so much fun together.

Well, back to Dick. He had a roving eye, which caused a lot of grief and fighting. Soon we were only seeing each other occasionally. I'd always cared more for him than he had me. Everyone told me I was nuts to put up with him, but they didn't understand what made me tick. Since I didn't expect *anyone* to love me, his bad treatment was fairly easy for me to take. Eventually we broke up, but as I was still hooked on him, when he invited me to go to a party with him, I went.

From the time we walked through the door at the party, I knew why he had wanted to be there so badly. He wanted to see another girl there and hung over her all night. Humiliated and hurt, I got drunk for the second time in my life. I don't remember it, but apparently I made a scene. I vaguely recall Dick putting me in his car. The next thing I knew, it was morning, and I was in my bed at Billie's. Dick was standing in the corner of the bedroom.

Billie was shaking me awake, and she told Dick that since he was the one who had gotten me drunk, he could jolly well take care of my hangover. I was still mad at him, and when I told him so, he told me that, in that case, he wouldn't tell me what had happened before he brought me home. Apparently we had made love, if you could call it that. I didn't see him again for several weeks. When I did, it was only because Billie had told him I was pregnant.

Boy, what an uproar *that* created! Everyone urged us to get married immediately. But he didn't want to, and, surprisingly, neither did I. Billie's husband, Ray, was really upset and hurt that I would bring such drama into his home. He wanted me to leave, and I didn't blame him a bit. So Mother let me move back in with her and Charmaine.

At around five months into the pregnancy, I began having severe pains in my stomach and suffering hearing loss. Thinking I was miscarrying, Mel came over and took me to the hospital. It turned out to be the result of the quinine pills Mother had been giving me and had nothing to do with the pregnancy. She had claimed the pills were vitamins. The doctor gave me a relaxant, and I slept until late the next day.

When I woke up, Mother told me that Dick was there to see me. Surprised, I staggered out of bed and to the door. Dick said he'd called earlier, and Mother had told him about the trip to the hospital. She had bawled him out, saying that it was all his fault. He went on to say that if I hadn't lost the baby by the following Tuesday, he thought we should get married. I wasn't sure what the following Tuesday had to do with anything. I guessed he wanted to give it a week to be sure he wasn't marrying me for nothing. Ha!

Some proposal. But I said OK, and the next Tuesday we went to city hall in Martinez and got hitched by a justice of the peace. Peace? Hardly! If peace and I hadn't exactly been best friends *before* I married Dick, we were total strangers after.

CHAPTER TWENTY-FIVE

The art of living is more like wrestling than dancing...

—Marcus Aurelius

"We moved in with his mother," I told Miss Callahan, "who announced that since Dick and I were married, *I* could look after the family.

She confessed that she had been biding her time until the boys grew up before she left their father, but since I was there, she didn't have to wait any longer. As it turned out, though, Mr. Elling and Tommy, Dick's younger brother, moved out and left his mother, Dick, and me to live in the family home. To be more accurate, *I* lived there. Neither Mrs. Elling nor Dick was there much.

Dick was constantly off with friends, while I was left alone. Tommy, sweetheart that he was, would come over, and we'd go for walks or just sit around, listening to music.

He replaced my own brother, who was still in Oklahoma. I loved him very much.

Things weren't going well at all in our odd little household. A disturbing red flag of warning shot up for me when one night, during a quarrel, Dick slapped his mother. His own mother! She slapped him back, and he hit her again. Shortly after that, she sold the house, so Dick and I found a place to rent in Concord.

By that time, I was seven months into my pregnancy and still hadn't seen a doctor. My mother, divorced again, had a new boyfriend, who had a fit when he heard that I hadn't been getting medical care. He arranged for me to see a doctor friend of his.

Dr. Fisher hadn't taken on an obstetric patient in seven years, but he reluctantly accepted me as a patient. I liked him immediately, and he seemed to like me, too, not just as a patient but, since he had never married, maybe as a daughter as well.

He was as blunt and bold as he was nice. Once, when he was shopping at the department store where Mrs. Elling worked, he told her to tell her "son-of-a-bitchin' son" to be more considerate of me, and he said to her that being pregnant at seventeen was hard enough on me without Dick being an idiot.

Things steadily got worse. Dick went around mad a lot and started shoving me around. After throwing one of his tantrums, he'd leave for days, only popping in to change clothes. I never knew where he was, and Dr. Fisher was afraid that when I went into labor, I'd have no way to the hospital. We didn't have a phone or car, nor did we have a TV or radio. I'll always remember that time as one of the loneliest of my life, as I was cut off from everyone by the fact that I was married and pregnant.

None of my high-school girlfriends were allowed to associate with me, and I didn't know any other married girls my age. Even if I had, I wouldn't have been accepted, because I didn't really have a husband in the traditional sense, since he was gone all the time. It was the same old feeling of not belonging anywhere, of still being the oddball.

At night I had two sources of entertainment. Since we lived on a busy street with another busy street intersecting it, I'd turn out all the lights and pretend that the shadows on the walls made by passing cars were horses. Voilà, instant western movie. Crazy, huh? If you get lonely enough, anything amuses you as long as it moves.

The other thing I did is even more embarrassing. This house had been a two-story home before some enterprising fellow had divided the upstairs from the downstairs and turned it into two separate apartments. The original stairs were in my laundry area. They led up to a sealed door, which acted as a divider between the first and second floors. By creeping quietly up the stairs and sitting on the top step with my ear to the door, I could hear the voices of the people living above me. Little did those faceless voices know that they were entertaining a very lonely girl. No distinct words were heard, but the murmuring sound of people conversing offered a strange companionship. Pretty pathetic. I can still remember the ache I felt.

One night Dick came home with four of our friends, and when I begged him to stay home, he got mad. He yelled some pretty nasty things at me, which in turn made *me* mad. Next thing he knew, my glass of iced tea was flying at him. Due to my lousy aim, the glass hit the wrong guy, ricocheted off a table, and broke. In a fury, Dick hit me. The next day I called Mother from a pay phone to ask if I could stay with her until the baby was born. She said I could, and the only time I saw Dick after that was when he brought my piano to my mother's.

"And was that the end of it?" Miss Callahan asked.

"No," I replied, "I wish it had been." I gave birth to Ricky on November 22, 1959. Mother located Dick somehow, and he showed up at the hospital. Boy, when I saw Ricky for the first time, I felt like I'd performed a miracle, which I guess I had, because all babies are little miracles to me.

Judging by the way Dick acted toward Ricky, I thought maybe things would get better between us. He was wild over his son and didn't want me to go back to my mother's house, so I agreed to move in with him and his mother in her new house. Dick was fairly attentive for a few days, but then he started staying out all night with friends again—or so he said. It turned out he'd been living with another woman while I was pregnant, and she started making threatening phone calls in the middle of the night. He had broken off their relationship, and she claimed that I was the cause. While I maintained that a wife and baby were as good a cause as any, she didn't see it that way. When I confronted Dick, the fighting started again, and so did his disappearing acts.

My focus was on my precious son. I loved him so much. And you know what? This baby, this tiny, little human being, only wanted me. I mean, no one else could make him happy. Can you imagine such a thing? Me! The center of someone's world. That put a new light on everything. The mother that this baby loved couldn't be treated like trash. His mother had to be treated with respect. My way of thinking about myself began to change.

When my father-in-law told us about a little cottage for rent just across the field from him, Dick and I rented it. It was a cute little place. Someone had started to build a house on a piece of property in the middle of a field of walnut trees. The garage had been built first, and then, for whatever reason, the house never got built. The garage was sold and turned into a rental cottage. Since it was originally intended to be a garage, the rooms were oddly shaped. One long, dark-paneled wall divided three-quarters of the rectangular shape. This made a long, narrow bedroom on one side and a long, narrow living room on the other. The end walls of these rooms could have been raised and opened with just the removal of a couple rosebushes. It was, after all, a garage door. At the other end were the kitchen and a little bathroom, and I do mean little. You had to step into the shower in order to have enough floor space to shut the door. An attached laundry area housed my wringer washer.

One of many drawbacks in renting this place was that it was six miles from town. Once more, I was cut off from civilization, with no TV, no car, and no phone. Well, you take what you can afford.

My father-in-law was very kind; he surprised me with a radio to keep me company. Dick continued his absentee-husband routine, but this time I couldn't have cared less. I had Ricky! He was my whole world. On nice days, I would put him in a buggy and walk a mile to visit my grandma.

Tommy, Dick's brother, often walked with me. Like Dick, Tommy was tall, with the same dark, curly hair and full, pouty mouth, and he was as breathtakingly handsome. Physical appearance was all they had in common, though. Quite *unlike* Dick, Tommy was shy and easygoing, with a sweet, gentle disposition. He seemed oblivious to all the girls who fell all over him and got teased a lot about it. His response was a slow, easy smile. He was so much more compassionate than you'd expect a fifteen-year-old to be and expressed affection easily. Along with my father-in-law, he came over frequently to play with his new nephew and to see if I needed anything. It wasn't as lonely as before.

Once, when Dick had been gone for ten days, I don't know what got into me, but I painted Dick's wheelbarrow black with big, red polka dots. Without even waiting for the paint to dry completely, I dumped all his belongings in it and pushed it out to the front of the cottage and left it there. He didn't show up for another few days, and by that time, all his clothes were a little on the dusty side. Did I mention that in addition to a dust-ridden walnut field, the cottage was surrounded by dirt driveways? When my father-in-law came over, he couldn't help but notice the bizarre yard decoration and roared with knee-slapping laughter. He said, "You know that's going to make him mad, don't you?" I told him yep, but I didn't care. We laughed for years over that.

Dick did come home and *did* get mad, but after hurling some obscenities my way, he just grabbed his dusty clothes and left.

Several months had passed when I began seeing a nice man named Jim. He was nice looking and very good to me, but I wasn't ready for anything serious and was still in a big mess. A divorce was harder to get back then, and besides, I didn't have money for a lawyer. I'd gotten on welfare and was better off financially than I had been when I'd had to depend on whether or not Dick felt like working.

Also about this time, having turned eighteen, I received some money from a trust fund my father had set up through the army when I was born. At last I could finally buy a secondhand television, and my father-in-law loaned me some additional money to buy a clunker of a car. I was still lonely, but the car and TV eased a little of that loneliness.

One night, I went to a party, along with Ricky, and met up with Jim. Dick was there with his buddies and tried to start a fight with Jim, so I left. Jim showed up at my door shortly after I'd been home, and I told him I didn't think we should see each other anymore because it would only cause him trouble. He accepted that and was just leaving when Dick and his friends charged up the sidewalk. Dick stood by while one of his friends beat Jim up. Dick told Jim he was coming home to, as he put it, make things right so that we could be a real family. I think that translated to mean that his other woman had thrown him out and he had nowhere else to go. Like a fool, I took him back.

The following Sunday was Easter, and Dick, Ricky, and I went to a dinner party with his mother. The hosts kept pressing wine on me while making toasts, and I got more than a little drunk. That night I also became more than a little pregnant with Binky. Everyone was pretty unhappy when they found out I was expecting again. Our marriage was too rocky to be adding another child.

During this pregnancy, Dick was more husbandlike but still had terrible fits of temper. He hit or knocked me down several times. I wondered how the baby within me could possibly survive.

My own attitude about having another baby wasn't too great until I laid eyes on her for the first time. She was my dimpled darling. Shortly after she was born, we moved into town and rented a little house just down the street from the hospital where Dick worked as a dishwasher. We had barely unpacked before he started leaving for long periods of time again, and when he *did* come home, I was eager for him to leave again.

In addition to being afraid of his temper, I was afraid I'd get pregnant again. We were perpetually broke, which frustrated him. Additionally he was frustrated because he wanted to sing professionally but didn't know how to get started. It was hard for him to find a decent-paying job without any work experience or a high-school diploma. What skills he had weren't salable.

I got a job sewing upholstery for minivans and hired my friend JoJo to watch the babies. Dick was jealous of the money I made and poked fun at me a lot. He called me a dumb Okie and made fun of my accent. Nothing I did pleased him, and I was so tired that I admit I quit trying.

I've never known why he lost his dishwashing job, but lose it, he did. At the same time, I was laid off from mine. The tension between us worsened. I became so depressed I stopped cleaning the house or doing much of anything but halfheartedly taking care of the babies. I paid a visit to Dr. Fisher, who said I was on my way to an ulcer and urged me to leave Dick. He tried to reassure me about my abilities to no avail.

"Barbara," Miss Callahan interrupted, "why did you hang in there like that with this person who mistreated you so?"

"I vowed I'd never be like my mother," I explained. "I really wanted to make that marriage work, but I failed."

"I think that saying you failed is a little too strong for these particular circumstances," she chided. "What made you finally leave? Or did he leave you?"

My body shuddered at the memory.

"I hate to think about that even now. Dick had been out drinking with his friends, and when he came staggering through the door, he got mad just because I was still awake. Maybe he felt guilty; I don't know. He stomped over to where I was sitting in this ugly, lime-green leather club chair that had wooden arms. He towered over me and growled out words I couldn't even understand. At six foot six, when he towered, he *really towered*! I didn't want to hear any of his nastiness and tried to get up. He pushed me back down in the chair and yelled something at me while he slapped one side of my head and then the other. My head rocked back and forth; my tears flew. Then he started shaking me.

"All the noise woke Ricky up, and he came wandering out of his room to see what was going on. When he saw his father standing over me, he yelled out, 'Don't hurt my mommy!' over and over. He cried and screamed and then grabbed Dick by a leg and tried to pull him away from me.

"Dick reached down and threw Ricky's little body across the room. This seemed to sober him up a little, because he walked over to another chair and just fell into it, putting his head in his hands. Trying to compose myself, I crawled to Ricky, who was lying where he had landed, crying and whimpering. I gathered him into my arms and sat on the couch with him, rocking him in an effort to soothe and quiet him. I told him over and over that everything would be all right.

"All the while, I knew I was lying to this baby. Nothing would be all right, ever, if I didn't make it so. I put Ricky back to bed and returned to the living room. I told Dick that if he was quite finished with me, I was going to bed. There must have been something in my tone of voice that clicked in his brain, because he followed me into the bedroom and said, 'It's over, isn't it?' I told him yes, it was and we'd be out of his life the next day.

"The next morning I got the kids ready and drove to the rental office of a place that rented out former military-base housing. I don't know why I thought to take extra clothes and snacks for the kids, but I'm glad I did. The managers of the duplexes informed me that a deposit was required by six o'clock that evening in order for me to rent the last place they had available. On their advice, I went to the welfare department, only to be told that they couldn't open my case until I had been separated from Dick for a specified time. I told them about the beatings and everything, but they were adamant about their rules. After a lot of futile pleading, I told them I'd have to spend that time in their offices because I had nowhere to go. They didn't believe me, but I settled down on a bench with Ricky and Binky, along with some of their toys. When I was still there at five minutes to five, they set aside their rules, and I left with a check."

"Persistent, weren't you?" Miss Callahan laughed. "Why do you suppose that the young girl who fought the welfare system so successfully is now afraid to go out her front door?"

"I think life killed her off, and I took her place."

We both laughed.

"Anyway I moved the next day. Dick and a few of our friends helped. Our breakup upset them. I'd never seen that bunch so subdued, and I assured them that Dick and I would try to work things out but that living apart until we did would be best."

Turning to look out the window, I joined Miss Callahan in wondering what had happened to that determined young girl.

"So that was my first failure," I continued. "Nineteen years old and already on the road to being just like the mother I'd disapproved of—divorced. I'd reached a dead end. Then I went on to surpass anything my mother had ever done."

"How so?" Miss Callahan asked.

"Well, at least my mother didn't go off and have two illegitimate babies."

"That would be Butch and Joanie?" she asked.

"Yes."

"You seem to feel pretty bad about that," she noted. "Why don't we get all *that* out in the open?"

"Oh, boy." Reluctance made me shift uneasily. "I sure hope you're right in thinking that all this talk about the past is going to help figure out the panic and dizziness. This is hard. I don't like to think about the past, much less talk about it."

"I know," she pressed. "But, believe me, the only way I can help you is to know all about you."

"OK." I let out a long sigh.

"Well, as far as Butch is concerned, there isn't that much to tell," I began. "Dick and I had been separated for quite a few months. As I've told you, I was on welfare, and the kids and I were doing quite well. We hardly saw Dick, which was predictable. I had made friends in the neighborhood and was at one of their houses one day when Ernie, one of our high-school friends, came over to tell me that—Miss Callahan, I want to quit for today. I'll tell you about this another day."

Tears welled up in my eyes, and my throat ached, choking off my ability to speak.

"Come on, Barbara," Miss Callahan gently urged. "You've got to stop burying these painful things. Maybe it won't hurt as much as you think. What happened? What did Ernie tell you?"

"Dick's brother, our beautiful Tommy, was dead. And with all due respect, if you don't think this hurts to recall and talk about, you've got a tougher heart than I do. I couldn't believe it! I had just seen him two nights before. He and some friends went to a party at the house of some guy he didn't even know. This guy started bragging about what a quick draw with a gun he was, and they jokingly challenged him on it. The guy took his gun and made a makeshift holster out of a dish towel. He told Tommy to hold his hands apart, chest high. He said he would have the gun drawn and at Tommy's chest before Tommy could clap his hands together. Well, he did all right. He shot Tommy in the heart. Ernie said that Tommy just looked surprised and fell into the guy's arms as if to embrace him."

Every muscle in my body grew taut as I told her this. Control was slipping away, but I hung on.

"My father-in-law was asking for me, so Ernie had come to take me to him. He was also asking for Dick, but he was nowhere to be found. In a daze, I packed up the kids, and we went to Ernie's house first. Our plan was to phone everyone we could think of who might know where Dick was. We hadn't gotten far into our plan when Dick came sauntering up the driveway; he had been in jail for robbing a gas station.

"When word of Tommy's death reached the police department, they released him without telling him about his brother. Envious of his ignorance, I watched him amble up the drive. Agonizing over what to say, I walked down the drive to meet him. I finally got out what had happened, and, oh, how I hurt for him. He fell across the hood of Ernie's car and beat his fists on it and screamed Tommy's name. I envied him again because of his ability to let his grief out. I couldn't cry or anything. My own grief stuck in my chest and refused to show itself."

"It seems you had already mastered the art of suppressing painful experiences," Miss Callahan noted.

I nodded as I replied:

I kept thinking I had to be strong for Dick and couldn't afford to break down. I took him to his father's house, and they grabbed each other like they'd never let go. Dick and his dad had never been close, but this bonded them like nothing else could. The days that followed were terrible. We couldn't add to my father-in-law's grief by telling him about the robbery, so I went to the district attorney's office and talked him into fining Dick rather than jailing him again. The attendant at the gas station made a statement in which he said that Dick was not the one with the gun, and since Dick had no priors on his record, the DA agreed to a fine and probation. I stayed with Dick and his dad for a few weeks after the funeral, but it wasn't a very happy atmosphere for Ricky and Binky. As much as they loved their grandpa, they wanted to go home.

Dick said this had taught him that life was really about family and he wanted us to get back together as soon as his dad was stronger and didn't need him. I agreed and went back home to wait for him. Months passed with no sign of Dick moving in with the kids and me, so I decided that while I waited, I would go back to school and get my diploma. I moved to an apartment in Pittsburg that had a high school close by and enrolled in evening classes.

The apartment complex was full of single people. The three other single girls with one or more children were, of course, the ones I gravitated to. Above me lived a single guy whom no one seemed to know much about. I met him through the kids, who were outside playing on the lawn when he came home from work one day. Overhearing them talking to someone, I went to the door to find out who it was. They introduced me to their "new friend," Gil.

An initial appraisal of him told me he was Mexican, in his late thirties, with the dark, curly hair and dark eyes that I found attractive. He was short in height but tall on sarcastic humor, one much like my own. It also seemed he was a little on the lonely side, because he stopped in at our apartment quite often after work just to say hi and play a bit with Ricky and Binky. Since they didn't see their father at all anymore, it was nice to have them relate to a man.

Gil had just recently broken off a three-year affair with a married woman, who had six children. Gil wanted her to leave her husband, but she wouldn't. I knew he'd been seeing someone because I'd hear them yelling at each other. That they'd broken up was no surprise.

He had asked me out several times, but I'd always said no. I still believed that Dick and I were getting back together. Besides, I was focused on school, the kids, and the occasional night out with the girls to go dancing. Then, one summer day, I took the kids to a drive-through ice-cream place, and just as I turned into the parking lot, Dick's car pulled in just in front of me. There he was...with another woman. She was all snuggled up to him, with her head on his shoulder.

My stomach lurched, and I almost vomited. I told the kids I'd forgotten my wallet and needed to go back to get it. I backed the car out so that Dick wouldn't see us and returned to the apartment, where I stalled awhile to allow time for Dick and the woman to leave. The kids yanked on my skirt and whined for their promised ice cream as my head spun. Again, as so many times before, I had to fight hard to keep my emotions under control. I couldn't let the kids see my fury and hurt. We went back for their ice cream, and when we got back home, they trotted off to play while I sat on the porch, trying to keep the top of my head from blowing off. Gil chose that time to come down the stairs and ask me out again. When I said, "Sure, why not?" he nearly fell over. He naturally assumed I'd say no, as I usually did.

I don't know how I thought going out with Gil was going to hurt Dick. But I did, and that's all I wanted to do...just lash back at Dick. What an idiot! I couldn't believe I'd been waiting for him and going to school to better myself while he was running around again, after all we'd been through. So I went out with Gil that night, got drunk, and got pregnant. I'm the only person I know whose hangovers last nine months! No wonder I don't drink.

"It must have devastated you to learn you were pregnant," Miss Callahan asserted.

"Yeah, I was pretty upset, and I wasn't the only one. There was one good payback moment during my pregnancy, though. I wasn't aware that Dick even knew where I lived, but one evening, out of the blue, he popped in just as I was getting ready for school. He flopped down in a chair and let those long legs stretch out over half the small living room. When he'd first come through the door, I had been in the kitchen, my lower body hidden by the counter, and when I came around the corner, his eyes about popped out of his head. He took a hard look at me and asked, 'Isn't that a maternity smock you're wearing?' I told him yes, it was. He stuttered, 'But, but, it's been...' And he sat there, obviously trying to work out how long it had been since we'd been together. Flippantly, I told him not to fret, since it wasn't his. He turned the oddest color and looked frozen...like he'd been turned to stone. I asked him, 'What's the matter? Don't you like the monster you created?' I sincerely felt he'd been a big contributor to the person I'd become.

"It was his turn to be furious, and he called me all kinds of filthy names. I just looked at him wearily and said that if he was quite finished, I needed to get to school. Telling him about the ice-cream incident effectively shut him up, and he stormed out. There was no turning back, and reconciliation was out of the question. Since he wanted nothing to do with me, he wanted nothing to do with his children, either, and none of us saw him again, except for one unpleasant hour three years later at a party."

"And what about Gil?" Miss Callahan asked.

"Gil and his lady friend had gotten back together before he even knew about the pregnancy. The very day I realized I was pregnant, he came down to say hello. He had on a new painter's hat and asked me how I liked it. I said I liked it just fine but that it seemed a little big. He agreed that it was, and I told him that he needn't worry; his head would probably swell to fill it out. He came back at me with some wisecrack about 'swelling something on me,' and I said he already had. He asked me what I meant, and I told him, 'My stomach.'"

Remembering that moment caused me to pause. There must be 1,001 ways to tell a man you're pregnant with his child. I chose one of the worst.

"That's how we always communicated, sarcastic humor. It was awful! He kept asking me what we were going to do. Very icily, I told him that *we* weren't going to do anything but that *I* was going to have a baby."

"Was there ever any discussion about marriage?" Miss Callahan inquired.

"Not much. For one thing, I was still married to Dick, and for another, while Gil seemed kind of excited about being a father, he had his other woman to consider. One morning he called me up to his place and showed me some sales ads in the newspaper. He wanted us to go buy some maternity clothes for me. I thanked him for the offer but told him no, I didn't want anything from him. I was so cold and hard. I was afraid *not* to be. If I had let any softness come through, I'm afraid I would have begged Gil to love me, take care of me, and stick by me through the pregnancy and maybe after, but I feared his possible rejection. My behavior certainly wasn't warm and lovable.

"As people found out about the baby, they had one response. Abortion! There was no way I would do that. Everyone, including Dr. Fisher, was against me having that child. Dr. Fisher strongly urged me to place the child for adoption, but I couldn't bring myself to consider that, either. Anyway, with my harsh defensiveness, I managed to turn Gil against me completely. I really did have warm, tender feelings for him and longed to show them, but I was scared to death he'd trample them. Dick had. Still sorely wounded by Dick's unfaithfulness and Tommy's death, I was afraid that Gil would be unable to return those feelings, and that would have crushed me.

"I strongly suspected that if I allowed myself to cry, the tears would be blood. My emotions were shredded. Feeling I needed a fresh start, my friend JoJo urged me to move to San Leandro to be close to her. She and her husband had moved there recently because of his job. It wasn't just that JoJo wanted to look after me. It was also that San Leandro was a bigger city than we were used to and she had no friends there. I gave in to her urgings and moved, but I quickly got so homesick for familiarity myself that I called Aunt Billie, and she helped me move back to Concord. Once there, I took in ironing all that summer to save up to replace the car that had pooped out on me months before and waited for the baby to arrive. With help again from Aunt Billie, I did get a car and went back to night school; I was still determined to get an education.

Cool evenings sitting at a desk were sure more appealing than hot days spent standing over an equally hot ironing board.

"When Butch was born, I was so glad I hadn't given him up. Once again, I was overwhelmed at how much love a baby can conjure up in a mother's heart. By that time, too, I was accustomed to having children without the support or love of the other parent. Ricky, Binky, and I absolutely adored this chubby-faced, cheerful baby.

"I went to see Gil after Butch was born, and when I told him he had fathered a son, he broke down and cried. Like me, he wasn't as hard-hearted as he pretended. He asked a lot of questions about Butch but would not see him. He even came to our house once with his lady friend but wouldn't come in, saying he just wanted to know where we lived. And that's the story of Butch. Can I go now?"

Miss Callahan looked at me strangely, but I didn't care or know why. Nor did I ask.

"Yes, of course," she said slowly. "I guess this was a lot for you today. Tomorrow we'll talk about Joanie."

Her parting words shot a lightning bolt of pain through my temples.

Cooking dinner that evening provided a welcome diversion from my thoughts. I'd invited Pat to eat with us, and once we'd eaten and the dishes were done, I settled down on the sofa to watch TV with him and the kids. The images flashing on the TV screen couldn't capture and hold my attention, though. Knowing where Miss Callahan wanted our next session to go kept distracting me. The next logical topic was Joanie's father, and I didn't want to go there. The sessions were wearing me out, with no significant benefit. Every time I tried to go somewhere, the fear of having a panic attack still scared me to death.

I decided to cancel our next session and then another and another. Missing three appointments, however, didn't alleviate the apprehension, and the court order still hung over my head. I was just putting off the inevitable. It took four days for me to keep my next appointment, and I did so sheepishly.

To my surprise, Miss Callahan didn't even seem upset about the missed appointments. She acted as though we'd met just the day before. The resentment and anger I felt about having to be there would have outmatched any upset on her part anyway. At best, I was sullen. The part of my life on the agenda that day was such that I scrambled to think of any way to skim over it.

Unsure of where to begin, I opened with, "Have I mentioned the scream that lives in me?"

"No, I don't believe you have," she replied, positioning her notebook in her lap. "Are we going to talk about the scream today or Joanie's father?"

Little dark clouds formed in my brain as I tried to blot out all feeling. A welcome fog rolled in to settle on my emotions. That was good; no sharp bolts of pain penetrated. If I could maintain the lack of feeling, I could manage.

Attempting blandness, I explained, "His name was Joe. He and the scream are pretty much the same entity. The scream started out as this tiny, little whimper. Then it seemed to feed off the sad things in my life and grew, like when Tommy died. When I lost Joanie's father, I thought it had reached maturity, and I had to fight hard…so hard…to keep it locked inside. It came very close to escaping when I was in that mental hospital, but, no, it's still locked deep within me. I wonder if it will ever go away. I figure if I let it out, I'll be locked up for sure. People can't just go around letting screams run all over the place, now can they?"

CHAPTER TWENTY-SIX

The heart will break, but broken live on.

—*Lord Byron*

"No, I suppose they can't," Miss Callahan agreed. "Perhaps there is another way. Let's talk about Joe today and deal with the scream another time, OK?"

My chair endured some uneasy shifting. "What happens if I can't keep it in while I'm telling you about Joe?" Her answer would decide whether or not I told her about him. "What would you do to me? This isn't just an idle question; I really need to know."

"Well, I won't lock you up, if that's what you're afraid of. As a matter of fact, I'm wondering if you let it out, maybe it would just go away and not bother you anymore," she encouraged.

The sigh I exhaled could have knocked trees over. "I wish I could be sure." Then I tried to get enough air back into me to get through this. Air was a precious commodity to me and hard to come by when anxiety hit.

"When Butch was about three months old, we moved into a small house built behind a larger house. I liked this place because we were off the main street, which made it a safe place for the kids to play. The Mexican family living in the front house had several children, so my kids had a lot of playmates handy. However, wouldn't you know it; my kids didn't *like* those children and preferred to go across the street where another Mexican family lived with *their* six kids. So much for choosing a safe place for them to play. So I would walk them over and go back for them later.

"That's how I met Ramona. She and I became friends, and over several cups of coffee and stacks of delicious homemade flour tortillas, I pretty much told her everything about myself, hoping she would want to be friends with someone like me. She did! If nothing else, we had children and poverty in common. We hadn't lived there long before Ramona became pregnant with baby number seven.

"In her third month, one of her daughters ran into my house, crying that her mother wanted me. I ran over and found Ramona in bed, pale and looking funny. She thought she was miscarrying the baby. I grabbed the two oldest children and put them in charge of the younger ones, mine included, and rushed Ramona to the doctor. She did indeed miscarry only moments after I got her there. She was so upset, just falling apart. I took her home and fixed her up in bed, and she asked me if I would explain to the children what had happened, which of course I agreed to do.

"They were all upset but found comfort in the fact that the baby was in heaven. That was their idea, not mine. I let them keep their illusions, but I was still skeptical about heaven because of my father. Anyway for a little over a week, I went to Ramona's every day to care for her. Early in the morning, I'd get her older kids off to school and then stay with the younger ones until they returned.

"One morning as I walked around the front house, heading for Ramona's, I felt someone watching me. The windows to that house lined the walkway, and I thought I saw a figure passing from one window to the next as I made my way to the street. When I told Ramona and her husband, Jesus, that someone had spied on me, Jesus laughed and told her something in Spanish, and chuckling and shaking his head, he sprinted out the front door. Just as I was leaving, he came back onto the porch with...well, I don't know what to tell you what *with*. What I saw was more than a mere man; he was a beautiful creature, too beautiful really to be just a man. I instantly went deaf and dumb.

"Jesus told me in his broken English this was 'the spy,' and he howled with laughter. The creature looked puzzled as to why Jesus was laughing so hard and just stood staring at me with a glazed expression. I knew for sure I was blushing. My face turned red hot. Jesus said something to him that I couldn't understand, and then it was the creature's turn to blush. So there we stood, blushing at each other."

Pausing, I remembered that first encounter with Joe with quiet, familiar sorrow.

"What's the matter, Barbara?" Miss Callahan asked. "You suddenly look as if you're not feeling well. Can I get you something?"

The fog threatened to roll out and let the pain in.

"Is it the scream?" she gently probed.

I nodded and tried to achieve total numbness again but failed miserably.

"If I can just keep my eyes from being pushed out of my head from the pressure building up there, I'll be fine." My weak effort to joke failed, and I was miserable. I decided I'd just have to get through this as best I could and went on.

"You know? I loved that man on sight, and he felt the same way, according to Ramona. She told me later that he was a cousin from Mexico visiting the family across the street. When he had first seen me out the kitchen window, he was intrigued. He had run over to Ramona's to ask about me. She told him everything she knew, and I do mean *everything*. I guess that should have upset me, but actually it was a relief, because I didn't have to explain anything to him later. That would have been an exercise in futility anyway, because he only spoke and understood the slightest bit of English. He'd told her he was impressed by three things: my hair, my children, and my devotion to her. He thought I was a woman of great courage. Ha! If he could only see me now."

The pressure in my head grew, but I continued:

Oh, how I wish he *could* see me now. I wish we could see each other, hold each other, lean on each other the way we did in our brief time together.

Anyway, we spent a lot of time at Ramona's house, where we'd mostly just sit and look at one another since the language barrier was pretty thick. Ramona acted as our translator and laughed when she translated the name Joe bestowed on me, Little Tail, because I was so thin. A few months later, I moved back to Pittsburg. Joe and Jesus helped me move all the heavy things, and in the weeks that followed, Joe helped me paint the apartment.

After the painting was finished, the three of them continued to show up often. I hoped that was Joe's idea. Turns out, it was. Ramona started subtly hinting that it might not be a good idea to get too involved with Joe. When I asked her why, she said she couldn't tell me. Well, just add "blind" to that deaf-and-dumb stage I had experienced, because I couldn't see any reason why I shouldn't get "involved" with him.

I loved him more each time I saw him. He was very old-fashioned by American standards and shyly asked me if it would be OK to visit without Ramona and Jesus. Of course I said yes. His visits inspired me to check out recordings at the library to learn Spanish, and, in turn, I attempted to teach him English. Verbal-communication challenges didn't prevent me from seeing how terrific he was with my children.

Since Butch was half-Mexican, I expected he would be Joe's favorite, but Joe proved that theory wrong. Kids were kids to him, and they were crazy about him. Every time he came to see us, they would haul out every toy they owned to share with him. He would play with them for hours. Every picture I have of him to this day is of him playing with them.

One night, after the kids were in bed, he tried to tell me that he wanted to marry me, but it came out in his poor English as him saying he wanted to spend the night. I jumped off the couch and ordered him to leave. Angry tears poured down my face as he stood in front of me and looked letdown and confused. He asked me to excuse him and rushed out the door. He was back within fifteen minutes or so, all smiles, and, boy, when Joe was all smiles, those bright, white teeth set in his dark-complexioned face blinded you. He told me, "Telephoned Jesus. No spend night. Spend forever! Me be your *marido*, uh... husband?"

I didn't know whether to laugh or cry, so I did both. I was so excited, but there was a flaw in any happy plan to marry Joe; I might have still been married to Dick. I'd filed for a divorce but hadn't been able to notify Dick because I didn't know where he lived by that time. The attorney had told me he'd put a notice in the newspaper and if Dick didn't respond, the divorce would be granted by default. Being the moral nonconformist that I was, I never followed up.

So Joe moved in with me, and we lived as a married couple. Even without a license and ceremony, ours was so much more of a marriage than what Dick and I'd had. Joe was everything I'd thought a husband should be, and I was finally something more than a good mommy; I was a good wife. It amazed me that he was so happy with me.

Sometimes after we made love, I would stay awake just to look at him, unable to believe that such a man loved me. And the kids! Oh, my gosh, they obeyed him with just a look. It broke their hearts if they thought he was unhappy with them, so they were always on their best behavior when he was home—unlike the rest of the day.

The smile that memory brought faded as a new thought occurred to me and brought my narration to a halt.

"The scream again?" Miss Callahan asked.

Softly, I said, "No, I was just wondering why the kids seem to have forgotten him. They loved him so much, and yet they never mention him. They haven't, since shortly after he was gone."

"I think you've always been the focus in their lives," she offered. "Maybe as long as *you* were there, they didn't think much about anyone else. After all, a lot of people have come and gone for them."

The truth of what she said made me concede her point. "I guess you're right, but it does seem strange. Oh, well, anyway," I said and shrugged and went on. "Joe worked in highway construction, and the job took him out of town often. He'd be gone for three and four days at a time. I tell you this so you'll understand the rest of this saga. Joe and I had decided we wanted to have a baby and set ourselves to that loving task.

"One day when Joe was out of town, I went to see Dr. Fisher, who confirmed my happy suspicion that I was pregnant. I was so excited! The day Joe was due back, I baked a cherry pie, got fresh corn tortillas from the Mexican grocer, and fixed Joe's favorite dinner. Ha, just like *The Donna Reed Show*, huh? I spent all day cleaning and fixing myself up for his arrival. I could hardly wait to tell him about the baby.

"It had just turned dark out when I saw headlights through the front window. A smile of happy anticipation spread across my face. Then there was a knock at the door, so I knew it wasn't Joe.

Disappointed, I opened the door to a man who, if he'd had a window in his stomach, I swear to you, could have been a building. Mind you, Dick was six feet six inches tall, so for people to appear tall to me, they really had to be tall.

"This mountain of a person asked if I was Barbara Elling, and I confirmed I was. Then he flashed a badge at me that identified him as a federal agent! I gave a nervous laugh and asked him what he wanted. He asked if a Juan José Robles Becerra lived there. I told him yes; he wasn't home at the moment, but I expected him any time. Much to my surprise and annoyance, he pulled the screen door open and moved me aside with his forearm as he insisted I allow him to search the apartment.

"Indignation kicked my annoyance aside, and I asked him why and for what. He said he worked for the immigration department and that Joe was in the United States illegally. He was there to arrest Joe! I told him no way, that there had to be a mistake. He moved one side of his sports coat aside to reveal a gun. My eyes nearly fell out of my head! With one hand on the butt of his gun and the other clamped around my wrist, he pulled me along with him as he did his search...a very thorough search.

"Butch woke up with a cry when his crib was abruptly moved, so the agent let go of my wrist and stood looming in the bedroom doorway while I soothed Butch back to sleep. He then steered me into the living room. My hands kept going to my stomach, as though to comfort our unborn child. The only way I kept from becoming hysterical was to tell myself that Joe would clear up this terrible mistake as soon as he got home.

"Not in the habit of entertaining federal agents, I didn't know what to do while we waited other than offer him a cup of coffee. He refused the coffee with thanks and gave me instructions on what to do when Joe got there. He said I was to answer the door; he would be behind it, and I was not to say a word to Joe, or else. I shuddered to think of what the 'or else' meant and kept assuring him he would see what a mistake this all was."

Miss Callahan looked concerned when, unable to sit any longer, I pushed myself wearily from the chair. "Uh, I need to walk."

"OK, how 'bout a stroll to the water cooler?"

"Sounds good to me."

Out in the hallway, we each grabbed a pleated paper cup from the cooler, filled the cups, filled them and paced up and down the hall in an attempt to lessen the tension running from my stomach to my throat. With that bit of relief, we returned to her office, where my pacing continued as I recounted that night:

We saw car headlights flash across the front windows of the apartment, and I knew it was Joe. The agent hurried behind the door, wrapped his hand around the butt of his pistol again, and motioned for me to open the door. I thought, at last we can get this over with, get it all straightened out, and went to the door. I opened it and forced a big smile at Joe. I started to speak but then remembered what the agent had said, so I just kept smiling and didn't answer Joe's greeting. Instead I sort of inched away from the door into the middle of the living room. Joe opened the screen and came toward me; he was smiling that gorgeous smile. He didn't seem to notice anything was wrong, and as far as I was concerned, there wasn't! This was *my Joe*! He wouldn't do anything wrong.

Joe reached me and was in the process of taking me into his arms when the agent spoke to him in Spanish from behind the door. I only understood his name. I stood there, smiling like an idiot and waiting for Joe to laugh or something. After a few seconds, I blurted out, "Can you imagine? He thinks you're an illegal alien!"

The look on Joe's face buckled my knees, and he looked like someone had suddenly stolen his entire bone structure. He shrank. His shoulders slumped. His neck didn't seem strong enough to hold up his dear head, and it fell forward. Tears streamed down his face while the agent continued speaking to him in Spanish. I wouldn't have comprehended what he said if he'd spoken in English, because the whole scene was so incomprehensible.

It was crazy! Joe raised his head slowly and told me he was sorry. *Sorry!* The agent seemed to be asking Joe questions, to each of which Joe answered yes. Then the agent turned to me and explained in English that someone had reported that Joe was in the United States illegally and had given my name and address. I felt sick, and Joe looked just as bad. I went to him and held him tight. At first, he seemed unable to gather the strength to return my hug, but when he did, we just stood there, hanging on to each other for dear life.

Optimism is curable, or so I've heard, and mine got cured real good that night. The pain was similar to when Tommy had been killed. We talked to the agent for quite a while and asked if there was something we could do so that Joe could stay. I told him about the baby and thought what a terrible way it was to break the news to Joe. It wasn't what I'd had planned at all.

Funny how you keep doing normal things under extremely abnormal circumstances. With tears falling, I cut and served pie. I served coffee, because what's pie without coffee? So strange. This agent could offer us no hope, however, and merely said he was truly sorry. He shared that in his job, he was often attacked physically as well as verbally. He said no one had been so nice to him in his role before, and he thanked us for that. I believe if he could have turned his back and walked away from us, leaving us be, he would have. The man who had originally come to take my Joe away was not the same man who left with him. His whole attitude had changed, and I believed he regretted what he had to do. I guess Joe and I and our obvious feelings for each other touched him.

Strange, isn't it, how people hit-and-run each other emotionally? That man had a tremendous impact on my life, and yet I only saw him twice. That kind of hit-and-run is oh so legal and yet as devastating as being smashed by a car or a bus.

After they'd finished their pie and coffee, the agent said it was time to go. At the finality of his words, I felt like the witch when Dorothy threw water on her—simply shriveling away. I looked at the agent and asked if he had a family, if he had someone who loved him more than life. Sobbing, I pleaded with him again to please help us. I told him we'd go away. He could say he never found us. I would have groveled at his feet if it would have helped. But all this was for nothing, because there was no way out.

Joe asked if he could look in on the kids before he left, and the agent agreed and followed Joe from room to room. I tried so hard to be brave so that Joe wouldn't feel any worse than he did, but, God, how it hurt. Joe looked in at Ricky and Binky, adjusted their covers, and touched their cheeks and hair. Then he went to our room, where Butch slept. Butch woke up and reached for the only daddy he'd ever known. Joe picked him up and cradled him while Butch playfully smacked Joe's cheeks with his chubby little hands. I had to leave the room; any self-control I had left was slipping away.

Then it was time to let go. Joe came over and touched my tummy, where his child was growing, unaware of all the trauma Mama was going through. He said nothing would keep us apart if we didn't let it, and I agreed. The agent walked Joe to his car, and I watched them drive away. If the pain had been bad before they left, now, when I was unable to see Joe's face, it was not to be borne."

"Why are you clutching your chest? Are you in pain?" Miss Callahan asked, looking a bit alarmed.

My reply was a near whisper. "Pain? Yes, pain. I need to keep it pressed in."

"Can you go on?" she questioned.

My head bobbed in an assenting nod. "The moment they left, I thought I would cease to exist—not die, just stop *being*. I quickly peeked at the kids and then ran to the laundry room to use the pay phone to call Ramona. I was screaming at her before she even answered. Somehow she made out a little of what I was hysterically trying to tell her, and she, along with Jesus, came over.

"They were very upset themselves when they arrived. Ramona explained that this was why she had warned me against getting involved with Joe. She and Jesus had known all along but had been protecting Joe. I could only pace the floor, moaning and crying.

"Then there was a knock at the door; it was the agent again. Joe had asked him to turn back so that he could give me his paycheck and medical-insurance card. I looked out, and from the light shed by the lamps in the parking lot, I could see that Joe was handcuffed to the steering wheel of the car. I demanded that the agent take those ugly things off him and tried to run to the car, but Ramona held me back. So much for staying in control. If I have ever really been crazy and deserving of being locked up, it was then."

Feeling drained, I sank back into my chair as the words poured out:

The next few days passed in a blur. The agent told me that he would be taking Joe to Soledad prison, and I could see him there the following Sunday. Ramona and Jesus went with me. Joe was locked up in a world of gray iron and steel like a criminal. I guess in the eyes of the law, he was a criminal, but I saw him through different eyes and resented his being treated that way. He told me they were going to fly him to the interior of Mexico, and he would have to work his way back to his family home in Tijuana. I told him I would meet him there. He argued there was a better way, but I wouldn't hear of it.

I left there still feeling terrible, but at least I had the hope that this wasn't a final good-bye after all. A few weeks later, Joe's father, Antonio, contacted me, expressing joy at the news of the baby and sorrow that loving his son had caused me such grief. He said the children and I were welcome to come stay with the family to wait for Joe.

He didn't need to coax me. After selling both cars and most of our furniture, I packed toys and clothes and, kids in tow, boarded a bus for Mexico. Jesus and Ramona sent me off with dire warnings. They cautioned me to keep a close eye on the kids, because Anglo children were highly profitable in the kidnapping trade. It was 1964, and though most of Mexico had recovered from the revolution, border towns were short on jobs and long on people desperate to gain entry into the *Estados Unidos*. Tijuana was plagued with criminal activity and such severe poverty that whole families often lived in old, rusted-out, abandoned cars. It brought to mind the Joad family in *The Grapes of Wrath*. The prolific dirt and dust still stand out in my mind.

Wanting to be near the border, Joe's family, like many others, had given up a productive farm they had owned in Jalisco to move to Tijuana. They'd had high hopes that their children would cross that border to get well-paying jobs, with the added consequence of better lives in general.

I was impressed with how helpful people in general were to me. Most who saw me struggling with luggage and three small children offered assistance. It could have been a difficult trip, but all in all, it didn't seem so bad. After all, I was going to see Joe again.

The worst part of the trip occurred when we got off the bus in San Ysidro. It was a long, hot walk to cross the border, and a strong wind blew dust that stung our skin. With three trunks and three kids, I was doing quite a juggling act. Three kind men came along, each taking a trunk and a child's hand, and led me into Mexico. Recognizing that the gringa wasn't faring well, they also helped me get a cab.

For the first time since I'd started out, I began to question the wisdom of this move. I didn't speak the language and felt helpless. I managed to get to the family house, though, and, boy, the sight of it made me feel even more unsettled. The front of it was on solid ground, but the back half of it jutted out over some sort of deep gully, with only wooden poles propping it up. Quite a sight. Joe's father rushed out to greet me and just about hugged me to death. His mother, however, was cool, and I suspected right away that our being there was a problem for her. Given that there were two sisters and a brother still living at home and given their poverty, I guessed maybe she had mixed emotions about more mouths to feed.

They put the kids and me in Joe's room, which made me nervous because it was one of the rooms held up by those poles. The floors were roughhewn wood planks, so I was concerned about putting Butch down. He wasn't walking yet, and I worried about him crawling. His little knees would have been full of splinters. In addition to that, there was nothing between the far-below ground and the underside of the floor, and the planks had some fair-sized gaps between them. They were not exactly airtight and were some pretty-good finger and toe pinchers.

A few days later, one of Joe's brothers-in-law took me to meet with the border patrol and then on to the immigration bureau in San Ysidro. I tried to get information on Joe's whereabouts but had no luck. Again, I was warned about the possibility of kidnapping. We just had to wait.

While we waited, I learned what "roughing it" really meant. Laundry was done outside along the backside of the house. The downhill slope was so steep you just about needed goats' feet to keep from sliding to an untimely demise. I'd always joked that housework could be fatal, but that really drove it home. Water was heated on the stove and then hauled outside, where diapers were scrubbed on an old metal washboard. My citified hands were pretty well chewed up in no time.

It was during one of those joyous scrubbing days that I got my kidnapping scare. The kids were all outside with me, and I'd gone just a few feet away from where they were playing to dump a tub of rinse water. When I turned back, Ricky was nowhere in sight. I grabbed Butch and hurried to the front of the house to look up and down the street. No sign of him. Antonio heard me calling for Ricky and came running. He went one way, and I went the other, all the while calling for my son. I stopped a man walking my way and tried to ask if he'd seen a little red-haired boy, and thankfully he understood my pidgin Spanish and told me he'd just seen Ricky at *la tienda*, the store. No kidnapping— just a precocious little boy in search of a candy bar.

Three weeks crawled by before the day I looked down the road and saw Joe walking toward the house. I ran as fast as I could to meet him, and we grabbed each other like drowning people grabbing at lifelines. It felt so good to be held by him again. But Joe treated me differently in Mexico than he had in our home in the States.

The image of a man and his behavior in Mexico differed greatly from anything I was accustomed to. He acted indifferently toward me, not touching me and not paying attention to me the way he usually would. It confused me, and I reacted badly. He spent a lot of time in hushed conversations with his mother, which I found curious. A couple of times, he went off with his brother-in-law and didn't come home all night. I'd been so lonely before Joe got there and was hurt when his presence brought little relief. He did take me to a friend's house for a party one night, but not knowing the language only served to remind me of what an outsider I was.

Another three weeks passed, when one night Joe came to me and said he wanted me to go back to Pittsburg. He said he was worried about my not getting medical care and had devised a plan that would reunite us before the baby was born. After three weeks of this new, macho Joe, I didn't question him. He drove me to the border, and I boarded a bus back to the States. Sorrow and pain resumed their place in my heart, and I worried myself sick all the way home.

Ramona picked me up at the bus depot, and we stayed at her house for a few days. Then my grandmother suggested we rent her garage until I found something else, so that's what we did. My grandparents owned five small houses on their parcel of land, but they were all taken by other relatives. The garage was in no way renovated to act as suitable living quarters, so we slept among old tires and any manner of cast-off junk stored in there. It sort of suited the way I felt about myself—cast-off junk. Old beds were scrounged up along with bedding, and we made do. In the mornings, we would troop onto the laundry porch to use the toilet, and then I'd fix the kids something to eat in Grandma's kitchen. Back to the garage we'd go to get dressed and then pile in the car to go house hunting.

My mother's family is bigoted, and Mexicans are low on their totem pole. Yet Butch, who is half-Mexican, was one of their favorite grandchildren. Looking back, I wonder if they were concerned that Joe would show up, and they didn't like that idea. When I was a kid, the word "dumb" always preceded "Okie," and to this family, the word "dirty" preceded "Mexican."

A friend of mine turned me on to a duplex near her in Pittsburg, and even though it cost a little more than what fit my budget, we moved there as Joe had requested. The summer passed, and our child grew within me. We both hoped it would be a girl. In the meantime, Butch learned to walk, and Ricky and Binky joyfully rediscovered the cartoons on television they had missed so much when we'd been in Mexico. The days just came and went as I waited in limbo.

Once a week I'd write a letter to Joe and take it to Ramona to rewrite in Spanish before it could be mailed. Joe was faithful in answering, so at least I had something to cling to, some hope that our life together wasn't over. In early September, I received a letter, in which he wrote that he would be in Pittsburg on such and such a Saturday. He told me to put on the beans and stock up on corn tortillas.

I was so happy! All the lethargy I'd felt with the heat and pregnancy vanished, and I cleaned the house from top to bottom. I worked like a fiend, preparing for his homecoming. That Saturday came and went with no Joe. Two agonizing weeks passed before I finally heard from him. The letter was postmarked in a town in Mexico that I'd never heard of and couldn't even pronounce. It frustrated me to have his letter and not be able to read it. Not patient enough to wait through a drive to Ramona's, I went to a Mexican neighbor's house and asked if she would read it to me. Poor lady! We hardly knew each other, and if she'd known what that letter contained, she surely would have refused; I would have, if I'd been her.

Racking sob after painful sob vibrated through my body as she read. Joe had made it across the border to San Diego, but while he was standing in line to buy his ticket to San Francisco, the border patrol picked him up and arrested him. They flew him to Texas and put him across the border there, ensuring it would be a long trip back to his family. That pretty much killed his chances of crossing into the United States any time soon. He went on to say that he loved me with all his heart but that maybe it just wasn't our fate to be together. That letter was his good-bye.

I hurried to Ramona's and had her write a letter saying I would move to San Ysidro so that I could cross the border whenever I wanted, and we could still be together most of the time until we found a way to get him in the States legally. The letter came back, stating on the envelope there was no such person there and no one knew his whereabouts. And that, as they say, was that!

Miss Callahan looked at me a long time before saying anything. "And was that indeed that?"

The scream began to seep out. "How could he do that to me? How could he just give up like that?"

Anger yanked me out of the chair, and I paced like a caged animal, wringing my hands. All I could do was alternately moan, "It hurts! It hurts!" and yell, "How could he?"

The thought came to me that after crying throughout that entire session, the flesh of my cheeks was going to turn prune-like from being soaked in tears for so long. That thought made me laugh and laugh. I laughed until Dr. Wright came in and gave me a shot.

That shot flew me beyond calm and landed me in a stupor. Miss Callahan called Pat in from the waiting room.

"I'm afraid Barbara has just been through a rough ordeal," she told him. "Would it be possible for you to find someone to stay with her tonight? She's going to need help."

"As long as I'm around," he assured her, "she has all the help she'll need. I'll stay with her and the kids myself."

"And, Barbara"—she turned to me—"you've done great. Let's give you a couple of weeks off, OK?"

Pat gathered us all up, took us home, and put me on the couch. Butch kept coming over and, with his pudgy little finger, tracing the tears down my face while pleading, "Mommy, why you cry? Don't cry, Mommy."

That just made me cry all the harder. In my medicated, muddled state, I wondered if this was all going to end up with me unable to care for my children any longer. That I would be able to continue on was doubtful. I couldn't bear that thought. Things had to get better.

CHAPTER TWENTY-SEVEN

*To be suspicious is not a fault. To be suspicious all the
time without coming to a conclusion is the defect.*

—Lu Xun

After a dismal and subdued dinner, Pat got the kids to bed.
Halfheartedly, I helped him clean the kitchen and then went
to bed myself. He came in and tucked me in as though I were one
of the children.

"You get a good rest," he commanded gently. "Think about seeing Joanie this weekend. That always makes you feel better. I just
hope she's there this time."

Pat had taken me to Grandma's every weekend, but most of the
time, Bud and Mary would be gone or tell me that their daughter,
Margaret, had taken Joanie for a walk. They always said she would
be right back, but somehow she always managed to stay gone until
I had to leave. Finally I confronted them.

"Look," I challenged Mary. "I'm beginning to think you're deliberately keeping Joanie away from me. You've always understood

that Joanie staying with you is only temporary. In the meantime, I need to see my baby. I'd take her home today, but I need to be sure that when I do, the time is right and safe for her."

"Well, shore, I know it's only temporary," Mary assured me. "Margaret jes' likes takin'er fer walks and showin'er off to her friends, tha's all. I'm sorry, nex' time yew come, she'll be here. Yew jes' keep on a'gittin' help and git better."

My gut told me something strange was going on, but I was still so wrapped up in trying to understand what had happened to me that I didn't put out a lot of effort to identify it.

I assured Pat, "I'm just a little down from all the talk about Joe." A "little down" grossly understated what I was feeling. Having to relive that time with Joe ripped opened emotional wounds that devastated me all over again and reawakened the deep sorrow.

"Well, just to make sure everything is OK," he said, "I'm going to bunk down on the couch. If you need anything or just want to talk, I'll be here."

At some point in the middle of the night, I woke up sobbing noisily. Pat came in and took me in his arms to comfort me. Comfort turned into a desperate passion that physically led us to a place we shouldn't have gone, creating a tension between Pat and me. We weren't comfortable about what had happened and vowed it wouldn't again. I wouldn't know about the pregnancy for several weeks, and in the meantime, I had to keep more therapy sessions with Miss Callahan and was still dependent on Pat to take me.

Since there weren't any more skeletons in my closet to confront, I didn't feel as tense about my next session. All the painful history had been revealed, and I felt that, at last, we could focus on getting me well again.

"Hi, Miss Callahan."

"Hello, there." Her brown eyes searched my face. "How are you? Any better now? You really fought through a lot of tough stuff in our last session."

"Yeah, I guess so. I do feel a little calmer now, though. I apologize for the hysterics. What are we going to talk about today?"

"Well, I'd like you to take me the rest of the way, all the way up to the point when you first started getting dizzy."

That brought a frown to my face. "Oh, I hoped we'd be finished with the past." A sigh of disappointment whooshed out of me. "OK, where was I? Oh, yeah, Joe's gone."

Collecting my thoughts, I snickered. "We moved again, wouldn't you know? I got another place where we used to live in West Pittsburg. Remember the place I told you about when I first left Dick? Yeah, that seemed to be the best bet economically. This duplex happened to be a nicer place, though, and had a regular front and backyard, which was nice. I pretty much just existed until Joanie was born. I was content enough, given the circumstances. I guess when you don't expect anything, you're never disappointed. While I waited for the baby to be born, I rehearsed what I'd tell people if or when they asked about my kids and their fathers. I decided to tell them I'd been married twice, divorced once and widowed once, with two children from each marriage. I'd also tell them Joe had committed suicide."

"Did he really?" she asked, eyebrows shooting up to her hairline.

I stared at her. "Truthfully? I'm not sure. His last letter sounded like that was his intention. And shortly after I got that last letter from him, Antonio's letters stopped. Before that, I got a letter from him once a week. I've never found the nerve to write and ask. There was no point anyway. It was over, and I'd given it all I could. Ramona denies knowing anything, which I find hard to believe. After Joanie was born, our friendship suffered a—shall we say—disconnect."

Cocking her head to one side, she scrutinized me. "So you must have been a bit angry as well as grieved."

"Admittedly, I suppose I was. But mainly by that time, I realized that the kids weren't going to stay babies forever, and I was sure they wouldn't respect me if they knew how stupid I'd been. People were going to pity me either way, and at least along with the pity, they could throw some respect in the mix. It made perfect sense to me. I even told the kids that Joe had died, but they were too young to know what that meant exactly and didn't ask for details."

"Do they know the truth yet?" she asked.

"No, and they never will unless someone else tells them."

"OK," she urged. "Go on with your story."

"Well, there's not much more to tell that you don't know already. I woke up on October 12, 1964, in labor, went for the baby-sitter, and started out for the hospital. I drove to Concord because Ramona had said she would take me and be there for me. Thinking there was plenty of time, we had coffee and got her kids off to school and then started out.

"We'd just joined commuter traffic on Arnold Industrial Highway when suddenly we heard a 'ping, ping, ping,' and the motor just quit! We tried to flag someone down, but when cars would stop and drivers would see my condition, they would encourage us to find someone else.

"Finally a guy pulled over in a brand-new Stingray. I was sure *he* wouldn't want to transport me, but he surprised me by loading my suitcase in his car and squeezing me in; and I do mean squeeze. A Stingray would never double as an ambulance—no stomach room! The contractions had reached the point where I didn't care if I gave birth on the freeway, but it was nice to ride in relative comfort the rest of the way to the hospital.

"Joanie made her way into the world a mere ten minutes after arriving at the hospital, and like the other kids, I loved her fiercely. That love, though, came partnered with an intense pain. She was a tiny, precious angel and a miniature version of Joe."

Wanting to escape the pain of that memory, I rushed on.

"Not wanting to be away from the other kids too long, I went home the next day. They loved her on sight and quickly set about playing the roles of big brothers and sister. She had blue-black hair, just like her daddy, and the same eyes, so brown they were almost black. She still looks just like him. She's with an aunt and uncle right now; did you know that?"

"Yes, I saw that in your doctor's release-of-information form about you. How long is she to stay with them?"

"Not much longer now, I hope. I guess I'm waiting for some encouragement from you. I mean, do you think I'm able to care for my children?"

"Why, of course I do," she shot back, eyebrows raised. "Don't you think so?"

"To tell you the truth," I confessed, "I'm not sure."

Dreading the answer to the question on my mind, I leaned forward. "Miss Callahan, crazy people shouldn't be allowed to take care of children; do you think?"

"Are *you* crazy? Is that what you believe?"

"These anxiety attacks and dizziness sure make me feel I am," I claimed. "What if I am? What if I really am going crazy?"

"Barbara, let me reassure you on that score." She spoke with a firmness I hadn't heard from her before. "If you were going crazy, it's highly unlikely you would be aware of it. Being a mental-health professional, I strongly dislike the term 'crazy' anyway. I don't think you're losing touch with reality, and as far as I'm concerned, you could get Joanie back whenever you felt comfortable doing so. Don't leave that up to anyone else."

"I will. I really will. In fact, I have to. There's something odd happening with her that I can't put my finger on, but I feel something is wrong."

I took a moment to mull that over before going on. "At any rate, right after Joanie was born, I went back to night school; I was determined to change the course of my life. I knew it was going to be hard raising those children. When I got home from the hospital with Joanie, I took a good look around, and the startling reality of how outnumbered I was really shook me up!"

Both of us saw the wry humor in that fact and laughed.

"But the fright gave way to this fiercely protective feeling that absolutely nothing or no one was ever going to hurt my little family. Pretty ironic that the only threat to my family would be me.

"I studied math at Joanie's two-in-the-morning feedings and science during the six-in-the-morning feedings. Butch would always wake up when Joanie did, and he would wander into the living room, bearing Binky's little tin tea set, and pretend to serve me coffee. That always made me laugh, and I called it our air-blend coffee. He didn't get the joke. Cutest thing you've ever seen. Anyway, getting a diploma became the driving force of my life. I'd often heard nobody got anywhere without a diploma, and I vowed to have one soon.

"When the time came and I took the test for a general-education diploma, I flunked math and science by two points. Maybe Butch's coffee wasn't strong enough. Knowing what I was up against personally, though, the instructors allowed me to repeat the test without waiting the usual time period, and I passed math by one point and science by two. The instructors laughed and rejoiced with me because they appreciated what I was attempting to do. Soon I was going to all these job-training places set up by the state and learning how to look for work. I learned how to fill out applications, how to dress for interviews, and such.

"Then the county started an on-the-job-training program and placed me at the health department. That's when the world started moving under and around me. I saw my doctor, who sent me for counseling, and then I had to quit my job to go into a mental hospital. You know the rest of the story."

Wondering what would happen now that she knew my life story made me squirm with anticipation.

"Barbara Jo Elling, twenty-four years old." Miss Callahan studied me. "Quite a lot of life for someone so young. And since you *are* so young, there's still a lot of life ahead of you. So let me ask you, what do you want to do with it?"

"For starters, I want to stop the dizziness and panic attacks," I adamantly declared. "Beyond that, I don't know. I'll tell you one thing, though: no more reaching into the cookie jar for me."

"What do you mean by that?"

Leaning toward her anxiously, I needed to make her understand how earnest I was. "I mean I'm never reaching out for what people generally call 'happiness' again. Every time I do, I get my hand slapped. I quit!"

"You were reaching out when you took the job at the health department," she countered. "Maybe that's why you got dizzy, for fear your hand would get slapped again."

"Yeah," was my retort. "And it did."

With a bland expression, she suggested, "Maybe you slapped your *own* hand."

"Well, that's great speculation." Of their own volition, my eyes rolled. "So help me stop."

"I'm certainly going to try," she said. "In the meantime, I believe we've moved to the next stage of your therapy. How 'bout we take another break and resume two weeks from Thursday?"

CHAPTER TWENTY-EIGHT

*I have several times made a poor choice by avoiding
a necessary confrontation.*

—John Cleese

Miss Callahan's suggestion of a break encouraged me. Maybe it meant she thought I was getting better. Excitedly, I made plans to see Joanie that Sunday. During the drive to Concord, I rehearsed how I would tell Bud and Mary that I planned to take Joanie home with me soon. Recalling how childhood had been for me in that family, I knew it would be the same unhappy experience for Joanie. They might have felt it was best for them to keep her, but I knew better. Everyone knew Bud drank too much but ignored it.

Memories came to mind of Bud coming home drunk and screaming that big, black bears were after him. Grandpa would lock him in the barn. Whenever I went in the barn to gather eggs, I never saw the bears and wondered why Bud was the only one who saw them. It also made me wonder why they would send *me*, a small child, in there with ferocious bears. That didn't seem right. Alcoholism ran rampant in both sides of my family, and I didn't see that as a desirable place for Joanie. I'd seen only pain and unplanned children result from alcohol. I could understand them thinking I was unfit to raise her, but I didn't see how they thought they could do better.

As usual, upon arrival, the kids checked in with Grandma first to say hi. After giving her a hug and grabbing a biscuit, they charged out the back door. Just a few minutes later, Ricky came in crying because Uncle Bud wouldn't let him see Joanie and one of Bud's sons had chased him away.

"I told him I just wanted to see my baby sister," Ricky wailed. "But he told me Joanie wasn't my sister anymore, so I had to go away." He buried his face in my skirt and sobbed. "She still is my sister, isn't she, Mama?"

"Of course she is." I stroked his head in an attempt to calm him. "Don't worry, Son. I'll take care of it. Did you see Uncle Bud anywhere?"

"Yeah, he's out watering Grandma's roses."

Alternating hot flashes of anger and icy chills of alarm washed over me as I went out to the garden to question Bud.

I called softly to his back. He turned to me, and I asked, "Bud, is there a problem with Ricky seeing his sister?"

"Well, yeah, I reckn they is," he replied mildly. "The ol' lady has it figgered that Paula should stay on with us. She means to fight yew if she has to."

And there it was at last—time for the long-overdue clearing of air. "And how do you feel about all this?"

He turned back to the roses. "Lookee here, I don' much keer to kick a body when they're down, and I reckin yore as down as they come. But the ol' lady has 'er heart on keepin' that chile."

An ominous fear flooded my gut. "And what about *my* heart, Bud? My heart was set on keeping that child, too. From the first labor pain to when I got sick and trusted you and Mary with her until I got better, it was always understood that Joanie staying with you was only temporary."

His back still turned, he answered, "All I kin say is, don't make me hurt yew."

"What does that mean?" I asked, stiffly.

"Bobbie Jo, I'm ready to drop yew if'n that's whut it takes to keep 'er." His tone remained as mild as if we were discussing the price of beans.

Stunned shock almost knocked me over. A more commanding tone replaced the former soft tone of voice. "Bud, look at me."

He turned slowly and stared into my eyes. The tears that streamed down his cheeks belied his verbal blandness.

His pained expression added to my shock and caused me to take a step back as I challenged him. "Bud, you can't mean that. Surely you wouldn't threaten me with bodily harm. What have I ever done to you? I just don't understand."

"All yew need to unnerstand is ye're not gonna take that baby away. Mary wants 'er, and Mary'll have 'er. If'n she don' git to, she aims to leave me. They's thangs that happens in a marriage that mebbe yew don' know nuthin' 'bout. They's thangs twixt Mary and *me* yew don't know nuthin' 'bout. Yew jes' never mind, and leave us be. I'm a tellin' ya, ya ain't gettin' Paula back. Tha's all they is."

My jaws clamped together so hard my teeth hurt. Enough was enough! The shout I loudly hurled his way nearly stripped my throat. "Joanie, her name is Joanie."

At a near run, I headed for their house. Did I say "house"? Hardly. They lived in the very same garage Grandpa had wanted me to rent when I'd returned from Mexico. Very few renovations had taken place inside it, which did away with the need to do any housekeeping. A space had been cleared among the rusty farm equipment and greasy auto parts to accommodate beds, a sewing machine, and a couple of chairs, nothing conducive to stimulating homey, decorative touches.

My heart thumped hard against my ribs, and the struggle to appear calm was making me dizzy.

"Mary, I have to talk to you."

"Well, I'm listenin'. Go on and talk," she said.

"I just talked to Bud. He said you plan to keep Joanie, and I'm here to tell you, no, you *can't* keep her. You knew this was only temporary. You were the one who kept telling me to take my time, get things straightened out, and then take her home. What are you trying to do?"

Her lips were pinched together so tightly that I was surprised she could form words. "At first I wuzn't bothered in the least that yew'd ever git that chile. But lately seems like yew been gettin' stronger, and I figger maybe ye're startin' to believe yew kin take care of 'er. I love 'er now and don' aim ta let 'er go. She thinks I'm 'er momma now, and they's no room in 'er life fer yew. She has all she needs right 'chere with us."

Stunned and grabbing for a straw, I asked her, "What do Grandma and Grandpa think about all this?"

She made a guffawing sound. "Now, Bobbie Jo, whadda *yew* think? They want whatever their lil baby boy wants. Yew know that. And if'n I tell 'em Bud wants to keep that baby, then that's that."

It was difficult for me to sound demanding since my body's inclination was to collapse onto the ground. "Where's Joanie now?"

"Well, now, I don' reckin that's any of yer business, Aint Bobbie." She snorted mockingly. "She's with 'er big sister, and tha's all yew need to know."

Through jaws once again clenched, I warned, "Mary, you'll never get away with this. I'll fight you for her; I swear I will. If *I* don't get her, neither will you after the authorities investigate you and Bud. Maybe what's really best for Joanie is to be in a foster home. That would be a neutral place, and child-welfare services would make decisions on her behalf."

She planted her hands on her hips and cocked her head to one side to look at me defiantly. "Now how're yew fixin' to fight fer her? Yew scairt of yer own shadow. Yew'd never even be able to sit in a courtroom, nervous like yew are."

Her words reflected exactly my own doubt. I believed she was right and overlooked the fact that a judge had already declared me a fit mother.

Sensing my hesitancy, Mary looked smug. "Now if yew agree to some simple rules 'bout this, we could mebbe work somethin' out. Fer instance, yew jes' keep on bein' Aint Bobbie and git yer other kids to never tell Paula she's their sister, and yew kin keep on aseein' her. If not, yew try to take her, and I'll shoot yew down my own self."

"You mean to tell me you'd really *shoot* me?"

"Got it all figgered out." She smirked. "Yep, all figgered out.

Astonished and needing to think, I forced my shaky legs to walk back to Grandma's house. What had happened to that woman outside the door of family court who had been humble and eager to help me? The obvious answer was that the business of my getting well was taking too long and she had come to truly love my baby. After mumbling a subdued good-bye to Grandma, I rounded up the kids and drove home.

Pat was in Hawaii on a temporary-duty assignment, and not having him to turn to increased my awareness of just how alone I was. Driving the miles back to Suisun, I tried to sort out this new turn of events. Reflections played through my mind of the many times I'd heard of people facing problems and hardships and had attributed their circumstances to something they'd done to invite them. How wrong I'd been to evaluate their situations so harshly. Without walking in their shoes, who knew why their bad choices had been made? What reason or explanation did I have for mine? The answer was clear: a chronic lack of belief in myself and a mind-set that life was a scary wilderness that I didn't know how to navigate.

My newly found determination to get Joanie back faltered after the showdown with Bud and Mary. It became even dimmer when I glanced at the calendar on the way to the kitchen to fix dinner.

Oh, no! There's no way I can wait until Thursday to see Miss Callahan, I thought frantically.

CHAPTER TWENTY-NINE

We crucify ourselves between two thieves: regret for
yesterday and fear of tomorrow.

—Fulton Oursler

Fidgeting and perspiring, I waited for Miss Callahan to come to the phone. *I need a phone at home. These walks to the phone booth are going to kill me.*

Her voice finally came on the line. "This is Miss Callahan, Barbara. What's up?"

"I need to see you as soon as possible," I blurted. "Do you have any openings today?"

"I do, as a matter of fact," she responded. "Can you be here at two?"

"Yes, thank you so much. You're not going to believe this." Sobs erupted. "I think I'm pregnant! What am I going to do? Do you know what this means?"

"Barbara, please calm down. No, I *don't* know what this means. Tell me!"

Groans replaced the sobs. "It means I won't be able to fight for Joanie. They'll never give her to me now. I've played right into their hands. Can you imagine anyone choosing me for her over a respectable, married couple? It means I'm scared! If I can't make it through a grocery store, how am I going to survive all those doctor appointments and the hospital?"

"I'll see you at two," she replied. "We'll talk then."

By the time we reached the clinic, I was both panic-stricken and furious. After the kids were settled in the waiting room with blocks and books, I practically raced Miss Callahan down the hall to her office. Before the door was fully closed, I began choking out the details of my visit with Bud and Mary and then went on to moan, "I'm scared to death to think I may be pregnant."

"What scares you so much about having a baby?" she asked. "You've had four beautiful children already."

Her question struck me as being incredibly obtuse. "I was well then and not having these panic attacks. I can't imagine having the prenatal examinations and the blood tests and being trapped in the hospital."

"Why? What do you think is going to happen?"

"What do I think? Can you relate to not being able to *think* at all? That's what happens to me during these spells, or whatever you want to call them. All the little wheels in my head that create thought just quit. Everything in my head jams up, and my feet start moving. I need to run away. It's not a conscious choice. It just happens. How can I lie still during a pelvic exam? How can I run during a contraction?"

"I see." She nodded, though I seriously doubted she did. "Do you feel you should get an abortion?"

"Abortion?" I echoed stupidly. "Oh, no, I couldn't. I just couldn't. I'd be scared out of my mind."

"Well, you're scared anyway," she reasoned. "Getting an abortion would only mean you'd be scared for a shorter time."

Massaging my temples, I let her meaning soak in. "I know what you're getting at, but an abortion would only solve this immediate fear. Then I'd have to deal with possible regret, and I don't think I could handle that. I have so many things to regret already; I don't want to add another one."

Jolted by this unexpected event, I knew I faced a major setback in attaining the mental health I longed for. We ended our session with me using the clinic's phone to make an appointment for the following day with Dr. Galen S. Wooley.

Dr. Wooley's waiting room was nice enough, I suppose, with its plush beige carpet and comfortably upholstered chairs. Paintings of beach scenes adorned the walls. But they were still walls, and it took every ounce of strength to stay within them while I waited to be seen. Convinced I was going to choke to death, I opted to stand by the door. My feet were itching to run away. By the time the nurse called my name, my perspiring hands had nearly rubbed through the fabric of my pants' legs in an attempt to dry themselves. Barely able to walk, I hoped there was enough fabric left to render my jumping kneecaps invisible.

The nurse introduced herself as Jeannie. She was young, cute, and blond, with a combination of humor and kindness in her blue eyes. As I climbed onto the examining table, my own private little earthquake rumbled beneath me. When a fear-filled whimper escaped, I asked her for a wet paper towel.

"Sure, sweetie," she obliged. "Are you feeling sick?"

Starting to cry, I answered, "Not the kind of sick you're thinking. I, uh, have some sort of a problem that causes me to be scared all the time, which makes my face hot. A cool, wet cloth makes it a little bit better."

She took my vitals while I briefed her on the events of the past year and the fact that so far the therapist and I hadn't come up with a solution. When Dr. Wooley, bespectacled and bald, came in, the nurse passed a condensed version on to him. They kindly and patiently took their time with me, doing what they had to do to confirm my pregnancy. Wanting to reward them for being so good to the unworthy thing I knew myself to be, I promised to try to be a good patient. They graciously assured me that most of their patients were frightened and didn't like pelvic exams. Fright, I explained, was something I'd been taught not to show.

"You did fine, Barbara," Dr. Wooley assured. "I'll write you a prescription for prenatal vitamins and see you again in a week."

With the tension subsiding and the pregnancy a fact rather than a suspicion, chills shook me so hard my teeth rattled. I sat in my car, shivering, and wondered, *Now what?*

By the time Pat got back from Hawaii, my condition was obvious. After recovering from his initial shock, he studied the toe of his shoe for several minutes before saying, "You know, my divorce from Linda will be final soon, and, uh, well I could, uh, think of worse things than marrying you."

"No, that's all right; really, it is. You don't have to do that. You've done so much for us already."

"Look," he snapped, "it's not some favor I'm willing to do for you, like fixing your car. Can't you believe I care for you and the kids? I know we didn't plan this, and I know you don't love me. But why not give it a try?"

Cornered! All my fears took me hostage. In unison, they mocked me. *Come on; you can't get married. You'd have to go to court to make sure you're legally divorced from Dick, and you know you can't do that. Pat's in the air force. What about that? You might have to move a lot. He might even get stationed overseas; how would you handle that, you coward? You'd be committed to him. You were committed to Joe, and look how that turned out.*

Instead of aiming my frustrations at the fears, I transformed them into anger and threw them at Pat. He'd challenged me with what-ifs too numerous to face.

"No, no, no," I impatiently snapped. "Don't you understand? I don't want to get married. What I want is for you to get away from me."

Guilt was setting in, and I couldn't cope with it. It was still stuck in my mind that guilt put me in a mental hospital. I'd been unsuccessful at getting rid of guilt, so I thought I'd better get rid of Pat.

"Bobbie, honey, this is my child, too," he pleaded. "OK, we won't get married, but don't deny me my child. Let me stay with you. Let me continue to help you. When you feel better, we can solve all these problems together."

My head shook sadly. "No. Please, leave me alone."

It was his turn to get angry. "What do you intend to do?" he demanded.

"What do you mean?"

"Are you planning to do away with this baby?"

"No, I've thought about it, and I can't. Dr. Wooley and I talked about it, and he knows a couple who can't have children. The man, a pediatrician, is retiring from the air force soon, and the wife is a teacher. She can't bear children, and they want to adopt our baby."

Pat's head snapped back as though I'd struck him.

"No!" he cried in protest. "You can't just give my kid away like a record you don't want to hear anymore. Give it to me. I'll take care of it. I'll take him or her to my mother in Washington until I get out of the service. You can't do this to me. I won't let you."

The arguing went on and on until we finally agreed we'd go to Washington to meet with his mother and talk it over with her. That compromise calmed Pat enough to leave, and I fell into bed, exhausted. But sleep didn't come easily as I wrestled with doubt and sorrow and wondered what Washington would bring.

CHAPTER THIRTY

Courage, sacrifice, determination, commitment,
toughness, heart, talent, guts. That's what little girls
are made of…

—*Bethany Hamilton*

Pat's mother and grandmother were fine ladies, sweet and old-fashioned. They lived in a quaint and densely wooded area. Their backyard literally was a lake. To visit neighbors, who were few and far between, they used a rowboat. There was much to love about their home, and our visit was good, despite the hovering bit of understandable tension about the baby. As fine as these ladies were, though, they were more advanced in years than I'd expected, and neither of them was completely well or strong physically. It was impossible for me to imagine them having the energy required to care for a child; a younger couple would be much more capable. Also, there was no father figure. This child deserved a more well-rounded family. If Pat had been out of the service, there'd have been no question in my mind about where the baby should go.

But things being what they were, I still believed the couple recommended by the doctor was the best choice.

As much as I loved my children, I had grown in age and experience enough to realize that babies grow up. In time, they sense that their family is different and can resent it. My own erratic childhood had certainly caused me no end of resentment, and it was my prediction that my kids would resent theirs as well. I didn't want to do this to another child.

"Pat," I told him sadly when we returned home, "I'm so sorry about the way things have turned out for us. If I were emotionally well, I'd probably marry you and live happily ever after, if such a thing ever really happens. You're responsible and intelligent and have a wonderful sense of humor, and, more importantly, I can trust and rely on you. In fact, up until now, you've let me be totally dependent on you. You've let me grow and be strong when I felt capable and let me lean on you when I didn't. I appreciate that about you. That hasn't happened in previous relationships. I'm prepared to finish what I've started, so to speak, by raising the children I already have, but I have no desire to struggle through the dizzy spells and anxiety attacks with another one."

Sad and dejected, he went back to the base and left me full of remorse. This was the last conversation we had. Pat was shipped to Vietnam two days later. I never saw him again.

At that time, Vietnam was still referred to as a police action by the War Department. Husbands and fathers were dying over there, and it sure looked like war to the residents of Fairfield. While members of the military went overseas and died, either physically or emotionally, the rest of us stayed behind to protest or love in and drop out. The dropout group emotionally suited me. Amazingly enough, the world now seemed to accommodate people with my particular problem. Drive-up businesses reflected the hurried lifestyle that had become so popular. A shopper could just about do drive-up anything. Everything was geared toward speed. It was expensive but great for me. As much as possible, I utilized drive-up shopping, banking, and fast-food places; however, carrying and delivering the baby within me still had to be done the old, conventional way.

Shortly after Pat left, I moved into a dilapidated duplex formerly used as military-base housing. To avoid any questions the neighbors might ask if they noticed my condition, I hid in my home and waited for the arrival and departure of the baby. Binky started school that year—a reminder that, yes, my children were growing up and would soon ask some tough questions. I hoped I'd be ready for them. The kids didn't seem to notice my changing body shape, and there was no mention of a baby coming to our house. They did, however, ask about Pat. I simply told them he had gone to be a soldier.

The pregnancy seemed to drag on longer than the others. To help pass the time, the kids and I did a lot of paint-by-number pictures. For no particular reason, all of mine were of Jesus. Somehow those paintings brought on feelings of melancholy and hollowness. I assumed it was the dread of giving this baby away.

It was at the end of a routine examination when Dr. Wooley pulled off his rubber gloves and declared, "Barbara, you're two weeks past your due date. It's time we had this baby."

"Wha…uh, what do you mean?" I questioned. "I'm not in labor, am I?"

"No, you haven't started active labor," he replied. "But there's every indication you've reached full-term. Let's not drag this out. The adoptive parents are anxious, and I know the waiting has been hard on you. I suggest we go to the hospital and induce labor. Let's get this over with."

My body shook from head to toe. My own private earthquake was activated again. My hands flew to my stomach and felt the life in there moving around, and I blurted out my protest.

"No, not today. I can't. I don't feel good. I think I'm going to be sick. Please, let's wait a little longer."

"I can give you something for your nausea," he persisted. "It'll be fine. Inducing labor won't hurt the baby, and he or she will come quicker. I promise I'll take good care of you both."

My body slumped, and my mind sought reconciliation as I resigned myself to do this inevitable thing.

"OK, you win. When I put myself in the adoptive parents' place, I understand what you mean. This waiting must be as hard on them as it is on me. Would you please have Jeannie call my babysitter?"

My head grew heavy and fell into my hands. "I'm tired, just so tired. You're right; I might as well get it over with. Promise me one thing, though, OK? Promise me you won't let me be afraid. Don't let me pass out."

"What makes you think you'll pass out?"

"I don't know. Sometimes when I'm badly frightened, I feel like I'm going to pass out and not wake up. I'll just cease to be—not die, just stop existing. Just...please help me stay calm."

"I will," he said reassuringly. "I'll give you something to help you with that. Trust me; we'll take good care of you."

We left his office and walked out the back door to the emergency entrance of the hospital. He held the door open for me, and I'd gotten one foot in when the hospital smells changed my mind. My body abruptly turned, ready to run, but Dr. Wooley grabbed my arm.

"What is it?" he demanded, hanging on to my arm.

"I'm sorry. I'm sorry. I can't; I just can't," I whimpered, trying to get my arm out of his grasp. The scream demanded release. I had to get away. Dark clouds gathered in my head as I cried and begged him to let me go.

"Come on now," he coaxed. "Let's go have that baby. Come on. It's all right."

Hearing my whimpering and moaning, orderlies and nurses poked their heads out to witness the cause. They joined the doctor, pushing and pulling me into a room. Soon I stopped fighting as hard but was too frightened to cooperate much, either. As soon as they laid me on a bed, all resistance left me. As though playing peekaboo with the world, I placed my hands over my face in an effort to avoid the reality of what was going to happen.

The needle that pierced my arm was hardly noticeable. As the medication flowed into my veins, my body did a sudden sit-up and was on its way to completely standing. The propulsion nearly sent me through the window in front of me, but Dr. Wooley's arm stopped me. Grabbing his arm with both hands, I gripped it so hard he winced.

"You promised I wouldn't pass out," I yelled, "and I'm going to. I feel it."

"No, no, you're not," he said. "It's just the effects of the tranquilizer I promised you. It'll pass in a minute."

A nurse scooted on the bed behind me and pulled me into her arms. "Why, I believe I know who you are," she cooed. "Dr. Wooley called this morning and said he'd be bringing in a pretty, little redhead. You're Barbara, right?"

Dazedly, I nodded.

She assumed a singsong cheerleader voice, "Well, Barbara, I'm going to be your nurse while you're here, and I'm going to make sure that you're well taken care of. You just relax now, OK? Doctor is starting your labor induction now, and soon your baby will be here."

I mumbled that I wasn't going to *have* a baby. She was still behind me, so I couldn't see her as she slipped off the bed and stood. I don't know exactly what transpired, but someone must have indicated I wouldn't be leaving with this child. She dropped the cheerleader tone.

"This is a wonderful thing you're doing, Barbara," she said softly. "You must love this baby a lot to give it up to people who would otherwise never know the treasure that is a child."

On and on she talked in a soothing tone. The drug to stimulate labor kicked in, and soon I was in the delivery room. The faceless voice stayed with me the whole time and talked me through the whole ordeal. It was over quickly. Immediately upon its first cry, the baby was rushed out of the room, away. I didn't even get a glimpse of it. Empty. I was just so empty.

Lying there, I thought, *This is not the way it's supposed to be. When babies are born, people should be happy, not devastated.*

There was no joy, no jubilation, and no excitement. The only sound was my anguished sobbing as the doctor performed the usual postdelivery routine needed for my body, but there was no medical repair for my heart.

So that I wouldn't have to share my grief with others, a private room had been assigned to me. The sounds of babies crying and mothers cooing, saying the same things, making the same sounds I had made with each of my other babies, made their way through the walls, tearing my guts out. Another needle in my arm brought my new best friend, sleep.

When I woke up, the nurse had gone. Coaxing my legs over the edge of the bed, I peeked around. Not seeing anyone, I stood cautiously, and feeling steady enough, I edged toward the nursery. While I tried to appear nonchalant, my absolutely desperate need to see the baby propelled me down the corridor. My concern was that if the nurses recognized me as the woman who gave her baby away, they would throw up a roadblock before I made it there.

My mission went unhindered, however, and I made it. "It" was a girl, a very tiny, pudgy-cheeked baby with hair the same color as mine. The tag on her bassinet told me she weighed six pounds six ounces and was eighteen inches long. So pink and precious. My arms spread themselves of their own accord to embrace the window and ached to hold her. My arms needed that baby. All I could do was cry, and my throat-shredding sobs brought a nurse, who tried to take me back to bed. Falling to my knees, I begged her to let me hold my daughter. Instead, she knelt on the floor beside me and held me.

"Barbara, dear, believe me," she said, softly but firmly. "That would only make it worse."

"It can't possibly be worse," I pleaded. "Please, just let me hold her and look at her. I've changed my mind. I can't let anyone take her away. She's my child...please, *give* her to me."

Another needle. More sleep. Two days passed in a blur. When I finally became completely coherent, I asked for her again, but she had already left the hospital with her "mother and father." They had left a message with Dr. Wooley for me, saying they intended to give her the name I had chosen, Kate. Dr. Wooley also had a message for me. He delivered it during my discharge examination; I'd never carry another child.

Upon returning home to my children, I found that stroking their hair and nuzzling their cheeks held a more poignant joy than ever before. My eyes couldn't get enough of them. The sight, sound, and feel of them reminded me, though, that raising them alone would mean some hard and financially lean times along with that joy.

That reminder acted as a healing consolation about giving Kate up. Whereas my other children had to make do with just me, Kate would have a complete family. She'd never have to wonder if poverty would keep the Easter Bunny, Tooth Fairy or Santa Claus away. So while I carried a hard and heavy guilt in my heart for hurting Pat, I felt better about Kate and began the day-by-day healing that the passing of time affords. It was time to resume my quest for mental and emotional health *and* to figure out when and how to bring Joanie home.

CHAPTER THIRTY-ONE

*They always say time changes things, but you actually
have to change them yourself.*

—*Andy Warhol*

The inexplicable, irrational fear continued. I'd feel fine at home until I contemplated going certain places. A trip to the store was too awful to consider at times. A trip to any place of business was a nerve-racking experience. Medical visits were so ominous that the thought of them brought on flu-like physical symptoms. Almost any place outside my front door that required adult behavior was nearly impossible. It was as though a little kid in me was throwing horrible tantrums in protest of growing up. Playacting the role of an adult came easy, but achieving *real* adulthood escaped me. I was all child and parent, with no governing adult in sight. And the parent I was to myself differed from the one who parented my children.

Unable to handle the magnitude of stress heaped on it, my body rebelled. The protest began with more weight loss, and I dropped into the ninety-pound range again. Friends teased me that ten pounds of that weight was my hair. Being held captive in a beautician's chair to have it cut was unfathomable, so it was indeed on the long side. The next protest came in the form of acute mucous colitis. What pain! It easily equaled childbirth, without the reward of a baby when it was through with me.

I managed to find work as a motel maid, which was a good job for me. The constant moving involved in cleaning the rooms kept me ahead of the anxiety.

My life was strange and full of surprises. Some were pleasant, some not. One of the more pleasant surprises was meeting Garry Mumau. My car had refused to start, so I was pushing it down the street when an old jalopy pulled up alongside and out popped one of the skinniest people I can recall, other than myself. He had red hair and freckles and wore glasses as thick as soda-bottle bottoms. He helped me start the car, and to thank him, I invited him into the house for a glass of iced tea. We talked easily for over an hour, and I learned he was in the air force, stationed at Travis, and terribly homesick. By the time he left, he was no longer a stranger but a little brother.

A much less pleasant surprise came at me one morning when I got up to go to work and was seized with horrendous pain in the pit of my stomach. It dropped me to a fetal position on the floor. *Oh, great, I've gone and gotten an ulcer.*

Fortunately, Garry worked nights at the base, so he was able to take my call and rushed over to take me to the hospital's emergency room. A blood test showed an imbalance in my red and white blood cells, and the doctors decided to go on a surgical exploration. That threw me into a petrified state, but the enormity of the pain made my fear miniscule. A team of white coats stampeded me to a room for preparation. To physically describe the nurse who was assigned to me would be a gross act of unkindness, and her personality was worse. She slithered, rather than walked, into the room. Grabbing my arms, she stroked them and hissed in a style befitting Dracula, "My, what beautiful veins you have."

Hearing something a little more comforting would have been appreciated, but at least someone was pleased about something.

Coinciding with her entrance was a shiny head with gray hair creating a border around it just above the ears, which poked around the door to ask the bride of Dracula who I was and what kind of problem I was having. She told him I was being prepared for exploratory surgery.

"Do you know what they're exploring for?" he inquired.

"Well, no, at least I haven't been told," she stammered, looking flustered.

He walked briskly over to me and smiled. The kindness reflected in his eyes calmed me a bit. "I'm Dr. Parkinson," he offered. "I'm going to look over your chart here and see if I can help. Is that all right with you?"

My consent was a pained nod. The ER doctors came in, and Dr. Parkinson asked them if I had a family doctor that they knew of. They told him no and described the symptoms that had brought me there.

"I'd like to take over her case," he instructed them. "I think she needs to be stabilized first. She looks as though she's suffering some sort of shock. I'd like to get her on an even keel before resorting to surgery." With that, he shot me with some sort of tranquilizer.

Now that was my kind of doctor! For me to so instantly trust a doctor was rare, but I gladly turned myself over to him.

At his request, two nurses whisked me out of the emergency room and down a crowded corridor. The odor of disinfectant and alcohol caused my stomach to lurch. Buzzers and intercom exchanges created turbulence in my head. Within minutes, the gurney I rode on passed through a door into a blissfully quiet room.

The quiet didn't last long, though, as Jenny, according to her name tag, rolled a tray of scary-looking paraphernalia to my bedside.

"Hi, Barbara," she chirped. "I see you're one of Dr. Parkinson's patients. You're lucky; he's the best."

The medication blurred my vision and made it difficult to focus on her face as I tried to smile.

"According to the doctor's orders, one of the first things we need to do is to get this into your stomach." A long, clear plastic tube dangled from her hand.

Panic tried to present itself, but the sedative effectively squelched it.

"Now you drink this glass of water quickly," she instructed. "Take big gulps, and just try not to think of anything else."

With no small amount of doubt, I did as she said and swallowed the tube along with the water. She taped the tube to the side of my face and explained, "This will gently pump all acids from your tummy."

The squeak of more rubber-soled shoes diverted my attention as another nurse rolled in yet another tray filled with ominous gadgets and, to my horror, four syringes.

Jenny turned to the nurse and reported, "The Gomco suction is in place so we can get the catheter inserted and her IV hooked up. Are those the vitamin and antibiotic injections?"

Not wanting to watch their ministrations, I stared at the beige drapery with its large, green, palm-leaf print. More machines were brought in and attached to various body parts, and soon the sounds of clicking, beeping, and whirring replaced the quiet of before.

"There," Jenny announced proudly. "You're being fed, emptied, and detoxified. Your only job is to make sure you lie flat on your back and move your arms as little as possible. We've got everything else covered."

Strong sedatives relaxed my mind and body but didn't stop my buttocks from protesting the many injections of vitamins and other unknown medications. Seven days passed as I lay flat on my back with those tubes for constant companions. Four painful injections four times daily introduced me to a new brand of pain. By day three, when one of the nurses came to administer the shots, tears flowed quietly from my eyes into my ears. The back of my lap had developed knots from the previous injections and throbbed miserably. By day four, the nurse apologized as soon as she came through the door with the needles. She was so sympathetic that I made a sincere effort to be brave for her, but the tears flowed anyway.

Garry came to visit daily and reassured me that the kids were fine, even though they missed me. An acquaintance by the name of Fat Cat came once but broke down and cried when he saw my condition. He didn't come again. Miss Callahan came with forms for me to sign, which gave her permission to release details of our sessions to Dr. Parkinson.

On the seventh day, all the tubes were removed, and my palate was treated to a meal of soft, mushy food to test-drive my stomach. It was dull and lacked any gourmet flair, but the pain was gone; I felt I'd never been sick. My blood count was normal, and I was scheduled for discharge the next day with a diagnosis of acute pancreatitis.

Miss Callahan and Dr. Parkinson agreed that emotionally induced illnesses would undoubtedly continue to plague me due to the constant tension I lived with. They concluded that I should continue under Dr. Parkinson's care, as well as Miss Callahan's. While he maintained my body, she would work on the emotional aspects. They made a good team.

That emergency room hosted me as its guest frequently over the next few years, as I appeared with colitis, acute pancreatitis, and then emotionally induced arrhythmia. My heart had at last joined my other organs in waging a protest at the tension it was fed. Being full of various and sundry medications, I found it a chore to drag my skinny body from one day to the next.

That following November, after Ricky's tenth-birthday party, Butch climbed onto my lap and, after hugging me, declared, "You're the best mommy ever." Then, pulling my face closer to kiss me on the cheek, Butch added, "Mommy, why are your eyes so yellow?"

I hadn't felt well for a week, but I had chalked it up to something flu-like. Wrong. It wasn't the flu at all. It was hepatitis. Back to the hospital.

Having Garry in my life meant always having someone to turn to. It was Garry and a sympathetic friend of his who took turns staying with my children during my three weeks in isolation at the hospital. Ricky, upset at my leaving again, ran away. He rode his bike to the hospital and looked through every window he could reach until he found me. On that particular day, I was peaking as far as the color the hepatitis had turned my skin, and I looked frightful. After one look, Ricky took off. He was convinced that this time I was going to die. I spotted him peering in but couldn't get out of bed to get to him. All I could do was cry as I saw the revulsion and fear registering on his dear face. Garry scoured all of Fairfield, and when he found Ricky, Garry comforted him and convinced him to return home and told him I would be OK again soon.

Despite my heartache over being absent from my children again, that particular stay in the hospital was a well-disguised blessing. Being in total isolation the first week didn't allow me any visitors. That was the longest time I had ever been so completely alone. Time to think, and, boy, did I think! When I had first entered the hospital via the emergency room again, the doctor on duty thought I was too far gone to make it and pulled a sheet over me and rolled me into a corner.

"Oh, the poor dear," I heard a nurse murmur. "She must be in tremendous pain."

To the contrary, pain wasn't an issue for me at all—only an inexplicable peace. I later learned that 87 percent of my liver was damaged and a large percent would never regenerate itself.

Later, while lying in isolation, I questioned myself about how I felt about being on a first-name basis with death. What good had

I done in my life and what bad? What was correctable and fixable, and what wasn't? Was I getting one of those second chances, and if so, why? I pondered all the things in my life that Miss Callahan and I had talked about and their meaning. Mainly we had dumped badly on my mother, which was the fashionable thing to do in psychiatry.

But what did it all mean? Could I start all over and go for job training again? All I knew for sure was that I didn't want my life to continue down a road to nowhere. I was still scared silly of facing the anxiety attacks, but I decided to, at least, try going back to my goals of four years ago: get a job, get off the welfare rolls, and be a better example to my kids. No more living as half mom, half human being. I wanted to live a whole life and not waste a minute of it.

CHAPTER THIRTY-TWO

The human heart dares not stay away too long from that
which hurts it most. There is a return journey to anguish
that few of us are released from making.

—*Lillian Smith*

Three days before Christmas, I was released from the hospital weighing a new, rounded-out 135 pounds. Along with my new poundage, I returned home with a new attitude. All I wanted was to be functional. That didn't seem to be too much. I was still scared but determined, and it seemed that my sessions with Miss Callahan were finally paying off. The anxiety didn't seem as intense, nor did it seem to be present all the time. It became an off-and-on ordeal that allowed me some time to regroup between episodes.

This renewed strength must have reflected itself to Bud, Mary, and Grandma during my visits to see Joanie. Even though I didn't say anything threatening to them, they knew I was only biding my time until I felt sure enough about myself to safely bring my daughter home. The tide had shifted; it was their turn to be fearful. To resolve their fears, unbeknown to me, they put together a plan that prompted my cousin Denny to call me one morning.

"Bobbie Jo?" a man's voice rumbled into the phone. "Is that you?"

"Yes, who's this?"

"It's me, Denny Ray. Listen, if you tell anyone I called you, I'll say you're lying. You gotta promise not to tell I was the one who warned you."

Not in the mood for guessing games, I insistently asked, "Warned me about what? Denny, what's wrong? Is Grandma OK?"

Denny was Aunt Billie's oldest son, currently living with Grandma. He played a dual role in her life: favorite grandson and caregiver.

"Oh, shore, she's fine," he said impatiently. "It's Joanie I'm callin' about. All I'm gonna say is you better come and get 'er now— and I do mean *now!*"

My knees buckled, and I landed in a chair, clutching the edge of the kitchen table. The hairs on my arms and the back of my neck were like hot needles in my pores, as though I were being electrocuted.

Tension gritted my teeth. "Denny, what are you talking about? What's wrong with Joanie?"

"I'm a tellin' you. I cain't say nothin' more. You jes' better come get 'er."

Frantically, I urged him for more information. "What do you mean you can't tell me more?"

He sniffed and said, "Bobbie Jo, you know Grandma has always wanted Bud to have anything he wanted. She'd help him do anything. She told me if I let on to anyone what they're plannin', I'd be written out of 'er will. I've told you all I can."

He started to cry. His painful struggling was obvious. "You and me was always close, and my mama always loved you. I know you was always good to me, but I cain't tell you no more. I'm takin' a chance tellin' you this much, and now I got to go. Good-bye."

With that, he hung up. I didn't know what to do or think. Confusion threw me into a tailspin for a few minutes while I attempted to sort out what Denny had said. With my head spinning, I called the sheriff's department in Contra Costa County. The officer who answered said that in order to file a complaint, I needed to go to their office and file in person. After I told him how far away I lived, how Joanie had come to be living with these people, and how Denny had called me, he still insisted that I had to make my request in person. I tried to think of a way I could sneak into Bud and Mary's house and take Joanie without being caught. That they would do me physical harm was a firmly held belief. With no feasible plan coming to mind, I called social services in their county and told my story to an intake social worker, who agreed to go out there herself.

She called me the next day and said that she had set up an informal hearing in her office for Mary and me. The thought of an actively involved ally sent relief and hope flooding through me. *Now if I can only squelch any anxiety attacks so I can get through this.*

Shortly after I walked into the nondescript county-office lobby, with the predictable fake rubber tree, a Mrs. Whigan came out of the inner sanctum of offices and led me into her allotted space. Too nervous to sit, I paced while I explained the anxiety attacks. I told her it was better if I could keep moving, so she paced with me. She made no comment about my obvious discomfort. What I didn't take into account at the time was that anyone, not just me, would be discomfited at a time like that.

It wasn't long before Mary showed up. "Howdy, Miz Whigan," Mary said upon entering the room. Then she looked my way and said, "Hi, Bobbie Jo. How're yew?"

I bit back the temptation to ask her why she bothered asking and merely returned her greeting and kept moving. "I'm fine, Mary, just fine."

The meeting was as horrible as I'd anticipated. Mary cried and cried, whereas, as was typical of me when extremely upset, I remained dry-eyed through the whole thing. Mainly I felt angry, but as the meeting and the crying wore on, the anger began to subside, leaving me torn and confused. Mary really loved Joanie, and I hated that my lack of emotional wellness was causing her such torment. Listening to her side of the story brought on feelings of guilt about wanting my own daughter back. The sense of triumph and fierce determination with which I'd gone into the meeting began to falter. The line between what was right and wrong became blurred. One of us was going to have her heart broken.

"Look here, Bobbie Jo," Mary sobbed. "I know we done some awful things to yew. We didn't play fair, and I'm sorry. Jes' don't take'er away from us. Yew cain't take care of 'er the way we kin, and we love 'er so much."

"I'm sorry, too, but don't you think your statement is a bit on the ignorant side? What about *my* love for her? What about her brothers and sister? Don't you think we love her too? And threatening to kill me? How dare you?"

Back and forth we went until finally Mrs. Whigan cleared her throat and took over. "This is not an uncommon thing happening here. My concern is not for either of you; it's for the child. I'm going to request a full investigation of both parties concerned, and this department will decide who will attain custody. Legally, the mother has all rights to the child; however, in light of the circumstances, there seems to be some question about the ability of the mother to assume responsibility for Joanie-Paula just yet. Mrs. Dickerson, I will be in touch by the end of the week to make an appointment to pay a visit to your home and see the child. Mrs. Elling, due to the fact that you live in another county, I'll have someone from Solano contact you for a home visit. We'll end this meeting now, and I'll be talking to both of you soon. I do suggest, Mrs. Dickerson, that you do not go around threatening people's lives, no matter how strongly you feel. We must go about these things in a legal manner for the good of all. Good day to you both."

After contacting Dr. Parkinson and Miss Callahan to let them know a Mrs. Whigan would be contacting them, there was nothing left for me to do but wait.

Late Thursday morning, the phone rang, and I answered it eagerly.

"Mrs. Elling?" a woman inquired.

"Yes, I'm Mrs. Elling."

"This is Mrs. Whigan. I'm afraid I have some bad news. I went to the Dickersons' home this morning, and, well, uh, they seem to be gone."

CHAPTER THIRTY-THREE

Kindness is the language which the deaf can hear and the blind can see.

—*Mark Twain*

"Gone? Gone!" I echoed stupidly. "What do you mean gone?"

"I mean they've moved." Mrs. Whigan spoke around an obvious clog in her throat. "I checked in with your grandmother, but she wouldn't tell me anything. She's not willing to cooperate with us at all. She merely said that Paula is safe and that you'll never hurt Bud."

"I don't believe it!" A combination of raging pain and disbelief hit my head and gut and shot lightning bolts of pain through both. "This can't be real. Why would Grandma want to hurt me so? Did you talk to Denny?"

She let out a long sigh. "I tried to. I sure tried to. He won't tell me anything, either. I even questioned the neighbors. But no one saw anything, and everyone seemed genuinely surprised that they were gone. And what a mess! No wonder they didn't want me to visit them."

Tensely, I asked, "What now? What can I do?"

The ensuing pause told me her answer wasn't going to be anything I wanted to hear. "I'm afraid that's the worst part. This isn't considered kidnapping. It's called child stealing, and it's done all too often. The legal implications are not quite the same. In other words, the FBI cannot, will not, be called, and legally your investigative powers are nil. In short, there isn't anything to do."

The sense of utter disbelief intensified. "You know when I was in Mexico, waiting for Joanie's father to return to his family home, I was warned constantly that someone there, some banditos, might steal my children and sell them. We got through that fine. And now, right here in the United States, my daughter has been stolen, and I've no legal right to stand on. I have family members who know where they took her, and you're telling me the law will not help me get her back?" My voice rose to a hysterical pitch.

"I'm afraid that's correct," she admitted. "I'm truly sorry. This is small consolation, but this department had decided in your favor. What we needed to do was have Joanie made a ward of the court and returned to your care."

My heart had been feeding on a steady diet of anger and resentment for a long time, and after this phone call, it swallowed another mouthful. I had a sudden urge to go through Joanie's baby book and then remembered—it was gone. It went with her when I went into the hospital, how many years ago? A million? I felt so old and tired it could have been that long. No baby, no book.

It was 1970. I was twenty-eight. Five years had passed since the nervous breakdown. My mother had moved to Iowa with Ray, whom she had married soon after my move to Fairfield. My occasional visits to see Grandma dismayed Miss Callahan to no end. She thought I was a glutton for punishment for having anything to do with any of my family. However, the hope that maybe one day Grandma would slip up and give away some clue of Joanie's whereabouts caused me to continue my visits. In addition, aside from my children, Grandma was a staple in my life and the only family I had left. I would forgive her for anything, because the kids and I needed her. I even had some understanding of why she did what she did. She wasn't against *me*; she was just *for* her son.

The helpless pain of losing Joanie was pushed down and hidden away with the scream while I carried through with the promise I'd made to myself to change my ways after the bout with hepatitis. A vocation-rehabilitation worker placed me in another job-training program, initially doing assembly work. He explained that the kind of work wasn't the important thing. The primary goal was to train people to get up and be at a certain place at a certain time, stay there, and be productive for a specified period of time. It was essential to learn how to deal with people in the workplace and how to regiment my life. My life needed structure, but I hated assembly work and stuck it out only because what he said made sense. Making it through a full day without an anxiety attack chasing me out the door made me proud and increased my confidence.

After a month of that, I was transferred into the office to do clerical work. That was more to my liking. I perceived myself as someone of importance, running here and there, typing this and copying that. The people there had varied backgrounds; some were heading back into the workplace after going through withdrawal from drugs or the excessive use of alcohol. Some, like me, suffered mental or emotional hindrances. The one problem we all shared was that we wanted employment but didn't know how to manage our lives well enough to get a job and keep it. We lacked any concept of our intrinsic value.

The training there did me a world of good. Within a few months, I felt prepared enough to apply for a *real* job. A small answering service took me on, and, boy, it was tough. Being tied to a switchboard on swing shift wasn't a great career choice for someone constantly battling tension. It was high pressure and hectic. With my headset plugged into the switchboard, my compulsion to walk off anxiety was severely hampered by the earpiece jammed into place. Whenever a bout of dizziness hit, I'd bounce my leg, wiggle my foot, or do whatever else I could do to ignore it, and I would press on with the business at hand. The upside of working swing was the time I had with the kids in the morning before they went to school and having a few hours to do housework before going to work in the afternoon. Garry watched them after school, and I'd be home for their bedtimes.

Unfortunately, this didn't last long.

Francis Daniels, the owner of the answering service, was not a well man. He had suffered a stroke a few years earlier and hadn't completely recovered. One side of his face and an arm were paralyzed. While undergoing therapy in the hospital, he met and married Helen, a paraplegic. Despite his health issues, Fran was a wonderful man, full of life and optimism. Whether he married Helen as one of his many rescue missions, I don't know, but as positive as he was about life, she was equally negative. She was depressed most of the time and had attempted suicide several times. Shortly after I began working there, business slowed, and Helen began another painful slide into depression. Fran was under a lot of pressure, and I hated to approach him for time off.

"Fran," I began, "I hate to do this to you, but I need a couple weeks of sick leave. I saw a podiatrist this morning, who tells me I have a tumor in my left foot that has to be removed. I can wait as long as it takes you to find a temporary replacement, but then it really needs to be taken care of. The pain has gotten so bad I can't sleep."

Fearing he would tell me not to bother coming back, I sat there, holding my breath. Since I hadn't been there very long, I didn't feel secure about my position.

Knowing about my anxiety problem, he asked me, "How do you feel about this surgery? Are you nervous?"

"Well, at first I was scared to death," I confided. "During the first few visits to Dr. Cedar, I couldn't even sit still for more than a few minutes before an attack of diarrhea demanded a trip to the bathroom. It was hard for him, because he'd just start examining me and I'd have to run. The thing is, though—and this is different—he never makes fun of me. He's so nice to me and never gets impatient. His attitude makes me want to please him by being the best patient he's ever had.

"He says he doesn't understand my extreme fear but that it must be real, so he accepts it and looks for ways to deal with it. So, yeah, I'm scared and nervous, but I believe in this doctor. He knows that I'm not the tumor and I don't live in that foot. He claims he'll treat the fear first, which *is* me, and the tumor last. No one has ever talked to me like that before. It's a humbling experience. I'm so grateful for his attitude that I'd lay down my life for this man."

We laughed, and then I thought of a question. "Do you ever go through this with your disability? I mean, when people accept you just the way you are, do you find yourself feeling grateful?"

He laughed again. "I know what you mean, but more than anything else, I appreciate their good sense. Yes, it pleases me when people look past my drooping face and flopping arm to get in touch with the whole, intelligent human being I still am. I'm glad you've found such a doctor for your special needs. It takes a wise man to accept without understanding. That's important, isn't it?"

"Sure is," I replied emphatically. "That's a big part of my problem—the fear of not being accepted—and yet I can't explain to people what I don't understand myself. Uh, Fran, there's something else I'd like to know. Can I come back after the surgery? Will you be able to hold my place for me?"

"I'll make every effort to do just that," he assured me. "You just be a good girl for this doctor and get that foot taken care of."

Apprehension nagged at me when I left work that day, partly because of the surgery I faced and partly because of something I couldn't name.

Three mornings later, not so bright but very early, I reported in to Dr. Cedar. The Valium I'd taken to fortify myself calmed me enough to show up. My colon had already begun its rebellion against the tension it was fighting to absorb, and I was concerned about the predictable attacks of diarrhea I knew would follow.

"Well, you *did* come!" Dr. Cedar greeted me "We were going to start a pool and take bets on whether you would or not. Come on in, and meet the doctor assisting me today."

He didn't usually have an assistant, but when I had expressed anxiety of another hospital stay, he had agreed to do the surgery in his office, where I'd feel more comfortable. To do this, California State law required him to have another surgeon on hand.

Cautiously entering the room where the surgery was going to take place, I looked at the two of them amusedly. They were total opposites; Dr. Cedar's sandy-blond hair, blue eyes, and stocky build contrasted sharply with Dr. De Anza's blue-black hair, dark eyes, and slim frame. They both grinned at me broadly as Dr. Cedar declared, "Meet my partner in crime, Dr. De Anza. While I do all the work, he's going to tell you Italian jokes to keep your mind off what I'm doing."

The entire medical profession should be made up of doctors and dentists like those two. They dispensed humor, kindness, acceptance, and much more than medical treatment. They gave the impression that the only reason for their existence at that moment was to make me feel relaxed. Fear didn't stand a chance against all that caring.

After sterilizing my foot, they had to wait several times while I made my sojourns to the bathroom. Instead of getting angry with me for making them wait so many times, they remained cheerful and accommodating. Finally the Demerol they had injected began to take effect, and the tension eased up. They propped me up, per another of my requests. Lying down furthered my feeling of helplessness. A white sheet draped in front of me prevented me from seeing what they did with my foot.

After an injection of Novocain, the operation began. A pillow to hug, a transistor radio, and Dr. De Anza's jokes helped distract me. Once the tumor was removed, they proclaimed I was the best patient they'd ever had. After all I had put them through, that pronouncement struck me as funnier than Dr. De Anza's jokes. They were full of praise, and I was equally full of gratitude.

"So, that's it for you, young lady." Dr. Cedar removed the white sheet with a flourish. "Behold! The latest thing in fashionable footwear...one foot of gauze wrapping, pun intended. All that's left for you to do is to stay off that foot as much as possible for a few weeks to let the incision heal."

My body went limp with relief. "I'll never be able to thank you two enough," I gushed. "Because of your patience and kindness, not to mention the iffy humor, I just got through something I never thought I'd be able to. More importantly, I did it without being humiliated because of my stupid fear."

"Aw, shucks, it weren't nothin', ma'am. I'll send the neuroma to the lab for testing, but I'm pretty sure it's benign. So see you in a week, and we'll get those stitches out."

With my lips fixed in a giddy grin and my foot amply bandaged, I floated out of Dr. Cedar's office on an emotional high to return home. Shortly after I got home and reclined on the sofa, the grin was wiped from my face when Sandy, a coworker at the answering service, came to the door.

"Hi, kid," she said. "How's it going?"

"Sandy, what a nice surprise! You're so sweet to come see me." It was always a treat to see her pixie-like face. Her dark-red hair was even cut in a pixie style, and her green eyes always sparkled with a feisty twinkle, which made you wonder what mischief she was up to.

"Well, I meant to come by anyway, and this morning just moved my visit up a little." She kept looking at the floor and taking big sighs between words. She sounded exhausted, which wasn't surprising since she had an active two-year-old son and a baby girl just a few months old.

"Sandy? Is something wrong?"

"Oh, Bobbie, I'm sorry. I'm just so upset." Tears washed the twinkle from her eyes, and her face crumpled. "Fran was found dead in his chair this morning. He had another stroke sometime in the middle of the night and just *died*."

"No! Oh, no, no! What's going to become of Helen? Who's going to take over the business?" Tears of shock and sorrow streamed down both our faces.

"I don't know." She sniffled. "I don't think Helen is in any condition to run it. I'm really worried about her. Fran was the only thing that kept her going. I don't know yet what will happen."

In frustration, I declared, "I feel like it's partly my fault; he was running short handed because of me taking time off. Maybe he was trying to cover a shift alone, and it was just too much for him."

"Oh, stop it," Sandy snapped sharply. "It wasn't anybody's fault, especially yours. These things happen, in case you haven't noticed."

Duly humbled, I asked, "Do you know of anything I can do?"

"Not at the moment. Besides, you're supposed to stay off your foot for two weeks, right? I'll let you know about any new schedule. I'll tell Helen you want to come back as soon as possible, OK?"

"OK, and please give her my love."

But my love or anybody else's was not what Helen wanted. She wanted to die, and die she did, the next week. Sandy found her dead from an overdose of medication, ironically prescribed to treat depression. Life was hard for her before Fran died and unthinkable after.

The concept of not having them in my life was nearly impossible to accept. They would be missed terribly, as they had become like extended family to me and the kids. Their absence left a gaping hole in our lives.

The business, which was attached to their home financially as well as structurally, was sold with the house. There was no job to return to, and I had little desire to find a new one. That wind had been taken out of my sails just in time for a different gust to blow into my life.

CHAPTER THIRTY-FOUR

To know yourself as the being underneath the thinker, the stillness underneath the mental noise, the love and joy underneath the pain, is freedom, salvation, enlightenment.

—Eckhart Tolle

That wind was called Fat Cat. I'd originally met him while working as a barmaid at a combination nightclub and poolroom. He was a real-life pool shark and tended bar at a club across the street.

Fat Cat worked when he wanted to, and the rest of the time, he lived off his considerable pool-shooting talents and quick wit. He lived with, and off of, several different women. He was a heavily built man, weighing close to three hundred pounds, hence his name. As charming as he was fat, he had a cherubic face, sandy-blond hair cut like a little boy's, and blue eyes that sparkled with mischief. Men envied his prowess with women and gambling. Women enjoyed the way he made them feel special. He had an indefinable something that attracted women, even though they knew he wasn't dependable or looking for a commitment to any-one or thing. He defined the term "free spirit."

He had come in and out of my life several times, and I won-dered what brought him into it again.

"Hey, Twig," he hollered, calling me by the nickname I'd been stuck with since the rise in popularity of the extremely thin British model. "I heard you were laid up and thought I'd come by to see you. Boy, are you a mess."

There I was, in an orthopedic tennis shoe, my foot still swathed in bandages and my eyes so bloodshot from crying about Fran and Helen that it looked like I might bleed to death if I shed another tear.

"Thanks," I muttered. "Your generous appraisal is much appre-ciated. What's up with you?"

"Oh, nothing much. I'm just back from Reno. Talked to Sandy's husband, and he told me what happened. I'm really sorry."

"Thanks again."

Further conversation paused as he looked around the living room. When the carpet fell under his surveillance, he burst out laughing. That carpet was the joke of our family: indoor-outdoor synthetic material, multistriped in every color of the rainbow—that is, if the rainbow was made up of dark, drab garish hues.

"I'm sorry. I really am," he choked out as his large belly shook with hilarity. "I don't mean to make fun of your carpet, but I've never seen anything quite like it in a living room before."

"Laugh on, jerk." I giggled. His amusement was contagious. "It may be ugly, but it matches everything and nothing at the same time. I rather appreciate that it doesn't clash with the renter-white paint on the walls. It really blends well with the rest of the green, Early Ugly American decor."

He threw up his hands in mock surrender and grinned imp-ishly. "So wanna go dancing?"

"I think I'll pass," I said, laughing. "Maybe in a couple of weeks...if by then, you even remember you asked."

"All kidding aside," he offered soberly, "I am sorry. I know you must be feeling crummy. How 'bout a drive instead? We'll pretend we're on a date."

"OK, I can go for a couple of hours before the kids get home from school, but why 'pretend'?"

"Because you're really not my type."

That date lasted five years. There's no specific date or time that Fat Cat moved in with us. He just sort of eased into our lives and stayed. How or when exactly I came to love him, I don't recall, but that happened, too. His own strong feelings for me both alarmed and surprised him. Sharing the lives of three kids and a skinny half-child, half-woman was hard for him; taking over those lives was easy.

"Therapy!" he exclaimed one day as I was heading out the door to see Miss Callahan. "You don't need therapy. You just need someone to take care of you. You're just insecure; that's all. It shouldn't surprise you that life has scared the hell out of you. If I'd led your life, I'd be insecure, too. This therapy stuff is just junk, a way to make money."

"Look," I argued. "She got me out my front door. That's all I know and all I care about. She's been a good friend."

"Oh? And how's that?" he retorted mockingly. "Friends exchange information about each other. They don't just sit and ask about your life. Friendship is sharing, not just probing into someone's childhood. How much do you know about *her*?"

"You just don't understand," I replied defensively and charged out the door.

Driving to my appointment, I fretted over what he'd said and asked myself what really had happened over the past few years in therapy.

As usual, I had more questions than answers, and I suddenly felt a need to evaluate my therapy sessions.

What had I learned in five years? What messages had I gotten from all this counseling? Was I getting better? Worse? Same? Five years! That was a long time to go for appointments and talk about my mother and family. Five years was a long time to rehash, over and over, all the unkind things done to me by various people, a long time to go over and over things I'd done for which I lugged guilt around. And, no, I didn't know anything about Miss Callahan. We had advanced to the point of me calling her Barbara, but what else was new? I still had to gobble down fifty or more milligrams of Valium to get through a day without a panic attack.

For five years, I'd had my questions answered with *her* questions. That type of therapy was what the psychiatric professionals believed would help patients analyze themselves and their problems. They didn't give direct answers. They made you guess and then agreed with whatever it was you came up with as a possibility.

An example of a typical session would be the following:

Miss Callahan: What scares you?

Me: Being scared.

Miss Callahan: Why does being scared scare you?

Me: Being scared puts you in a hospital and takes your children.

Miss Callahan: Where do you feel scared?

Me: Anywhere I can't control the fear: stores, banks, most public places, doctors, dentists, and, well, anyplace I don't feel I belong.

Miss Callahan: Where do you not belong?

Me: Around good or normal people, in confining places or situations.

Miss Callahan: What is it about a store that scares you?

Me: Nothing. I mean, I know there's nothing there that will hurt me. I'm not stupid! But I get panicky and have to leave.

Miss Callahan: What's wrong with leaving? Isn't it all right for you to leave? Can't you look at the door and tell yourself that if you have to leave, you're still OK as a person?

Me: There's a lot wrong with leaving. In the first place, how am I ever going to get any shopping done if I can't stay in the dumb store? In the second place, no, I can't convince myself that I'm an OK person if I leave. People should be able to go shopping.

Miss Callahan: What scares you about the dentist?

Me: Nothing. I'm not afraid of the needle or the drilling or the scraping. I'm telling you the fear just attacks me. I'm the victim, and it's the assailant, but it's only at certain places. It knows where and how to get me.

And so on and so on. In the past five years, being able to talk to someone who wouldn't ridicule or shame me had made life easier for me, but I still wasn't totally functional. For a while, I'd be anxiety-free, and suddenly, without warning, I'd be just as bad off as ever. It was frustrating.

By the time I arrived at the clinic, I had decided that Fat Cat was right. That Miss Callahan cared was great, but was caring enough? In the time I'd been seeing her, fashion and hairstyles had changed at least ten times, but there didn't seem to be much change in me, other than becoming self-centered and overly defensive in order to protect myself.

"Hi, Bobbie." She smiled as I entered her office. "Have a seat. I'll be right back. I have something to show you."

Curious, I took my usual chair in her office and waited. She returned, looking like the proverbial cat after eating that canary.

"Ta-da!" she announced while waving a newspaper in my face. "You've wanted a name for what you suffer, and the psychiatric community, in its wisdom and research, has decided to give you one. I hope it makes you feel better."

As I accepted the newspaper she offered, my eyes fell upon the word "agoraphobia" in bold type. I said, "This does make me feel better and more hopeful. If what I experience has a name, then surely it has a cure. Great! Now what?"

The illustrious expert on the subject who had written the article for the medical section of the newspaper claimed there were hundreds of people in the United States suffering from agoraphobia. Wonderful news! I wasn't alone, but where were they? *Who* were they? I hadn't met any of them. I wanted to run to the window, throw it open, and yell, "OK, out there. Show yourselves. I demand that all you other people with agoraphobia come out in the open right now!"

Agoraphobia, according to the article, was translated from the Greek as "fear of the marketplace." That was the original definition, but it had been broadened to mean fear of open or unfamiliar places.

So now the illness itself was known, but the causes and cures were still evasive. The important thing to me was that while I was still sick, I wasn't crazy. Now if I expressed fear or anxiety anywhere, I could glibly look people in the eye and say, "Oh, I'm OK. I just have agoraphobia."

That was what I *thought*, but I was wrong. The first time I said it to a checker at a grocery store while attempting to leave without causing a fuss, her response was something like, "Agoraphobia? What's that? New kitty litter? Try aisle *B*, section two."

Merely having a label for the illness wasn't effective for me without public awareness, and that just didn't exist yet.

When I got home from my appointment, I told Fat Cat about the title.

"So what's it mean?" he asked, arms folded across his chest.

His challenging posture caused me to stammer. "Well, it means…it means…I feel safe at home but not anywhere else."

"You've known that for five years!" he exploded. "See what I mean? What good is all this counseling doing? You have a problem. Solve it."

"Just like that?" I snapped my fingers angrily.

He grabbed me and gently shook me. "Yes! Just like that. You have a life to live. Live it." He pulled me to him and held me close. "I know how frightened you get. I've seen you have an anxiety attack. But I'll help you. You just need someone to help you, to go places with you. You'll see; you'll be fine. You just put yourself in ol' Fat Cat's hands. I love you, Barbara Jo. I'd never let anything or anyone hurt you."

CHAPTER THIRTY-FIVE

*Change, like sunshine, can be a friend or a foe, a blessing
or a curse, a dawn or a dusk.*

—*William Arthur Ward*

Putting myself in Fat Cat's hands meant becoming his own private little Barbie doll. When he wanted to play and show off his new toy, fine, and when he didn't, he would go to the store for a loaf of bread or whatever and come back three days later. Sometimes he was gone longer, but he'd always come back with what he had originally gone out for. Life with him was crazy and unpredictable but one that suited me. Convinced as I was that I'd never have a normal life, this erratic relationship was fine with me.

When he *was* around, we seemed to be the perfect couple in a perfect relationship, with no strings attached. Once more, I was just drifting through life with no ambition, and he was the original good-time Charlie. For the most part, he was very attentive to the children and me. But, as with any other toy, when he didn't want to play with me, he put me in the dollhouse, and I stayed there until he wanted to play again.

My therapy sessions with Miss Callahan came to an end when at our last session I asked her, "By the way, how old are you?"

Her response disappointed me. "Why do you ask?"

Two can play this game, I thought and pressed on. "Does it bother you that I want to know something about *you?* I just wonder; that's all."

"Are you trying to identify with me?" she hedged. "Do you think maybe we're the same age and want to compare lives?"

Tears welled up in my eyes as I realized that, at least in part, Fat Cat was right. She had done so much for me, but we couldn't ever be real friends. We were cultures and worlds apart. Our entire relationship was based on my needs and subsequent gratitude once she helped those needs be met.

One incident that stood out in my mind was the time Dr. Parkinson ordered a series of blood tests for me; when I went to have them done, I couldn't face doing it alone. I wrote a note and put it in the mail slot of the laboratory door. The letter stated that I was too frightened and apologized for my cowardice. A few days later, Miss Callahan went back with me. When the phlebotomist approached me, my arms reflexively drew in to my sides, out of his reach.

After several repetitions of this, he got angry and demanded, "Will you stop acting like a baby? Let's just get this over with. What's the big deal anyway?"

Miss Callahan threw her arms around me protectively and sternly told him, "You know it's people like you who create people like her. Your attitude keeps psychiatry flourishing. Now send someone else in here to do the tests."

What a comfort she was. The message she gave me of "You're OK; the rest of the world stinks" may not have been ideal, but she did make me feel better about myself. She allowed me to stop taking the rap for everything and to consider that some of my problems were not self-inflicted wounds.

But it had been many years and many appointments. What else was there to say? I decided to give life with Fat Cat a chance without the safety net of therapy. Possibly I was a little embarrassed about living with him and feared her disapproval and judgment.

We moved out of the house with the carpet of many colors and into a newly built apartment complex. We were the first occupants in our apartment, and I reveled in the fresh wood smell of the kitchen, the new rust-colored carpet, and the two bathrooms with sparkling-clean tub-and-shower combinations. We filled the place with brand-new furniture. Since there were four bedrooms, the kids each had their own room for the first time in their lives. The boys were the proud recipients of maple bunk beds, while Binky's new frilly habitat received a white-and-gold four-poster bed and matching dresser.

The boys teased Binky about the dark-pink ruffled bedspread and coordinating sheer curtains in her room. They said it looked like a bottle of Pepto-Bismol had blown up in there. Fat Cat and I chose a Hollywood-style king-sized bed in black walnut with, of course, matching nightstands. For the first time in the kids' and my life, all our living-room furniture matched. We had a sofa and side chair in avocado green, with a dark-gold floral design woven in; an avocado-green recliner; and dark-cherry coffee and end tables. Walking in our front door filled me with delight, and housework became house joy.

Fat Cat still worked as a bartender when he worked at all, so he was with me during the day while the kids were in school. At night he was gone, which left me quality time with the kids. During the day, Fat Cat and I would go grocery shopping, and twice a week he accompanied me to a hairdresser. In the morning, he would take me in to have my hair washed and set, and because I couldn't stand the thought of being trapped under a hair dryer, he arranged with the beautician for me to wear the curlers out of the shop. He'd take me back in the afternoon to have my hair combed out. With him at my side, I did wonderfully normal things—things that everyone else did—but in an unusual fashion. Not every woman took her husband or boyfriend absolutely everywhere with her.

In the evening, while Fat Cat was at work, the kids and I watched TV, talked, and just hung out together. Happiness and a sense of satisfaction were mine to claim. For the first time in twelve years, I saw a movie in a theater. If I became anxious and needed to leave a place, it was fine with him. He didn't chide or scold me. To show my appreciation for him, I tried doing things with him that I wouldn't have for anyone else. We went to Disneyland, the horse races, nice restaurants in San Francisco, and camping, all with me feeling comfortable because of his laid-back attitude and ability to humor me away from feelings of fear or panic. Having an encouraging guardian and cheerleader did wonders for me.

The only flaw in our otherwise-idyllic life was Fat Cat's kidney disease. A flare-up of acute nephritis brought on horrible abdominal pain, high blood pressure, and vomiting, which understandably caused him to be cranky. He would become a completely different person—verbally abusive and frightening. He would yell at the kids to the point where I was afraid it would cause a rift between them and me, because I was the one responsible for his being in our lives. While we all cared deeply for Fat Cat and were grateful for all the good things he brought to our lives, the angry eruptions created an atmosphere of tension and uneasiness.

Once again, I became tired of being a child. Something in me wanted to grow—to experience independence. I'd made failure comfortable, but it was still failure. I needed to know that I could function in the world by myself, if need be. My children were growing up, while I remained a child. Sometimes I wondered who was raising whom. I also worried about the example I was living out in front of the kids. A possible solution to that came to me one day as I sat thinking about it.

"Church," I announced to Fat Cat. "That would be good for the kids. I need to take them to church."

Hauling out the phone book, I browsed through the yellow pages to find possible churches. For a small town, there was a surprisingly large number of them, which left me wondering which one was best for us.

My fingers walked through the pages and stopped at an address close to our home. *Now what? I guess I'll just call and see what happens.*

Having no idea what to say when someone answered, I hung in there and waited while the phone rang several times.

"Good afternoon. Fairfield Presbyterian Church," came a soft voice. "This is Sheri Witt. May I help you?"

"Uh, sure, hi," I stammered nervously. "I, uh, I don't know where to start. Uh, I have three kids, ages fifteen, fourteen, and twelve. Do you have any good things going on at your church for this age group?"

"Yes," Sheri Witt replied enthusiastically. "We have a wonderful youth group for just those ages. They have a lot of activities they enjoy while learning more about the Lord."

Something in me cringed at the words "the Lord." For some unexplainable reason, my face grew hot and flushed, which made me uncomfortable.

"Well, we don't have a regular church," I told her. "But my kids have always enjoyed any Vacation Bible School they've gone to, and I just thought that, what with them becoming teenagers and all, maybe they should be going to church regularly. I'd like them to know some good kids to hang around with."

"We would certainly love meeting you and your children," she said brightly. "We have two morning services every Sunday and a Sunday school between those two services."

After she told me the times of the services, a question I hadn't intended to ask popped out of my mouth. "Are there a lot of doors in your church building?"

"As a matter of fact, there are," she replied.

"This is embarrassing, but I've got a problem. I can't stand being confined, and it would help if there were lots of exits available if I needed to get out."

"Tell you what," she offered. "You'd probably be more comfortable at the later service. My husband, Pastor Witt, conducts this service mainly for people who want a more relaxed worship atmosphere. It's very low key and unstructured. It's also less crowded, so you might feel more at ease getting up to leave if you wanted. How does that sound?"

At the word "worship," the hot flushing and uneasiness returned. "It sounds OK. Mind you, I'm not even sure I'll come, but if I do, I just wanted to know."

After thanking her, I hung up and marched to the front door and called the kids in from outside. They rushed in, out of breath and curious.

"Guess where *you're* going Sunday?" I challenged.

"Camping? Whoopee!" yelled Ricky.

The other two guessed Marine World.

"Wro-ong," I singsonged and laughed. "You guys are going to church."

Their faces fell.

"Church?" Ricky snorted. "That's for sissies."

"Church?" Butch groaned. "Why do we have to do that?"

Binky just looked back and forth between them and didn't say anything.

"Yes, church," I said firmly. "It'll be good for you. You'll meet some nice kids your own age, and they have a youth group that does things you might like. I'm not sure if they go to Marine World, but maybe they go camping. You need to meet some nice friends."

"Then why aren't you going?" Ricky demanded. "You could use some nice friends, too."

Butch agreed that he didn't want to go among a bunch of strangers if I didn't go. Binky expressed the same sentiment. *Cornered!*

"Look," I placated. "You guys know it's different with me. I can't go."

They didn't let up. They argued, pleaded, and then threatened that they wouldn't go if I didn't. So when Fat Cat got home, I asked him if he would go with me. He agreed to go but couldn't understand this sudden, strong desire; neither did I.

Sunday morning, eleven o'clock, there we were, sitting together in comfy, dark-blue seats that formed a half circle facing the gleaming, light-oak pulpit. The pulpit stood directly under a huge cross that looked like it had been carved from the same log. Burgundy robes swished as the pianist hit a chord, signaling the choir to stand. They sang a beautiful rendition of a song I'd heard as a child but couldn't recall the name of. More swishing swirled in the air as they finished the hymn and resumed their seats on stage. An attractive man in a black cassock placed himself behind the pulpit and greeted the congregation. The hair he had left was black, and his piercing eyes matched. In sharp contrast, his smile was wide, white, and bright.

The light and beauty and comfortable seats didn't ease my self-consciousness and feeling that everyone there knew what a bad person I was. I'd made a terrible mistake, and vowed I'd never come back.

But then as I sat listening to Pastor Witt speak, something in me started loving it and hanging on every word he said. At the end of his sermon, he apologized to the congregation for running over his allotted time. He could have gone on further as far as I was concerned.

Over the next few weeks, the kids made friends there, and after reading about all the activities the youth group enjoyed, they eagerly joined in. In all that time, I hadn't filled out a visitor card or introduced myself to anyone. When I finally did relinquish my anonymity by filling one out, it was received by Pastor Witt as an invitation to visit our home. He and a delightful young woman named Charlotte called on us. Pastor was a wonderfully soft-spoken man, and Charlotte, a young, pretty, blond woman, was easygoing and warm without gushing. She made me feel her equal, which was normally no easy task.

We sat making small talk for some time before I thought, *Might as well get the worst over with*, since obviously their visit was to get to know me.

"The thing is, you see—well, I don't want to lie or mislead you. I'm living with a man I'm not married to. I don't know if you want me in your church or not. I guess I really don't belong there. All the people are so nice and good; I'm not. You wouldn't believe some of the things I've done. I've led a terrible life. I just want things to be better for my kids. I want *them* to go to your church. Is that OK?"

CHAPTER THIRTY-SIX

*Going to church doesn't make you a Christian any more
than going to a garage makes you an automobile.*

—Billy Sunday

Pastor Witt and Charlotte exchanged knowing smiles, smiles that said, "Here we go again," or "How many times have you heard this one?"

"Barbara," Pastor Witt began, "do you realize that Jesus died for you? He didn't die for 'good people'; he died to save us all. Our church, or any other church, isn't a rest home for saints; it's a hospital for sinners, and our sinful natures should be getting cured there. Have you ever asked Jesus to come into your heart and serve as your savior?"

"Oh, I seem to remember," I said, "that as a kid, when I went to church with Grandma, I did. But that was so long ago, and so much has happened since then—I mean, I expect God really loves little kids, but now that I've grown up and I am what I am, I have a hard time believing that I'm all that lovable to him."

Charlotte reached over and patted my knee while the pastor scooted his chair a little closer and looked intently into my eyes.

"If there was no sin in the world," he reasoned, "there'd have been no reason for God to send his son to save us, wouldn't you agree? But since Adam and Eve, there has been, and still is, sin in the world. He tried other methods of saving us so that we could make it into heaven to be with him, but when they all failed, he sent his son as a sacrifice to assume the burden of our sins. That makes it possible for us to be forgiven. Jesus has already paid for your sins. All you have to do is accept his sacrifice and claim him as your savior, and you'll be forgiven and saved."

Fat Cat came home about that time and joined us in the living room. The pastor turned his attention to him.

"We've just been talking about the forgiveness and salvation made possible by Jesus's death on the cross for us," he told Fat Cat, "and I'd like to ask you as well as Barbara, have you ever experienced a personal relationship with the Lord?"

Fat Cat squirmed in his seat and cleared his throat; he was obviously made uncomfortable by these unexpected questions.

"No, I can't say that I have," he admitted. "I believe that we all have our own God to worship."

Pastor Witt laughed. "That's a familiar statement. Would you be open to some Bible study that would challenge that belief and maybe change your mind? Would you be open to learning the truth?"

Fat Cat hedged. "I don't have a lot of time for such things. I'm pretty busy."

Pastor turned back to me. "What about you? As a child, what made you believe that God existed?"

It was my turn to squirm and blush. "You'll think I'm silly, but I could swear I felt him, felt something I can't explain. I believe he even healed me once. My Sunday-school teacher had promised little-bitty Bibles with gold edges on the pages if we attended Sunday school every Sunday until Easter. I wanted one so badly.

They were so beautiful, and I loved books of any kind. My grandpa took Grandma and me to church every Sunday, but he'd never go in himself. Grandma used to say she was going to have to pray him into heaven by the back door.

"Anyway, one Sunday I was sick with the mumps and had a horrible, ugly fever blister on my bottom lip. Grandma said I couldn't go to church looking like that, and I cried and cried. Grandpa finally said I could go and sit in the car with him. He told Grandma to tell my teacher that 'By God, she's here, and she's leavin' with one of them books.' They wrapped me up in blankets, and off we went.

"When we got there, the preacher, Brother Bacon, saw me in the car and asked why I wasn't coming in. Grandma told him I was sick and shouldn't go inside. He said that sick children were God's special favorites. He came out to the car and carried me into the church house. He asked the congregation if anyone wanted to lay their hands on me to pray for healing. Boy, I've never had so many people touching me at one time. They prayed for the longest time and—well, all I can tell you is that by that afternoon, I had no trace of that fever blister or the mumps.

"I was running around the house, bellowing, 'Yes, Jesus loves me!' at the top of my lungs. I couldn't explain it, but I got that Bible. Grandma was amazed. I was a real celebrity to her for a good, long while. Relatives and people visiting from the church said they couldn't figure it out, but God must have had his hand on me. My aunts and uncles said they didn't understand why God would bother with me."

Chuckling, I added, "They sure didn't see anything special in me. Anyway, that's why I believed in him then."

While relating this story, I had been unable to look at anything but the floor; I longed to be that little girl again, so sure God had his hand on her. My eyes stung, and I wanted to be alone to have a good cry. When I did look up, I saw that Pastor Witt had started that good cry without me. Embarrassment flooded me.

"I'm sorry. I didn't mean to upset you."

Pastor Witt sniffed. "I'm not crying because I'm upset. I'm crying because that was such a touching story and because I believe, too, that God did heal you and had his hand on you. Don't you think he still loves you? Wouldn't you like to feel the peace and sureness you did then?"

Suddenly Fat Cat slammed his fists on the arms of his chair. "Wait a minute; just wait a minute. What's going on here? What are you trying to do?"

The pastor looked flabbergasted and surprised, as though he'd forgotten Fat Cat was even there. Charlotte had been looking at her hands in her lap, but her head snapped up at this outburst. My hand flew to my mouth in shock, and I started to protest. But the pastor held his hand out to stop me.

"I'm sorry," he apologized, a look of concern on his face. "Why is this conversation so upsetting to you?"

Fat Cat stood up and shouted, "Because if he gets her, I lose her. Ever since we've started going to church, she's been different. Her head is in the clouds most of the time when we leave there. I just don't like it. I'll lose her!"

Recovering from his obvious confusion, the pastor asked, "Then why don't you follow her?"

With that, Fat Cat, with no reply, stomped from the room.

It was my turn to be confused, and indeed I couldn't sort out all the strange emotions rushing around inside. My head started to pound, and my skin felt clammy.

"Well, Barbara," the pastor continued. "What do you think? Won't you invite Jesus Christ to come into your heart to live?"

"I don't know how," I confessed. "If I do, would I have to give up all the friends I have now?"

"No, you wouldn't," he assured, "but I suspect you'll choose to after a time of spiritual growth. Change takes place gradually, until suddenly you find you make different choices for your life as you walk with the Lord. As far as how you do it, I will simply ask you again. Barbara, do you accept Jesus Christ into your heart to be your Lord and Savior?"

As if preparing to dive off a cliff into deep, choppy waters, I clasped my hands together and took a deep breath. "Yes. I do."

Tears, the nature of which I'd never experienced before, streamed down my face; they were healing, cleansing tears that washed the grit and grime of despair out of me and filled in the blanks they left with peace. No sobbing, no hysterics—just a flow of ease and calm.

"Father, we thank you for Barbara. We thank you that she has accepted your forgiveness and claimed salvation through the blood of your son, Jesus. Amen." The pastor then turned to me and said, "There is rejoicing in heaven for you right now."

"How are you feeling?" Charlotte asked, dabbing at her eyes with a tissue.

"I feel the way I did when I labored to give birth to my children. The pressure and pain seemed to come from everywhere and were so intense that the rest of the world was lost. There were only the contractions and me. As soon as my body released the baby, I felt absolutely and totally pain-free and emptied. I thought I'd float right off the delivery table. That's how I feel now—light, emptied, like I've just given birth." Softly, I giggled. "Is that why you call it being born again?"

They laughed with me and agreed I had a good point.

"Let's join hands and pray," the pastor directed. "Lord, we thank you again for Barbara. We thank you for your love for her. We thank you for the peace you have just granted her through your grace. We ask that you burden all of us with the task of helping her grow in your love. We ask that you be with her to sustain her through the times ahead. Father, I pray that this woman will grow to be a strong witness for you. I pray she will have the courage to share her conversion with others and to be an encouragement to them. We thank you for your son and the meaning his death on the cross gives to all of us. In his precious name, amen."

Imagine someone thanking God for me! The thought nearly had me floating.

The pastor stood, beaming. "Welcome to the family of God. We have to be going now, but we'll see you Sunday, right?"

"You bet." I giggled. "And *every* Sunday, whether you give me a miniature Bible or not."

The three of us embraced, and they left. The thought of dealing with Fat Cat didn't overly bother me. A shield seemed to surround me that unhappiness and worry couldn't penetrate. Going to bed, I had a warm glow in my heart.

How 'bout that? Jesus has already moved in and has started a cozy fire going. I guess he's making my heart a homey, more pleasant place to live. Hopefully that fire will spread to the rest of my life.

CHAPTER THIRTY-SEVEN

I am an employment hyena. I am happy to make a meal of what the lions leave behind.

—*Henry Rollins*

In my quest to live a lifestyle I thought would be more to God's liking, I made the common mistake of changing the externals in my life rather than the internals. In other words, instead of putting forth any effort to change me, I changed the things around me. One of those things was my relationship with Fat Cat. When I asked him to move out, he was furious but not all that surprised, given that he had predicted it. My haphazard life with him wasn't something I thought God would be happy about. My motive was well intentioned, but banishing Fat Cat so abruptly was unkind. The change in me wasn't his fault.

My Christian infancy was wonderful. There was something so ethereal about it. The rest of the world, with all its problems, seemed distant, as though God had put me in a protective bubble.

The bubble burst, though, when it came time for me to grow. While working around the apartment, I'd sing "What a Friend We Have in Jesus," but I didn't behave like much of a friend. Establishing relationships with friends meant spending time with them—learning about them. Neither of these things did I do.

My conversion experience was like having gifts under a Christmas tree. The gifts of mercy and grace had been given to me. They were mine, but they remained unopened and unused. The Bible studies I attended were made up of married women with whom I had nothing in common, so I stopped attending. Admittedly, most of my desire to get to know about the Lord was to find out what he could do for me. Prayerfully, I challenged him to heal my phobic problems, find me a husband, and bring Joanie back. He promised in his word that he would never leave or fail me, but since I wasn't supplying the fuel of sincere worship, that cozy little fire in my heart died down to ashes. Living a middle-of-the-road Christian life was neither satisfying nor effective. Consequently, I ceased feeling the glow of his constant presence.

In the meantime, the welfare laws changed, and the new laws required mothers whose children were in school to find jobs or enroll in a job-training program. No longer could I hide behind my emotional illness and collect welfare. In a panic, I ran to Miss Callahan.

"I want you to write a letter to the welfare department," I urged her. "Tell them I can't work."

"But, Barbara, you can work," she responded. "You know you can. You've gotten jobs before; why are you so concerned about it now?"

"Because when I got those jobs, it was because I *wanted* to, not because I *had* to. This is different; this is life or death. What if I fail? What if I have an anxiety attack and get fired? It didn't matter as much before because I knew I had welfare to fall back on. I won't have that safety net now. It's too scary. Please, write and tell them I may not be able to do this."

"I'm sorry," she replied. "I can't tell them that. Look, you don't want to have something like that as a recorded fact somewhere. Think ahead. Someday that could be harmful. You never know what turns your life may take that a document like that might affect. I can discuss this with your social worker, but that's the most I can do."

As it turned out, my social worker assured me that the main thing the welfare department wanted to see was effort on the parts of welfare recipients to better their lives and be self-supporting. She assured me that if at any time I was unemployed, I would still have them to fall back on, but nothing would go in my file with them even hinting that I was emotionally unable to work. Her reassurance sent me once again on a quest for gainful employment.

A property-management corporation hired me to sell home-maintenance insurance. This was good for me therapeutically, because it promoted a greater sense of ease with people; however, it paid solely on commission, which promoted financial insecurity.

A position as mail girl for Gensler Lee Diamonds, a retail jewelry chain, seemed a better option for me, so I applied and was hired. Wilma, one of the supervisors who hired me, shrugged off my confessed concern about my lack of experience. She said they hired according to personality and believed mine was ideal. She was confident that anyone could be trained to do the mailing portion of the job. In my opinion, this was a legitimate job because of the size and stellar reputation of the company. After all, they even had radio ads, complete with a catchy jingle.

With my low self-image, I was constantly amazed that everyone, from the president on down to my coworkers and supervisors, seemed to really like me. I certainly liked them and loved walking through that swinging glass door each morning. Filled with a sense of importance, I'd walk across the plush gray carpet that lay between cases of sparkling jewels to take my place behind the sales and credit-application counter.

They praised me often for the way I did my job. And whereas once upon a time, I had spilled my guts to anyone who would listen, Fat Cat had reprogrammed me to believe that surrounding myself with a little mystery was a good thing, so I reverted back to rarely divulging anything about myself. The people at Gensler Lee knew nothing about my background or phobic problems. If I did experience some dizziness or anxiety, I would say I had a touch of the flu or that it was the first day of my menstrual cycle. Fear that they would discover my secret and fire me was a constant. The fantasy image I projected was one of a modern woman, single with children, churchgoing, career minded, self-sufficient, and strong. What a joke! That might have been my exterior, but my interior was exhausted from the effort of keeping up that charade.

Every six months, like clockwork, I was given a raise, and within a year and a half, I was promoted to credit manager. The BNF Society, a sorority exclusively for credit managers, asked me to join them, which really floored me. Me? A sorority member?

Gensler Lee became my home away from home, so I had my job and my apartment in which to be comfortable and at ease. The anxiety attacks lessened in frequency but not intensity when they did occur. With periods of time passing between attacks, I was startled and even more frightened when one hit. With my newfound periodic calm, awareness of the timing of the dizziness grew. Every July, the dizziness and I celebrated the anniversary of "going nuts" and entering Stockton State Mental Hospital.

Fearful I was completely relapsing, I'd run back to Miss Callahan. It also seemed odd that the dizziness was more intense about every three weeks and not all the time. There seemed to be no answer to the questions my mind asked. Constantly being on the lookout for the dizziness undoubtedly brought on a lot of the anxiety from sheer tension. Unable to come up with any ideas or solutions with Miss Callahan, I sought answers from Dr. Parkinson.

"Doctor, I'm really puzzled about this dizzy-spell thing. I can go for a couple of weeks and not experience any discomfort at all, and then, out of the blue, I'm feeling nauseated and dizzy. I joined the choir, you know, and most Sundays I'm able to get up on the risers, something I never thought I'd be able to do, and sing my heart out. Then suddenly I can't do it. I've started sitting in an outside chair just in case I have a panic attack and have to run out the side door. People in choir are supportive and understanding, but it's embarrassing. Why do you suppose it only happens sometimes and not all the time?"

He stared at me thoughtfully and asked, "Have you been able to determine how close you are to the first day of your period when these attacks occur?"

"To tell you the truth, I've never paid attention. Why? What are you thinking?"

"I'm just wondering if maybe you retain fluid during your pre-menstrual days." He pulled a prescription pad from his pocket. "Some women do and find that it causes some dizziness and discomfort. Often they feel irritable and bloated as well. Let's get you on a water pill and see what happens."

Being on a mild diuretic did help somewhat. It felt good to have a physical cause for the dizziness, for a change, rather than being told it was all in my head. A bit of emotional comfort came from that new knowledge.

Life became pretty comfortable and full. I had my job, the kids with all the dramatic joys and heartaches teenagers brought, my middle-of-the-road walk with the Lord, and the various and sundry men I dated. Periodically, however, I'd become besieged with a longing to find Joanie. At those times finding her became an obsession. After exhausting every resource, I'd give up when no results surfaced, only to try again at a later date. One campaign to find her led me to the Legal Aid Society. The staff informed me they were not set up to handle such a case, but through much persistence and networking, I came in contact with a law student there to whom the issue and frequency of child stealing were so challenging that he couldn't resist playing detective.

He was willing to extend every investigative arm he had available on my behalf. He contacted welfare agencies all over the United States, concentrating especially on states around Oklahoma. He believed there would be a chance that, given my uncle's drinking problem, he might be unemployed and find it necessary to obtain help from family members there.

A frustrating number of times, he'd locate Bud and Mary and send a welfare representative to their home. An initial contact would be made and a date set for a return visit by a social worker, only to find that they had moved when he or she went back. Their home was a trailer, so they were able to move quickly. They were tracked down in various parts of Oklahoma, Kansas, and Arkansas. The only information about Joanie I learned was that she was alive and living in abhorrent conditions.

About this time, Pastor Witt was doing a series of sermons on the beatitudes. The Sunday he taught on "Blessed are those who truly mourn," his words really spoke to me. The key word was "truly." The pastor shared his opinion on what *truly* mourning meant. He pointed out various ways mourning was done in the Bible and contended that after *truly* mourning, crying, and wailing, one had to let go and let God take the bitterness of loss away and replace it with peace.

The kids and I had been invited to a BBQ after church, and I had every intention of going. But suddenly I had a sore throat and fever. The kids went on to the BBQ with friends while I went to bed. I fell into a deep sleep only to come abruptly awake, crying. The pastor's sermon that morning coursed through my heart and mind, and for the first time, I *truly* mourned the loss of my daughter.

Sobbing and wailing, I kicked in my closet doors and confessed to God how angry I was and how frustrated I was that, on top of all else, I had lost Joanie. Flinging myself on the bed, I punched pillows and carried on in madwoman fashion, until at last I felt emptied of the bitterness and anger.

Finally exhausted, I prayed aloud, "Father, I am so weary of this cat-and-mouse game with Bud and Mary. My attempts to do this on my own have accomplished nothing. As of this moment, I surrender Joanie's well-being and my pain to you. Your love is sufficient for her, wherever she is. My efforts to find her have probably caused her a lot of grief, because of the many times she has had to move in order for Bud and Mary to elude me. Thank you for the children you have given me to care for. Help me to remember whose children they really are. Please work your will in my life and Joanie's. Give me the peace to accept your will. Thank you and praise to you, in Jesus's precious name. Amen."

With my mourning over, I fell again into a sound sleep. When I awoke, the soreness in my throat had gone. A subdued calm replaced the usual frenzy that accompanied thoughts of Joanie.

Three weeks and two days later, I came home from work and checked the mail, and in the mailbox was a letter postmarked South Carolina.

Who in the world do I know in South Carolina? Full of curiosity, I opened the letter.

CHAPTER THIRTY-EIGHT

Secrecy involves a tension, which, at the moment of revelation, finds its release.

—Georg Simmel

Dear Bobbie Jo,

I'll bet you're surprised to hear from me. I'll get right to the point; I'm married to a man named Rob, who is in the air force. We're stationed at a base in South Carolina. Two weeks ago, Rob and I went to visit my mother and father. Things have been bad for them for a long time, but at least it used to be only my father who drank. Now my mother drinks as much as he does. They're both alcoholics. My mother is rarely home, and when she is, she's so drunk she can't do anything.

There is nothing I can do to help my brothers, but I couldn't stand seeing Paula in that filthy house any longer. So when my parents weren't home, we brought her home with us. I know you don't want her, but I'm hoping you care enough about her to take an interest in her well-being and let Rob and me adopt her.

I need an answer right away, because we need to get legal guardianship immediately. My mother knows we have her and has already threatened us. She went to the school last week and tried to kidnap Paula from the play yard. Paula's a smart little girl, and she ran to a teacher, who intervened. We need to hear from you right away so that if Mother tries anything again, we can sic the law on her. I don't know if this will mean anything to you or not, but Rob and I are both Christians and promise to give her a good home.

Sincerely,

Margaret

All I could do was clutch at my heart and chant, "Oh my God; oh my God."

The kids were playing basketball at the school yard across the field from our apartment, and I ran wildly over the rough ground, twisting my ankle and stumbling often and waving the letter above my head. They thought I'd gone completely bonkers, the way I ran at them, screaming, "Joanie, Joanie, I know where she is!" Breathlessly, I read the letter to them, and we grabbed each other to dance around in an awkward embrace. Oh, what joy!

We rushed back to the apartment, and I hurried to the phone in my bedroom. Pacing between the window and my bed, my fingers shaking furiously, I punched in the phone number Margaret had included in her letter.

"Hello."

"Margaret? Margaret, is that you? This is Bobbie." My words came out in a rush. "I just got your letter, and…oh, I'm so excited." Nervously and anxiously, I stood and twisted the phone cord round and round my fingers repeatedly: twist, release; twist, release. "Listen, I've been trying to find you and your family for years. Do you really have Joanie, uh, Paula? Is she OK?"

"Trying to find us?" she echoed. "Why were you trying to find us?"

On the surface, that seemed like a dumb question. "Well, to be more accurate, I've been trying to find Paula. When your folks took her, I almost went nuts. I've been searching for her off and on ever since. Didn't you know that?"

"No!" She gasped. "I didn't know that. My mother said you walked in one day and told her you didn't want Paula anymore, and that was that." She paused a moment and then continued slowly. "Then you don't know what happened?"

"No, what do you mean?" I asked.

She emitted a ragged sound, part sigh and part sob. "Shortly after Paula came to live with us, I ran away from home and pressed charges against my father for sexual molestation. When I couldn't take it anymore, I confided in a teacher at school about my homelife, and she took me to the authorities. I was made a ward of the state, placed in a foster home, and haven't been home since."

My knees gave way, and I sat down hard on the edge of my bed while she went on.

"I met Rob through my foster mother," Margaret continued, "and married him right after graduating from high school. He was stationed near where my folks lived, which is how I knew about Paula's situation. I know my folks can be rotten, but they *are* the only family I have. I visited them often. Now that you mention it, maybe you're the reason they moved so often. I never could figure that out. They would just get settled someplace, and all of a sudden, they'd be gone. I'd call, and the phone would be disconnected. I wouldn't even know where they were until Mother would contact me..."

As Margaret told her story, I listened and watched the sheer curtains billow in, blown by a soft, gentle breeze coming in the window. Absently, I pushed the billows back and then allowed the breeze to blow them into billows again and watched the dust motes reflected in the rays of sunshine.

Growing impatient, I cut in on her story. "Margaret, listen, the main thing is I do want Paula. I've *always* wanted her. I know you must have been told I was having some health problems, and that's true. Dizziness and panic attacks and a stay in a horrible hospital...They all had me so traumatized that I lost all self-respect and was confused and vulnerable. It was like being encased in a glass dome, just me and a bunch of questions. I'd look out from my glass prison and observe but couldn't break out to do anything about what I saw. Those were rough and confusing times, but I never wanted to give Paula up permanently, and—well, I'm sorry to say this—but especially to Bud and Mary. Then, just as I was about to take her, your folks ran off with her. Look, I can understand if you're suspicious about me—"

It was Margaret's turn to interrupt. "As a matter of fact, I'm not. I remember you from when I was a kid. When Mother told me that you said you didn't want your own daughter, I kept remembering the times when all the other adults couldn't be bothered with us little kids and you would let us jump off the edge of Grandma's porch into your arms over and over again. Ya gotta like kids a lot, the way you used to play with us." She chuckled. "I had a hard time believing what Mother said about you, but then I'd think that, well, people change." She drew a deep breath as she struggled with this turn of events. "Bobbie, have you really tried to find Paula?"

"Yes, Margaret," I assured her. "Once time and therapy shattered that glass, I used every means available to me, and some that weren't supposed to be. The thing that finally worked was prayer."

I shared with her the story of my truly mourning experience three weeks prior.

"Margaret, I can certainly understand if you have doubts about me. Tell you what. I'll make copies of the letters from attorneys and send them to you. Would that help? I'll also sign release-of-information forms from any source you want—doctors, social workers, and, well, anyone and everyone you want." My tone was urgent and pleading. "Oh, please believe me. I'll do anything to get my daughter back. No more scaredy-cat and no more beating around the bush and worrying about hurting someone's feelings."

As I sat on the edge of the bed, my body began trembling with…with what? A small inner voice scolded me. *Didn't you promise the Lord you would accept his will? Calm down, and let him work.*

Understandably, this new information created a lot of turmoil for Margaret. All she could seem to manage were several deep, ragged breaths and heavy sighs. After several moments, she said, "Bobbie, if—and I do mean if—Paula goes to you, it won't be easy. My mother will be on the warpath, and I don't know what she'll do. You have to be ready for that. Also, if she knows I've had a hand in sending Paula to you, you'll be the only family I'll ever have in this world. There isn't one person in our family who won't hate me and persecute me."

Suddenly a heaviness settled in on my chest. This wasn't just about me and my yearning for Joanie. The obvious pain this was causing my cousin made my heart constrict. Here was another collateral-damage victim in my war against emotional illness. As an attempt to comfort and encourage her, I sighed and gently offered, "Well, Margaret, just as those who truly mourn are blessed, so are those who are persecuted. Please jump! I'll still catch you."

CHAPTER THIRTY-NINE

The pain of parting is nothing to the joy of meeting again.

—Charles Dickens

After we wound through miles of red tape and underwent several thorough investigations conducted by social-service departments in both California and South Carolina, the decision was made. Returning Paula to her biological mother was best. Upon receiving the news, I sat at the kitchen table and sobbed out my relief and sorrow over all the years we had lost as mother and daughter, all the pain that my illness had caused so many people. The social worker handling South Carolina's end of things wrote me a personal note expressing her congratulations and good wishes. She hoped our story would be told someday as an encouragement to others.

Telling such a story held no desire for me. Having my daughter back and a life of normalcy would be enough. The only encouragement I had to offer would have come in the form of advice—in case of illness or incapacity, place your child with strangers rather than questionable family members.

Joanie, of course, was given the freedom to choose where and with whom she would live; she chose us. What courage for an eleven-year-old girl. What a shock it must have been for her to find out she wasn't who she had been told all her life. Her identity was in limbo. Joyfully but apprehensively, I spoke with her several times by phone as we waited for arrangements for her return to be made. Our conversations were mostly one-sided, with me telling her about her brothers and sister and assuring her we had always loved her, were so happy and grateful that she was rejoining our little family, and had always carried her in our hearts. She offered nothing in response and only answered any questions with a soft, timid yes, no, or OK. She gave no elaboration or information about her life to that point and had no questions about ours. She did express one desire, though; she wanted to continue being called Paula. No problem!

Pastor and Sheri Witt and I had drawn close after I had joined the church. Their son, Rob, and Ricky were best buddies, which brought Rob and the pastor to our apartment often, most frequently at dinnertime. The good news of Paula coming home had me eagerly anticipating their next visit. My belief that her homecoming was a direct result of his sermon and my subsequent prayer of mourning was firm and unshakeable.

Upon hearing the news, the pastor grabbed me and hugged me. "Barbara, I'm just overjoyed. Can I confess something to you?"

"Turnabout being fair play." I laughed. "Help yourself."

"Sometimes it's hard to counsel and guide someone from a background such as yours. I admit I struggle to relate to you, because I've never had any similar experiences. Trying to disciple single women, especially those who've previously been married, can be frustrating. I'm afraid I've cheated you, and I'm sorry. In the second book of Corinthians, Paul says God allows certain kinds of pain and trial into our lives so that we may become effective, sensitive witnesses in order to help others who might be going through the same thing. Women like you, in your particular situation, are the best witnesses to others. I'm hoping someday you'll write a book about your life to benefit others."

My hands flew up in mock despair. "Oh, no, not you, too! I've had a doctor, a psychiatric therapist, and a social worker suggest the same thing. And now you. I'll tell you the same thing I told them. I'm not a writer, and even if I were, I have no desire to go back in time and suffer all those things all over again. Thanks, but no thanks."

His brown eyes twinkled with amusement. "You know," he answered my protest, "God called Moses three times before he agreed to set aside his fear to carry out God's will for his life. Don't make God keep calling you without offering your cooperation, or you might miss out on a great blessing."

"The only *calling* I want to hear from God," I said and laughed recklessly, "is a loud 'come home and rest' after I've raised these kids. Besides, I'm so tired of fighting anxiety attacks and fearfulness; my best hope is just to survive. And now with Paula coming home, as glad as I am, it adds more uncertainty to all our lives."

CHAPTER FORTY

Anticipation, noun: the act or state of looking forward to
some occurrence

—Merriam-Webster Dictionary

The best part about Paula coming home was that she *wanted* to come. There'd been a lot of discussion and concern over whether or not coming home to us was the best thing for her. At least with Margaret and Rob, she had familiarity and someone to share memories with—good or bad. With us, it would be totally strange and unknown. As for me and the kids, her homecoming began changing our lives immediately.

Butch had to give up his bedroom since it was the closest to my room and the hall bathroom. We weren't sure what Paula's physical or emotional needs would be. Ricky had to give up his privacy, as his little brother moved in with him. We scrounged for and accepted donations of furnishings for her room: an old but freshly painted, white desk dresser; an equally old but serviceable dark-wood chest of drawers, courtesy of my good friend Livvie; and a frameless twin bed. Binky gave up the pink-and-white afghan I'd crocheted for her when she'd had chicken pox to serve as a bedspread.

I gave up tall, blond, blue-eyed Jon, a doctor and captain in the air force. He was no great loss. He was just another guy who proved that my mother's mantra of "a man only wants one thing" from a woman in my situation was flawed. Men also wanted companionship and maturity, girlfriends they could be proud to introduce to their families and friends. They wanted women who could share fun times and sorrow with equal aplomb. Upon meeting me and my children, men first admired us and then felt a need to rescue us. Fear and doubt, however, drove them away as they competed with my children for my affections and lost.

Dating was difficult for me as an agoraphobic. Where could I go with them besides bed? That may have been tacky behavior, but it was the only place I was sure of myself. Sadly, I thought the only thing I had to offer was cheap thrills. A recent trip to a shopping mall had proved that Jon and I would never make it as a long-term couple. An anxiety attack had sent me flying to the nearest exit in a total panic. Jon saw that as an unacceptable character flaw, and we had a bitter fight as I tried to explain the workings of agoraphobia. But he threw up a wall of ignorance and intolerance.

"The *real* problem with you," he had roared, red-faced with fury, "is that you're no lady."

Mustering up all the dignity I could, I answered him, "It all depends on how you define 'lady.' I define it as a woman who rises to meet any occasion she is faced with; in that event, yes, most of the time, I am a lady. I'm just a different type. That's all."

That kind of thing happened all the time, but I never got used to it. It hurt! It hurt a lot. I fought to be the kind of lady Jon and all the others wanted me to be, but the dizziness and panic attacks won the battle often enough to discourage me. Playing the role of party girl was much easier than trying to meet men's expectations of what a lady should be.

The big day finally arrived. Livvie picked up the kids and me to drive us to the airport in Sacramento. She had the most dependable car and, given my anxious state, was the more dependable driver.

Dependability could have been Livvie's middle name. She was the picture of confidence, with every hair perfectly in place, styled in her own creation. The front of her short, medium-brown hair was bleached white blond in a frame around her face, softening her otherwise-piercing brown eyes. The confidence she exuded physically didn't reflect the insecurities she carried inside.

To please her third husband, she'd had all her teeth pulled and replaced with perfect white dentures. To further please him, she'd had breast implants the size of small cantaloupes installed. None of her beautification efforts paid off, however, and soon after their daughter was born, he left her for another woman. It made me wonder what *she* looked like. To my mind, women didn't come any more gorgeous than Livvie and certainly with no better hearts.

During the drive to the airport, I shared the kids' excitement but was fearful, too. What if Paula didn't like me? What if one more child proved to be financially impossible? She sounded so timid and shy over the phone. Should I grab her and hug her as I wanted to do? Should I keep a little distance so that I wouldn't frighten her? Stress turned what should have been an absolutely carefree day into a near nervous breakdown.

Turning to the back seat, I quizzed the kids. "How 'bout you, Ricky? How do you really feel about your baby sister coming home after all these years?"

He just laughed at me and said, "Mom, will you relax and stop analyzing everything? What's to say? Sure, I'm glad."

"Binky?"

"Mo-o-th-e-e-r-r," she groaned, rolling her big, brown eyes. "It's fine. You're so silly. Of course I'm glad. It's great! Now I won't be the only girl."

"I guess I'm next on the hot seat," Butch wisecracked. "Can we afford her? I mean, we already have a hard time getting by. Oh, well, it'll be neato meeting my sister. No one at school believed me when I told them I had a little sister coming to live with us. They thought I was jivin' 'em."

Arriving at the airport, we hustled inside just as her plane was landing. The circular-shaped reception area startled me at first with the floor-to-ceiling windows surrounding it. One had the sense of standing right on the tarmac. Each of the kids claimed a window to watch the plane set down. To ease my anxious anticipation, I snapped pictures of their backs and thought how poignant a scene it was.

Rubbing my face with the palms of my hands, I took as deep a breath as my anxiety would allow and hurried to the gate she would be coming through. Once again, gratitude surged through me for the recent pictures of Paula that Margaret had sent. Without them, I might not have been able to recognize her. What a thought. How awful to think I might not recognize my own child.

The plane touched down, and passengers started filing by. Butterflies played Ping-Pong with the Valium I had taken earlier. And there she was!

Oh my God, she's so small. Didn't they feed her? So tiny, so frail looking, and so scared. She looks like a trapped, timid deer. Bambi.

CHAPTER FORTY-ONE

*Love is a binding force, by which another is joined to me
and cherished by myself.*

—Thomas Aquinas

Fearful of rushing Paula, I advanced toward her slowly after turning the camera over to Livvie. Paula had cleared the gate and stood off to the side with her head down, her long, black hair hiding her small face. Her long, slender hands were wrapped around the handle of a red-and-black plaid bag in a death grip. Kneeling in front of her, I gently pried her fingers loose to take those hands in mine.

"Hello, Paula," I said softly. "I'm your mother." Reaching up, I tenderly touched her cheek and choked out, "I didn't know you were so beautiful."

An inner struggle took place. Giving in to the urge to whoop and holler with joy and to scoop her up into my arms and give her the biggest hug she'd ever had was not an option. Something in her face warned me that this little one wouldn't welcome such exuberance. She didn't return the squeeze of my hands; indeed, she didn't move a muscle. Tears streamed silently down her face. I couldn't decide whether they were tears of joy or sorrow. Her face was unreadable, her eyes still glued to the floor. Looking over her head, I sought reassurance, direction, or guidance in Livvie's eyes, but they were hidden behind wads of tear-soaked tissue. No help there.

Lightly stroking Paula's hair and arms, I turned her toward her sister and brothers.

"Well." I attempted a more jovial tone. "Meet the rest of the tribe. This is your oldest brother, Ricky, your big sister, Binky, and the joker we got stuck with, whom we call Butch."

She smiled shyly at them and muttered, "Hi."

"I, uh, I'm not sure what's appropriate for a time like this," stated Binky, "but what I want to do is hug you."

With that, she grabbed Paula and nearly squished her. Paula didn't raise her arms to return the attack of affection and seemed pleased but embarrassed. Her head went back down, eyes looking at the floor, as soon as Binky released her.

"Hi, Sis," Ricky ventured, giving out a nervous chuckle. "I sure hope you like us, because we're all there is." He gave her a quick, self-conscious hug.

Always the clown, Butch cracked, "Don't look like you eat much. That's good. As long as you don't like the same kind of cookies I like, we'll get along fine."

There was no hug from him; instead, he gave her a brotherly punch in the arm. That brought on a full-fledged smile. She looked him right in the eyes and gave him an ear-to-ear grin. My hand flew to my mouth as I fought an urge to throw myself at her feet and beg her to forgive me for all she'd been put through.

Later, I told myself. *Bedtime is crying time; don't do this now.*

Comic relief kicked in as Butch handed Paula the heaviest suitcase, while he took the smallest and headed for the car. Ricky and Binky scuffled over the remaining two pieces of luggage, each claiming to have wrist injuries making them unable to carry anything heavy. Giving out a loud "Hey!" I rounded them up and distributed the load more evenly, according to age and strength. Paula stole sidelong glances at me to see how I was handling the melee. My methods seemed to meet her approval, because I could have sworn she giggled. Livvie continued to snap pictures all the way to the car, and then we headed for home.

The weeks following Paula's homecoming were terrible for many reasons. Where was the happily ever after written about in fairy tales? There was a tension with her in our midst. What was it? Guilt? Old pain represented and relived with her presence? There was no specific issue to pinpoint, but the very air in our home was like trying to breathe syrup.

The vacation time I had taken from work flew by quickly. I enrolled Paula in school, but she refused to go. These weren't verbal refusals; she just wouldn't move. Separation anxiety was perfectly understandable, but I knew that the sooner we got into a regular routine, the better. We were all making our way through the adjustment and eager to get our household back to normal.

Paula only had a few suitable outfits for school, and somehow she always managed to get them stained, ripped, or so mussed they weren't wearable. She vomited so often that I finally took her to a doctor for something to calm her stomach. I'd never seen a child so acutely stressed. When I finally returned to work, I'd inevitably only be there a short time before the school would call to say Paula was sick and needed to go home. I'd get her and take her back to work with me. This continued for several weeks before Butch cornered me one day.

"Mom, you've got to do something. We're really having a rough time at school; no wonder Paula doesn't like to go. None of the kids believe her when she tells them she's my sister. They make fun of her and call her a liar. They tell her they've known us for years and if she really is our sister, how come she hasn't lived with us before. It's awful."

The Lord does indeed work in mysterious and wondrous ways. The girl who had worked as my assistant quit. While we were in the process of interviewing applicants for her replacement, Sandy moved back into town from Philadelphia. She and her family had moved there a couple years prior, but she was now back and in need of a job. With high hopes, I asked her to come in and apply, but I couldn't promise she'd be hired. The final decision-maker would be Betty, my supervisor.

"In looking over Sandy's application," Betty said with a wistful tone in her voice, "I sure wish she wasn't married."

Her statement elicited a chuckle. "What does her marital status have to do with anything?"

"Well, it's just that I think she's a talented girl with too much smarts to be a mere mail girl. If she weren't married, I'd hire her as a credit manager in our Palo Alto store. We just lost another girl there. It's a real problem store, and it needs someone good and tough in there to pull it out of the slump it's in."

"How 'bout me?" I suggested. "I don't know if I'm tough, but I'm experienced."

"What do you mean?" Betty's eyebrows shot up.

"How about hiring Sandy for the Fairfield store and sending me to Palo Alto?"

"You're kidding, right?" The eyebrows shot up even higher. "Would you really do that? What about the kids? How do you think they'll feel about it?"

"Can't hurt to ask them. How soon do you need a decision?"

"Yesterday, of course." She laughed. "Let me call Lee Follett and see what our illustrious president thinks about this idea. Can you talk to the kids tonight and let me know sometime tomorrow?"

"Sure," I said, hoping my level of confidence would catch up to my excitement.

Betty hopped on the phone to Lee immediately and reported his delight with our proposition. I went home to present my case about this move to the kids.

As I drove home, a little voice in my head said, *Boy, you've got a lot of nerve asking these kids to make yet another huge change in their lives. You're putting an awful lot of faith in their love and trust for you. You better hope they see this plan in the same hopeful light you do.*

The kids had spent their most secure and meaningful years growing up in Fairfield, and now I was going to ask them to give up everything familiar to move seventy-five miles away.

My power as the parent, I knew, was potent, a power with influence that needed to be used with extreme caution and care. This move could prove to be one of two things: a solution to the problem within our family or another bad decision that would blow up in my face. More than a few flutters rippled through my stomach as I entered our apartment and called out to the kids.

CHAPTER FORTY-TWO

Children are smarter than any of us. Know how I know that? I don't know one child with a full-time job and children.

—*Bill Hicks*

"Hey! Anybody home?"

Four heads poked out from doorways down the hall and gave me varied greetings.

"So, how's the Elling bunch doing today?" I inquired.

"We're all drunk and on drugs, listening to rock 'n' roll." Ricky spoke for the group.

"Very funny. If your next play is a comedy, you should get the lead." I smiled. "Would all you funny people stagger to the living room and grab a seat? I need to talk to you about something."

"Uh-oh," Butch groaned. "Well, you're smiling, so whatever it is, it can't be too bad."

"Yeah, but," Binky warned, "that smile looks suspicious to me."

Paula didn't verbally respond; she merely looked at them appraisingly.

"So here's the deal," I began after they were seated on the edges of their chosen places.

Painting what I hoped was an appealing picture, I presented my proposition.

In a lightly coaxing tone, I said, "I know this is asking a lot, but it would be an opportunity to make a fresh start as the family we are now, not the family we were before Paula came home. If you're all dead set against the idea, we won't do it. Or we can give it a try, and if you hate it, we'll move back here. I don't want anyone to carry around feelings of resentment toward your sister if this move turns out to be another one of your mother's infamous good ideas gone wrong."

Stealing a glance at Paula, I saw her eyes widen and fill with tears. "It's OK, honey," I told her. "We're just tossing around an idea. So what do you all think?"

They all relaxed, flopping back in their chairs, slouching there, and looking at one another for any opinions. Ricky, of course, had one.

"A bigger town would probably have a bigger theater-arts department at school," he mused. "That'd be cool." Ah, something appealing to my budding actor.

"They'd have a bigger sports program, too," Butch, my avid basketball player, added. "That would be *really* cool."

Binky, my fashionista, exclaimed, "Hey, all my clothes would be new again 'cause no one's ever seen 'em." Turning to Paula, she added, "And don't worry. We want you to be happy, so whether this works or not, it's worth a try. I'm not going to resent you for it. Mom's right; this will give us all a new start."

"Paula," I asked, "what do you think?"

She ducked her head, hid behind her hair, and shrugged. I took that to mean it didn't matter to her.

"What about you, Mom?" Ricky looked at me solemnly. "Will this fresh start mean you're going to make some changes?"

"I don't understand what you mean," I replied.

"What I mean is you're gone a lot. We're all glad you're not so housebound anymore, but you go out way too much. When you and Livvie aren't hanging out at that cocktail lounge, you're at choir practice or somewhere with your new boyfriend, Lee. He's a nice guy, and we don't mind sharing you with him. But why can't you be home more with us? You used to gripe about the way Granny Chris left you alone a lot; now you're doing the same thing."

The truth of his words was like a hornet sting to the brain. Stunned and flustered, I turned to the other kids. "But when I'm home, you only seem to need each other and your friends. I'm like a chair that's good to have if you want to sit down but is left empty and alone when you're off and running."

"That's not true, Mom." Binky squirmed a bit before hopping on the truth-to-Mom bandwagon. "We know you work hard at the store. We know you work hard here, too, but it always feels empty when we get home from school and you're not here. Then you get home, fix dinner, and eat, and then you're gone again."

Butch sat, head nodding his agreement, while he studied the floor for a moment and then slung his offbeat humor into the subject. "Yeah, the only time we don't want you here is when we're trying to get away with something."

Paula continued to hide behind her hair and said nothing.

Breaking the tense silence that had fallen upon the room, I cleared my throat uneasily and responded. "Ouch. I'm not sure what to say. I guess I've been pretty selfish. Since you're all older now, I've thought you didn't need me as much. Now you've made me think back to my own teen years, and, yeah, you're right. My need for friends shouldn't take away from my being Mom. All I can say is I'm sorry. I'll try to find more of a balance." My forced laugh sounded a bit hollow. "I guess that's another potential positive about moving to a new place. You guys will still have each other and make friends in school. I won't know where to go and will have no one to go with, so you'll be stuck with me more anyway."

After more discussion about the how, when, and where of this intended move, our meeting was adjourned. My still-stricken feeling must have shown on my face and caused Ricky to give me a rare hug.

"I didn't say those things to hurt you, Mom. I'm just a little nervous about the move."

Binky followed suit. "Me either, Mom. We do need you, though. It just feels better when you're home."

They all retreated back to their rooms to continue whatever they had been doing, leaving me to marvel at the trust and loving honesty they had just expressed. *I may be doing an OK job of raising them after all.*

The next two weeks defined "hectic." After training Sandy for my position, I was given a week off work to find a place to live. The schools and neighborhoods near the store in Palo Alto that were affordable were atrocious. We had lived in undesirable areas before, and I wasn't about to ask my kids to make a move backward, especially at their ages.

Unable to find a place in that week, I had to start work in my new store, which meant commuting a total of 150 miles each day, quite a challenge for someone subject to bouts of vertigo. In the mornings, I'd leave long before the kids were awake, and often didn't get home until long after they were in bed. It wasn't a great way of affirming for them that this move was a good idea.

Widening my search circle, I finally found a decent three-bedroom, two-bath town house in San Jose I could afford. Open-backed stairs greeted you immediately upon entering through the front door. These led up to the bedrooms and bathroom, which marched down the short hallway. Hanging a soft right through the front door introduced the living room, and a hard right led into the kitchen. All rooms had the requisite rental-beige drapes, beige-variegating-to-brown carpet, and off-white walls.

At first sight, I thought I'd gone color-blind; it was that bland. A sliding glass door at the end of the living room opened to a small, blank patio, perfect for assorted sports gear and skateboards. The cement courtyard leading from the street to the front door was clean and pleasing to the eyes, softened as it was with a variety of dwarf shrubs.

The move began. Garry Mumau had been discharged from the air force the previous year and gone home to Washington. He'd moved back to California just in time to help me make moving arrangements and, more importantly, to load and drive the rental truck. Once again, my good friend came to my rescue.

This move was a big step for an agoraphobic person. Fairfield was such a small town, while San Jose was large and scary. The progress I'd made was impressive, even to me. By this time, I was able to walk down city streets and grocery shop alone, albeit not always comfortably. Public buildings, such as the department of human services and the enrollment office at the middle and high schools, didn't intimidate me as much as they once had.

Driving the twenty-plus miles to and from work, however, was a problem. The murderous traffic was harrowing. As long as I stayed in the far-right lane, I did OK, but occasionally I needed to pull off the road to right my equilibrium. Scouting out and using back roads rather than the freeway proved helpful, but I still showed up for work and at home with seriously frayed nerves.

A huge part of my job was collecting payments on delinquent accounts, and despite the difficulties caused by the commute, collections were going well enough to earn me a commendation and much-needed bonus. The store was out of the red for the first time in years.

The move did wonders for Paula. She finally claimed her rightful place at home and joined the track team at school. To say she ran like the wind is such a cliché, but that's exactly what she did.

The other three did well also and together signed up to take classes in musical-comedy production, stage-set construction, and drama. Ricky and Binky landed parts in the first play that took place after entering these classes. Butch, my aspiring carpenter, found a place for his woodworking talents building scenery. The three of them filled the air in our house with tales, quotes, and anecdotes by or about their esteemed teacher, Mr. Sorich.

True to my word, I went straight home from work every night and stayed there through homework, any needed script memorization, and bedtimes. To further promote closeness and as an avenue for family sharing, I placed an old card table, along with a few jigsaw puzzles, under the stairs in the living room. Two or more of us gathered at that table and talked as soon as dinner was over.

There was a great church just down the street from our town house; it offered an opportunity, other than school, for the kids to make friends. I immediately joined a Wednesday-night Bible study but didn't attempt to form any friendships. Still feeling stigmatized by the attacks of panic and the restricted lifestyle forced on an agoraphobic, I snuck in the back door, sat in the back row, and left before the closing prayer.

Life at home was good, even if a little lonely at times. Life at work was never lonely but not so good.

As the Christmas season drew near, so did the volume of credit applicants wanting to open accounts. It seemed as though the entire populace of Palo Alto was intent on gifting the lucky men or women in their lives with jewelry. To accommodate these shoppers, the store stayed open until nine o'clock, seven days a week, instead of the usual six o'clock, six days a week. Including commute time, this turned my customary eleven-hour workday into fourteen. Again, I was leaving for work before the kids were up and arriving home after they had gone to bed. It was brutal!

The generous Christmas and monthly collections bonuses I received were passed on to the kids. Unable to find the time to do any Christmas shopping, I gave them each a hundred-dollar bill, and they shopped for themselves and each other. They had a blast, while I felt left out and dismal.

Four months into this fresh start, the commute to and from work, the pressure of meeting my money quotas, and all the frenzied activity the move had involved began chipping away at my energy level. Tiredness penetrated my very bones. Dragging myself out of bed to face another day became a major chore. Tired as I was, though, I vowed to attend every performance of the kids' play. With that vow came a flood of concern and worry that declared war on my already-puny confidence. How big was the building? Were many people going to be there? Could I find an aisle seat in the back? How many milligrams of Valium should I take beforehand?

As a phobic person, I always carried two things with me to assuage panic and maintain my comfort level: a can of cola and a cigarette. These were like appendages to my body. Opening night of the play was no exception, and, boy, when I set sight on the size of the theater, I particularly needed my feeble crutches. While walking toward the entrance, I nervously popped a Valium. Paula gave me a look but made no comment.

My worry about it being crowded was well-founded; it looked like the inside of a sardine can. And whereas in Fairfield, jeans and a sweater were perfectly acceptable attire for attending a play, that was not the case in San Jose. The women wore long skirts or slacks with soft, feminine blouses and blazer jackets. Their high-heeled boots contrasted sharply with my moccasins. The men were decked out in suits or slacks and sports coats.

In order to sit in the back row, I hung back near the entrance and held Paula hostage with me, while all the rest made their way into the theater. Nervously, I took a few sips of soda. Hanging back also gave me a chance to take a few puffs off the cigarette I felt a great need for.

The cigarette had barely made it to my lips when a young man charged up to me and snatched both cigarette and drink from my hands.

"Drinks and smoking are not allowed in my theater," he snapped and kept charging right on by.

"Well what in the world? How rude!" I exclaimed as I watched him whisk away. "I wonder just who he thinks he is? I always smoked and drank a soda at the high-school theater in Fairfield."

"Yeah, Mom, that was rude." Paula giggled. "But this isn't anything like that gym in Fairfield. This looks like a fancy movie theater."

Momentarily, I put my indignation aside and appraised the elegantly papered walls with large, framed playbill prints hung intermittently. The deep, green carpet with abstract slashes of autumn colors screamed, "I'm new. No messes, OK?"

Sheer orneriness seized me as I spied a table loaded with doughnuts and coffee. Childishly, to vent my annoyance at this cocky person, I reached out and snatched a doughnut.

"If he thinks of this theater as his, he probably has the same feeling about the doughnuts," I fumed to Paula as I chomped off a big bite. "Humph, that'll show him." But I was careful not to get any crumbs on the carpet.

My stall tactics worked, and we found perfect seats: back row, on the aisle, and near the door. The play was great, as were all the student performers. When Ricky was greeted with thunderous applause during the curtain call, I was a little surprised. He had always been well received at the high-school plays in Fairfield, but there he had been a big fish in a little pond. He was now playing in a very big pond and apparently quite successfully.

With the play over, Ricky took Paula and me backstage to meet his teacher, the infamous Mr. Sorich I'd heard so much about. We entered the greenroom, and I gasped. Mr. Sorich turned out to be the cocky young man I had encountered in the lobby. My face felt a change in complexion color. Mr. Sorich was completely unruffled when we were introduced; he just muttered something I couldn't make out and dashed away.

When doing theater in Fairfield, Ricky had a friend and self-appointed costumer, Frank Billeci. The second night of the play, Frank made the trip to San Jose to escort me and watch the kids perform.

Frank and I were standing, chatting in the lobby of the theater, when who should come up, pushing himself between us, but Mr. Sorich. His uninvited intrusion astounded me.

"Hi, I'm Jerry Sorich," he said, completely ignoring the fact that he'd almost knocked me over. "I hear you have a great collection of costumes."

They yakked for a few minutes, with Frank peering over Mr. Sorich's shoulder at me with an expression that clearly said, "What's with this guy?"

The third night of the play, the love I left behind in Fairfield came to join me for the show. Lee was hardly the theater-going type, but he sincerely liked my kids and shared my pride in their accomplishments. Even a strictly outdoor kind of guy like Lee understood that being the male lead in a play was hot stuff.

As soon as the applause died down after the last curtain call, Lee could hardly wait to tell Binky how hysterical he thought her stage makeup was, heap praise on Butch for his scenery construction, and, of course, congratulate Ricky.

By this time, Paula and I knew all the right doorways leading into the inner sanctum of the theater, so with Lee in tow, we went in search of my theater rats. We hadn't encountered the rude and incorrigible Mr. Sorich before the show, but when we entered the greenroom, there he was, the creep. He stood just inside the door, yelling at what I hoped was the top of his lungs. A louder volume would have split eardrums. He was yelling about gum on stage, among other infractions, and threatening lives if it ever happened again. Upon completing his tirade against the kids, he spun on his heel, kicked a desk, and charged toward the exit, right where I stood. For the third time, he nearly knocked me over.

"Really!" I exclaimed indignantly to his retreating back. "This is too much." Turning to find Ricky at my side, I blurted out, "To tell you the truth, what you all see in this man completely escapes me. He has got to be the rudest individual I've ever had the displeasure of meeting."

"Now, Mom," Ricky cajoled. "He's a great guy, really. Oh, yeah, and don't bring a date tomorrow night. On the last night of the play, there's a cast party after. Mr. Sorich says you can be a chaperone. Neat, huh?"

Sarcasm flooded my retort. "Sure, real neat. A fun night with an angry Godzilla is just what I need."

By closing night of the play, I had gained some confidence and an acceptable level of emotional comfort with the theater building. Stepping around the potential pitfalls of snaking cables and wires in the darkened backstage had become second nature to me, but a *party?* A party involved other kinds of potential pitfalls. Could I comfortably and confidently step around those? Was my getaway uniform of overalls, a turtleneck sweater, and moccasins suitable attire for a chaperone? These questions tormented me all through the final act of the play that night.

As requested, I went alone and sat alone. The curtain calls began, and I jumped from my seat to join the standing ovation for Ricky when he was introduced. When the cast called out for the director to join them onstage, I turned my gaze to the door leading from the lobby to the auditorium. Mr. Rude and Crude, Jerry Sorich, his straight, brown hair flopping into his eyes, trotted down the stairs toward the stage. His face never seemed to lose the grim expression I had come to think of as his trademark look.

For the umpteenth time, I thought, *Yuck. You, Mr. Sorich, are a cocky, conceited individual who should take a lesson or two on how to treat people. I hope you get what's coming to you one of these days. Boy, would I ever like to teach you a lesson.* Not very Christian thinking.

With the show over, everyone filed out to the parking lot. The kids had wanted to ride over with a classmate, so I was on my own. Mr. Yuck strolled over to my car and said the first civilized words I'd heard him utter.

"That's my MG over there," he said, pointing to an orange, convertible sports car. "If you want to follow me to my house, I'll be leaving in just a minute."

My reply was icy. "Thanks. I'd appreciate that since I don't know my way around here very well."

Still filled with apprehension, I followed him to a nice ranch-style house. Upon entering the living room, I immediately sought out the kids. It was my intention to stay as close to them as possible in order to feel comfortable in the crowd of noisy, adrenaline-pumped teenagers. They, however, had different plans for me. They pawned me off on the more awkward, less than popular stage-crew guys, and next thing I knew, I was dancing with them.

Needing a break to catch my breath, I went in search of coffee. A short, curly-haired blond woman seemed to know her way around the kitchen, so I approached her.

"Hi, would you happen to know if Mr. Sorich has any coffee made?"

She looked up at me, patted my arm, and replied, "Oh, my dear, you're much too young to be drinking coffee. Wouldn't you like a soda instead?"

Baffled, I gave a short laugh. "I beg your pardon? I'm more than old enough to have a cup of coffee." Holding out my hand, I introduced myself. "I'm Bobbie. Three of my children were involved in the play."

Her head jerked back as though surprised. "I'm Mrs. Sorich, Jerry's mother. With that long, TV-star hairdo and the way you're dressed, I thought you were one of the kids. You look too young to have teenage children."

Hmm, and you look too nice to have given birth to a Neanderthal like Jerry.

Ultimately, Mr. Sorich did get shown a thing or two and that lesson I'd thought he deserved…I married him.

CHAPTER FORTY-THREE

*If you want to sacrifice the admiration of many men for
the criticism of one, go ahead; get married.*

—Katharine Hepburn

Drinking a shot of gasoline with a side order of lit matches appealed to me more than the idea of a relationship with Jerry Sorich. But days later, when he asked me to come to his house to balance the income and expense accounts resulting from the play, I agreed. Doing something useful for the kids' school made me feel good.

"*Que pasa?*" He greeted me at his door, a grin flashing under his moustache. "Come on in. Want a cup of coffee?"

"Only if you promise not to knock it out of my hand." A sarcastic reply referencing our first meeting was irresistible.

Disconcerted, he replied, "Huh?"

"Never mind." I let him off the hook. "Coffee sounds good, thank you."

As he walked away into the kitchen, my eyes performed a head-to-toe scan of him: tallish, thinnish, and hippieish. His jeans and blue chambray shirt were faded and worn, but they looked clean enough. The brown slip-on, zip-up ankle boots affirmed that he would rather be on a street corner playing a guitar and singing folk songs than in a classroom teaching teenagers theater arts.

The clinking of spoons and sputtering of the coffeemaker came from the kitchen as I looked around his living room and laughed inwardly. His furniture was clearly purchased from the Dumpster Emporium. It was nice to know that a lofty, single, college-graduate schoolteacher had decor worse than a lowly single-mother, high-school-dropout bookkeeper.

Carrying two thick restaurant-style mugs, he made his reentry into the living room. "Here ya go," he said, placing the mugs on the coffee table. "Hope it's not too strong for you."

"I'm sure it's fine. Let's have a look at those numbers you need to justify."

"Yep, got 'em right here," he said. Grabbing a thick manila folder from the tabletop, he opened it quickly and then just as abruptly closed it. Several bits of paper floated around a bit and then landed willy-nilly.

Amused but bewildered, I said, "I'm pretty quick, but I'm not that quick. Did you want me to balance these or not?"

"Oh, it doesn't really matter. The ticket sales are accounted for, and I have all my receipts for anything the school had to buy. All I have to do is submit all this to the district office, and they'll take care of it."

"Then I'm a little unsure about why you had me come over."

"'Cause now I can honestly tell the district I had someone else look at the numbers," he explained, "and I wondered if you'd like to do dinner and a movie sometime."

Stalling, I picked up my coffee mug and sipped while I thought of what to say. I still had strong feelings for Lee, but that relationship would never go anywhere. That was one of the reasons it hadn't been that difficult for me to move so far away. And even though Jerry was eight years younger than me, I supposed we could hang out together as friends. Maybe he would be less obnoxious on a purely social level. Besides, he probably just wanted a friend, too, someone he could date with no strings until he found someone his own age, someone with a more similar background.

"Sure, that sounds good." My answer set in motion a very unlikely pairing of persons.

Almost everywhere Jerry and I went, the kids went along. We had picnics on the beach in Santa Cruz, went to various movies and plays put on by other high schools, and had frequent BBQs at his house. Butch, my little carnivore, particularly liked those. That Jerry included the kids didn't particularly impress me, though. From the beginning, I believed Jerry was dating a family and not me as a woman. We did, however, have a lot of late-night coffee dates at a nearby café that began to alter that belief.

Jerry started sharing things about himself the way a person does when on the verge of making an emotional investment in someone of the opposite sex. I was taken aback as the messages I received from him began to change.

"You know," he confided during one of those coffee dates, "I've just about accomplished everything I set out to do. I guess the only three things left that will complete my happiness are to get married, have kids, and have an elephant onstage in one of my plays."

Since we'd been inseparable from our first date, I wondered if this was a hint of a marriage proposal. Unsure of his meaning, I teasingly told him, "I hate to see anyone with unfinished goals. So I'll marry you if that's all you need, but I'm much too old to have your children. You'll have to find someone else for that little chore. As for the elephant, I'll grab one for you on my next safari expedition."

"The way I see it," he responded just as lightly, "you've already had the kids. Now all we have to do is get married and forget about the elephant for the time being."

This conversation, with little variation, went on for a couple of months. I decided to find out once and for all if he was serious.

"Jerry," I asked, "have you ever heard of agoraphobia?"

"No," he replied.

"It's a problem I have. It's an emotional disorder or handicap that brings on panic attacks. It makes it extremely difficult, if not impossible, for me to go certain places or do certain things. Because of it, I think it would be grossly unfair of me to stick someone with it. I mean, I don't think I'll ever marry again. I believe my life will consist of raising the kids as best I can and going back to school. At some point, I want to get some kind of degree that will qualify me to work with troubled children. After that, I'll sit back and wait for grandchildren, and that suits me just fine. If I could give you more of an explanation, I would, but I can't explain something I don't even understand myself."

"But," he protested, "you go places with me and the kids all the time."

That was true. I had gone places with him that were out of the ordinary for me. Maybe it was because I kept telling myself that our friendship wasn't important or threatening enough to cause anxiety. That the kids were always with us was undoubtedly a positive factor as well. However, I couldn't deny that lately my anxiety symptoms had been less severe. It was feelings of depression that were on the rise.

For weeks, my job had been unbearable. All those new credit accounts that the home office thought were so great to open at Christmas now had to be collected on. The increased sales raised my monthly collection quotas to an unrealistic high. Too many of the new accounts had fallen into delinquency, and I grew weary of making phone calls coaxing and coercing money from people who didn't have it. Or if they did have it, they sure didn't want to use it to pay on their accounts.

Feeling incredibly weary and defeated, I woke up one morning unable to force myself to go to that store another day. The very thought of it filled me with a sickening, paralyzing dread. Whatever I'd had that Gensler Lee could use had been depleted. The Girl with the Heart, as Gensler Lee's radio jingle called its credit managers, had apparently run out of heart.

Hastily and in tears, I scribbled a letter of resignation and took it to my neighbor Penny, whom I had recently hired as my assistant. Flabbergasted, she agreed to give it to whatever supervisor might visit the store that day.

The kids were shocked to come downstairs and find me sitting in our rocking chair and sipping coffee.

"Ma, don't you know what time it is?" Ricky demanded.

"Are you sick, Mom?" asked Binky, a worried frown clouding her face.

"Yes, Ricky. I know what time it is, and, nope, I'm not sick." I studied their faces to see how they would react to the news. "I quit Gensler Lee."

"You what!" Butch flung his arms over his head. "Are you jivin' us? How are we going to live?"

Paula sat on the corner of the sofa and hid behind her hair. She looked tense but offered no comment or question.

"I know; I know," I placated. "It sounds scary, but we'll be fine. I've put a plan together, and I'll go to social services today and discuss it with them. I've heard that if I go to school, we can get financial assistance, so I'm going to check into it. If that's possible, I really think I'd like to get a degree of some sort. If it's *not*, I'll find another job. Go on and get ready for school, and we'll talk again when you get home."

Looking concerned and doubtful, the four of them climbed back up the stairs. "I sure hope you know what you're doing," Ricky muttered. He wasn't alone in that hope.

Once the kids were off to school, I got dressed and went to the closest city college and enrolled. At the same time, I applied for a financial grant. The admissions counselor was sure one would be awarded. From there, I went to the welfare department and told them of my plan to return to school. Thankfully, they assured me that my benefits wouldn't change as long as I was in school.

Going to Jerry's house that night, I anticipated his delight at my decision. When I told him what a busy little bee I'd been that day and what I'd accomplished, his reaction was definitely not one of delight. His jaw dropped slightly, and his brow furrowed.

His lack of enthusiasm confused me. I said, "I don't understand. Of all people, I thought you'd be glad for me."

"Oh, I admire your decision," he assured me, fussing with his moustache. "It's just that...well, if we get married, I can't support all of us on my salary alone. I was counting on your salary as well."

"You mean you're really serious about all this marriage stuff?" I asked incredulously.

"Of course I am. What did you think?"

"Uh...I guess I haven't been thinking at all. How silly of me." My enthusiasm ebbed away, and while I tried to joke, the laugh seemed to be on me.

A mild tension sprouted up and wrapped itself around our moods. Wanting to escape the awkwardness, I said, "Jer, we both need to get up early, and I have a full day tomorrow. So I'm going to head on home. I have a lot of details to take care of yet about school and all."

He made no protest about ending our evening earlier than usual. We hugged briefly and said good night.

Driving home, I mentally evaluated our relationship and sorted through my feelings about him, us, and marriage at large. I had grown to like him. He still had those obnoxious, abrasive tendencies but didn't target the kids or me with them. We were so different in so many ways. He'd been raised in an idyllic home with devoted parents, while I...well, I had not. He liked calamari and escargot, whereas I was strictly a beans, corn-bread, and fried-taters gal. The kids liked him and had fun with him. He was steady. He loved me. He was dependable. He accepted my relationship with the Lord, and if nothing else, I felt a deep sense of loyalty toward him. Where exactly the loyalty thing came from eluded me. Maybe I didn't love him the way I had Dick or Joe or even Lee, but I decided the possibility was there. From a purely selfish point of view, that he loved *me* tipped the scales in favor of pursuing a future with him.

Again, it seemed as though God were performing some of his mysterious work in my life. Out of the blue, my landlord told me I'd have to move because he was selling the town house. Simultaneously, the lease was up on the house Jerry was renting. His roommate had plans to move out of the area, which left Jerry to find a place that he could afford on his own. It seemed that renting a house together was the practical thing to do. Since summer had just begun, there was no fear of discovery by his students or other faculty members who might disapprove of such an arrangement. The district would surely frown on a teacher living with the mother of his students.

We agreed to live together until the following September, when the school year started. If marriage wasn't a definite plan by that time, he would move out, and the kids and I would keep whatever house we found. We discussed it with the kids, and with trial marriage being such a popular concept at the time, they weren't too shocked and even agreed eagerly.

We found a great two-story, five-bedroom, three-bath house not far from where we already lived. The kids were delighted with the place. They each had their own room upstairs. Jerry and I took the bedroom downstairs at the end of a short hallway off the kitchen. The backyard was the size of a football field, and immediate plans for a garden were made.

The move was only the first of a rapid succession of events. I found work as a receptionist for a construction company and turned my back on college. Shortly after that, Steve, a very dear and longtime friend of the Sorich family, suffered a heart attack. When we went to visit him in the hospital, he was facing bypass surgery and was severely depressed.

"Well, old man," I teased him, "I certainly hope you're out of here in time to dance at my wedding."

His face brightened as he asked, "Are you two really going to do it? When?"

Oh, no, I didn't expect him to ask me for specifics. I only wanted to cheer him up.

Jerry caught the meaning of my uncertain, imploring look. Totally unruffled, he asked Steve, "When did you and Alice get married?"

"The twenty-fourth of September," Steve declared.

"Twenty-fourth of September, huh?" Jerry responded. "And my birthday is the twenty-fourth of October, which means that if we get married on your anniversary and one month before my birthday, I shouldn't ever forget my own anniversary and wind up in the doghouse. What do you think, Bobbie? Want to shoot for then?"

"Sure." I laughed nervously. "Why not? They've been married for over thirty years; it must be a good wedding date."

Steve cheered up considerably, which was the important thing. He not only recovered from surgery in time to dance at my wedding, but he also acted as my father and gave me away on September 24, 1977.

Because of the panic disorder and agoraphobia, I worked up a full load of anxiety planning the wedding. Playing it safe by going to Reno or Las Vegas to get married would have been my choice. Try as I might, I couldn't imagine getting through a formal ceremony without getting dizzy and nauseated. Jerry and his family, however, wanted a fair-sized, traditional service, and their word was pretty much law. Their desires were understandable, and making them understand mine seemed too daunting. They didn't comprehend the extent of my disorder, so they didn't see it as a big deal.

To me, the whole thing was a very big deal. I'd just started yet another new job at a real estate–title company that involved a world of unfamiliar, demanding duties. Topping that with preparing the guest list and the invitations, lining up a minister, and ordering the cake and flowers layered stress on stress. Making Binky's and Paula's peach-and-white eyelet bridesmaid dresses in addition to sewing my own dress of solid peach eyelet nearly sent me over the edge. Never had the hands on a clock gone round so quickly, nor had calendar pages turned so fast.

On the big day, though, I didn't have an attack severe enough to send me running out the side door of the church sanctuary. But trembling and feeling wrecked, I repeatedly mumbled to Steve as he coaxed me down the aisle, "I can't do this. I can't do this." He just beamed and kept tugging me along.

Once we were in front of the minister, everything became a blur while I concentrated on breathing slowly. Finally it was over.

Binky was the first to reach me after the pronounce-you-man-and-wife bit, and she laughed as she hugged me. "Mom, you did great, but it looked like you were standing in the center of an earthquake."

My new sister-in-law, Patti, was next. She was laughing, too. "The skirt of your dress was shaking so hard. We were all looking to see where the wind was coming from."

My ragged retort was, "Ha, that's nothing. You should have seen my jumping kneecaps."

Our wedding reception was fun and went off without a hitch. Our wedding night was a different story—no fun at all, with a huge hitch.

In our cozy motel room in Carmel, I came out of a sound sleep horribly sick to my stomach. Terrorized, I paced around the room.

A groggy Jerry propped himself up on one elbow. "What is it? What's the matter?"

"I don't know," I said breathlessly. "Help me; I think I'm going to be sick. I think I'm having a heart attack; it's beating so hard and fast."

But I wasn't having a heart attack, and after a bit, my heartbeat slowed, and the nausea passed. Feeling foolish, I chalked it up to the tension of the day and the hectic preparations of the previous weeks.

We returned home from our short honeymoon and resumed our usual schedules. Daily, we all went to school and work. Daily, we all met back at home to eat dinner and do home and house-work. Nightly, I woke up panic-stricken, sweating, and sick, run-ning for a door through which to escape.

At first I blamed it on the new job, so I quit and found another. That didn't solve the problem, and the nightly routine continued, which added sleep deprivation to my already-tension-racked body. A doctor I found in the phone book suggested two things: find a good friend to talk to and eat nothing for four hours prior to bed-time. It was an inexpensive enough prescription but ineffective.

So far I hadn't had any luck finding a sympathetic doctor in the area, which left me with a longing for Fairfield, Miss Callahan, and Dr. Parkinson. I had gone to the local mental-health clinic for a refill of my Valium and couldn't believe my ears when the staff physician told me he wouldn't write the prescription for me. Even after I recounted my medical history and listed the various medi-cations I was accustomed to taking, he wouldn't budge.

"Barbara," he said, dark eyes looking at me earnestly, "in the past, we doctors were trained in such a way that when a patient came to us with a complaint, we did something. If that meant pre-scribing nothing more than a placebo, that's what we did. More and more, however, we're beginning to believe that the best thing to do if we don't find a physical reason for a complaint is to do nothing. You appear to be functioning all right, except for this nightmare problem. I see no reason to medicate you."

"But I'm not having nightmares." My insistence fell on deaf ears.

All he had to say, as he stiffly walked me to the door, was to come back to see him every two weeks to let him know how I was do-ing. By my third visit, when he couldn't even remember my name, I disgustedly told him he would never be bothered with me again.

"Just so you know," I told him angrily, "so suddenly depriving my body of my medications has been a hellish affair. My vision is sometimes so blurred I have to hold completely still until it rights itself. My skin burns constantly, as if someone has poured gas on me and set me on fire. My stomach has always been sensitive, and now it's worse, even though I'm only eating the blandest of foods. If you're a married man, your wife can tell you that women don't usually think of shopping for new clothes as a dreaded chore. But if that shopping is because you're being scared thin, it's no fun at all. God help her, if she's dependent on you for help."

As I slammed the exit door in his astonished face, my anger vanished, and a mournful wailing flooded my gut. *Now what?*

CHAPTER FORTY-FOUR

*The good physician treats the disease; the great physician
treats the patient who has the disease.*

—*William Osler*

"Unbelievable!" Dr. Sjoberg exclaimed furiously. "It may be unprofessional for me to speak ill of a fellow psychiatrist, but advising a patient to discontinue Valium cold turkey, without medical supervision, is unthinkable."

Bernie Sjoberg came highly recommended by my social worker when I called to tell her about the fiasco with the doctor at the clinic.

"Let's lay out a better plan for you, OK?" He continued briskly. "I'm going to write a new scrip for your Valium. I want you to continue taking it as needed for the time being. You'll need to schedule weekly sessions with me while we taper you off. My hope is that we'll fix the reason you need it in the first place."

Heaving his stocky body out of his comfy leather chair, he walked around the desk to take a seat in the chair beside me. His blue eyes shone with compassion under his thinning blond hair. "I also want you to get a complete physical exam. We don't want to overlook any possible underlying physiological cause for your panic attacks." Reaching out to pat my arm, he assured me, "We'll get this figured out."

But we didn't. There were no new revelations or logical reasons for the panic attacks that woke me every night.

Dr. Sjoberg's recommendation of a physical exam was a good thing, though. The teachers union provided Jerry and me with the one-stop-shopping medical insurance, otherwise known as an HMO. The upside of that was I didn't have to shop for a doctor on my own. The downside was that all fields of medical practice were housed in one huge, ominous building.

The obstetrics-gynecology department was on the third floor. Due to my aversion to elevators, I used the stairs, so I arrived for this phase of my physical already breathless and tense, with flu-like symptoms coming on. After I checked in with the receptionist, a nurse escorted me to an examining room. Once she had gifted me with a dignity-robbing hospital gown and given me the predictable instruction to undress completely, she left. With hands trembling and perspiring heavily, I barely managed to unbutton my blouse.

The examination table, with its familiar stirrups, reminded me of how helpless I'd be as soon as I lay on it. Every muscle in my body was taut and quivering, nerve endings on fire. Nausea and colon cramps tore through me as my body threatened the old diarrhea routine. Breathing was shallow and difficult. Air couldn't make its way to the bottom of my lungs. My ears plugged up as if I were at a much higher elevation than only three stories above ground. In short, I felt lousy. But I couldn't just stand there naked, so I slipped into the gown and onto the table; I was determined to stick it out and get it over with.

Perched on the edge of the table, I clutched the paper sheet over my lap to dry some of the perspiration from my hands. Trying to think of anything other than what my body was doing, I tried to focus on the posters on the wall depicting cross-section photographs of the female anatomy or babies in utero making their way through the birth canal. A nice picture depicting fields of daisies would have had a more calming effect.

A rap on the door told me the doctor had arrived. "Hello, Barbara?" he inquired.

Fearing I'd be sick if I opened my mouth, a nod was the only reply I could manage.

Satisfied that he had the right patient, he closed the door, grabbed a rolling stool, and sat down. "I'm Dr. Phillip Miller; nice to meet you." He held out his hand to shake mine, but I couldn't let go of the sheet. "Uh, right," he said and withdrew the offer of a handshake. "Let's see, you're here for a routine pelvic exam. Is that right, or is there a particular complaint?"

As I tried to answer him, the room started spinning, and I began falling up! It felt like my personal gravity had disappeared. Lying back on the table, I turned my body toward the wall, trying to find something to grab and hold on to to keep from floating away.

"Oh, oh, no." Finally finding my voice, I gasped, "I'm sorry. I'm so sorry. I don't know what's happening to me. Water, oh, please, can I have a sip of water? Can I have a wet towel? Hot! It's so hot in here. I can't breathe." Words of near hysteria and distress shot out of my mouth like short bursts of gunfire.

While I imagined this doctor would call hospital security or men with straitjackets, he calmly and unhurriedly brought me a paper cup of water and pressed a wet paper towel into my hands.

Very softly, he said, "I don't know what's happening, either, but whatever it is, it's OK with me. You're OK with me. I'm just going to sit here with you, and when you feel better—and I'm sure you will in a moment—we can either go ahead with the exam or you can come back another time. Whatever you choose is all right, OK?"

Shame collided with great relief as he told me I had a choice. Having a choice meant I wasn't helpless after all. His gentleness and acceptance were a soothing balm on my mind. The ensuing calm allowed me to really see him for the first time and to appreciate the reddish-blond hair and the kind blue eyes that topped high, prominent cheekbones. His full mouth neither frowned nor smiled. His face held a matter-of-fact expression, as though he encountered this kind of behavior every day.

The intensity of the panic attack decreased, and while I still dreaded the examination, I found that I wanted this man's respect. As with Dr. Cedar, I wanted to repay his kindness by being a good patient.

Still massaging my face with the wet paper towel, I told him, "I'd like to go ahead with the exam, if it's all right with you. I'd also like to give you an explanation for my behavior, but unfortunately, I can't. I've been like this for a long time, and don't know why. I'll behave now. I promise."

"Why are you apologizing to me, Barbara?" he asked. "I'm sorry you had to go through that, but it didn't directly hurt me. You can do or be whatever you need to here, with no apology. It's OK... really."

He did a quick and thorough yet gentle examination. Once finished, he tried to take one of my hands, but I had them tightly clasped together. So he gently massaged an arm while he told me the news.

"In my estimation," he said, "you're about six weeks pregnant."

At his words, I knew how General Custer felt at Little Bighorn with all those arrows flying at him. Mine were emotional arrows, each one in direct conflict with the one preceding it. Joy, fear, excitement, terror, wonder, and self-doubt attacked my senses.

"Barbara, wide eyes are becoming on you, but they don't really convey how you feel about this news," Dr. Miller commented.

Struggling to sit up, I told him, "I was told I'd never carry another child." My voice took on a husky whisper. "I don't know how I can do this. I mean, what if I go crazy in the process of having this baby?"

Understandingly, he questioned why I had those concerns, and I explained about my fear of fear and its negative impact on a huge part of my life.

His response offered some assurance and comfort. "Well, perhaps we can lessen that fear of yours by agreeing that I think you're OK. I don't see you as crazy in the least little bit. Being here does seem to create terrible tension for you, but we can take our time and wait for you to feel at ease before we touch you. I'll try to prepare you at all times for what I'm going to do and what I need you to do. I believe you're going to be fine. Maybe in time, you'll start believing that, too. Whaddaya say? Wanna have a baby?"

The smile I gave him was uncertain. I sure hadn't expected this!

My announcement that evening shocked Jerry and the kids. Looking around the room at my four teenage children, I tried to visualize a baby in our midst. I couldn't. Apparently neither could they, judging by the disbelieving looks they gave one another.

"Well, in the future, if y'all are making too much noise, I know how to hush you up," I nervously teased.

Mildly sick from the pregnancy, I soon became filled with the never-ending wonder that a small human being was forming inside me.

Around this time, I began seeing a psychiatric social worker named May Gere, whom we'd met at church. As a woman, she was everything I wanted to be: witty, energetic, and strong but not cold or unfeeling. She was an impish woman, both in stature and personality. Her snow-white hair, cut like a little boy's hair, added to her impish look. To me, her most important quality was that she was a Christian.

Upon hearing that labels for my ailments encouraged me, she quickly gave my nightly problem a name: night terror. What an intimidating label, but it certainly suited the symptoms.

May and I worked hard to discover the cause; however, one crisis after another kept cropping up and competed for our attention. Family issues moved our focus away from the phobias and night terror. She found herself constantly endeavoring to just keep me going from one day to the next.

In the third month of the pregnancy, I started spotting blood. A trip to Dr. Miller confirmed that I was losing the baby. The only thing he could do was put me on strict bed rest and wait and see. Despite three weeks flat on my back, the spotting turned into flowing, and it was obvious that the baby hadn't survived.

Initially I'd been unsure that I wanted the baby, but when I was confronted with losing it, I felt crushed. I fought against the surgical procedure to remove any remaining tissue, but the danger of infection was such a threat that the dilation and curettage could not be put off. When I pinpointed exactly what my fears were, Dr. Miller decided to do the procedure in the emergency room as opposed to the surgery center. He also decided to do it only giving me a local anesthetic rather than putting me out completely. Bless him. My anxiety level mattered to him, and he always seemed to know how to minimize my emotional discomfort.

The day of the procedure presented Jerry with his first serious confrontation with my phobias. He didn't care for it at all. While I had been restricted to bed at home, he had patiently taken care of me, but his patience had run out. He was relieved that it would soon be over and didn't see why I was trembling and stalling, treating it as a big deal.

"Why in God's name can't you just do this and get it over with?" he exploded. "I'm tired! I can't take this anymore. Just do it!"

Dr. Miller leaped from his stool and, grabbing Jerry by the arm, turned him toward the door to the lobby. "I think it would be best for you to wait out there," he suggested.

Jerry's anger filled me with shame. My very soul cringed at his words. "Oh my God," I cried to Dr. Miller, "what made me think I could be married?"

Due to my crippling nervousness, I was unable to walk, so Dr. Miller put me into a wheelchair and wheeled me to emergency. He administered Valium intravenously and did what he had to do.

When I was wheeled out of surgery, I raised my arms to Jerry for a hug and felt destroyed when he wouldn't even look at me. Again, I wondered how I could expect someone to understand me when I couldn't understand myself.

We didn't talk about that incident much, if at all, and tried to resume living our lives as before. But the whole ordeal carved a scar onto the face of our marriage. It was ugly and left me lonely. Physically, I went through the motions of being his wife; emotionally, I retreated from him behind a wall of defense.

A month later, I was pregnant again. We hardly dared to hope I would carry the baby to term. But a strong heartbeat was detected, and just shy of five months, movement was perceptible. It seemed the Sorichs were indeed going to have a baby.

Since I'd made so many trips to see Dr. Miller, I began feeling more comfortable with the building that housed him. The closer I got to my due date, though, the more apprehensive I grew and the more I doubted that I could manage the labor and delivery. The night terror continued, and since I was working full time, a nap during the day was not an option. Getting enough rest just wasn't possible. My nerves were shot. It was a horrible time. Falling asleep only to be jolted awake, sick and terrified, was wearing me out. Dr. Miller had originally urged me to quit smoking and stop the Valium, but then he decided that anything offering me any semblance of comfort was fine by him.

During one of my routine prenatal visits with him, I voiced one of the many concerns plaguing me. "Would you be able to tell I'm a Christian if I didn't tell you so?"

"Why do you ask?" he hedged.

My admission just fell out of my mouth. "It's one of the things that bother me about being the way I am. My wish is that just by observing me, people will know I'm a Christian and love the Lord. But I'm afraid this illness hides that part of me."

He merely looked at me with a sad expression and shrugged, offering no reply.

Throughout the pregnancy, it was challenging for May and me to concentrate on the cause of the night terror, because life was so constantly beset with other urgent issues. The as-yet-unspoken-of trauma Paula had experienced in her early childhood, combined with discovering that she wasn't who she thought she was, raced up from her subconscious to painful, angry consciousness. She would cut school or, if she did attend, wouldn't come home after. Two or three days might pass without a word from or about her before the mother of a friend would call to tell me she had found Paula hiding in a closet. After several months of being placed on restriction, she ran away completely.

Jerry and I fought over the kids constantly. I felt he didn't understand their issues and was just being insensitive to all of us. The pregnancy had us feeling stuck, though, so we limped on without much faith at all that our marriage would survive.

We tried group family counseling with May, but she was unable to prevent our family from falling apart. Circumstances weren't ideal for the addition of a baby. I felt like a wad of overused and abused Silly Putty.

That summer, prior to her senior year of high school, Binky delivered a shocking blow. She went to visit a friend in Fairfield, and about the time she was due to come home, she called to say she wanted to drop out of high school, get a job in Fairfield, and live there.

Having graduated, Ricky also wanted to return to Fairfield to work and live with a friend.

Butch had originally had the best relationship with Jerry, but they became constantly at odds with one another. They argued and fought incessantly.

"How can I even consider being happy about this baby?" I wailed to May during a session. "Just look at my family! The one thing I prided myself on was that as a single mother, I'd managed to keep our family together, and now just look what's happened. I should never have gotten married. It was too soon. I should have waited until all the kids had grown and gone. And now to raise another child, knowing I've already failed with four…"

May did her best to point out that these things happened under much-better conditions than ours had been, but despair threatened to eat me alive.

Concerned about my emotional state, Dr. Miller asked a young woman by the name of Cynthia to call on me. She was a labor coach, training at the hospital to become a midwife. Dr. Miller wanted us to get acquainted before the onset of labor so that I would feel as though I had a special friend to help me through delivery. As it turned out, she was with me, and he was not. Labor began on December 11, 1978, while he was on vacation.

Cynthia was wonderfully sweet and gentle. Thin as a rail, with long, straight, blond hair, her physical presence was hardly noticeable. The soft quality of her voice was intended to soothe and relax, I supposed, but to me, relaxing meant giving up control and letting my guard down. Relaxing meant becoming vulnerable, thus giving fear and dizziness an open gate through which they could attack me. Loud, raucous joking would have suited me better. Having her with me served the purpose Dr. Miller hoped for, though. She did a terrific job of running interference for me with the hospital staff. They had a routine they followed that didn't fit me and my panic. She dictated my needs to them in no uncertain terms, and I totally put myself in her hands. The staff obviously respected her and obeyed her every request concerning me and the birth of our child.

Natural childbirth was new to me. The labor was, well, laborious. But I knew what to expect, so it was fine. But the delivery was a bit more hectic. As soon as I was able to push that baby out to claim a life of his own, we discovered why delivery had been so difficult: he weighed nine pounds ten and a half ounces. For my small frame to accommodate such a moose was a miracle. Robert Simon Sorich blasted his way into the world, blond, blue-eyed, and angrily screaming loud enough to intimidate the most seasoned, experienced hospital staff…and mother.

CHAPTER FORTY-FIVE

A woman who gives any advantage to a man may expect
a lover but will sooner or later find a tyrant.

—Lord Byron

With a new baby, my sessions with May and the night-terror problem got put on a back burner. In fact, since Simon demanded a bottle every two hours, sleep was so brief the night terror had no time to build.

From the time I had gotten pregnant, other than the fear that I wouldn't be able to control myself during labor and delivery, I had been fairly functional and free of panic attacks. Six months after Simon was born, however, the dizziness began launching surprise attacks that both jolted and depressed me. The night terror had been tough, but at least it had allowed me to function during the day, not a bad trade-off as far as I was concerned. Back into therapy I went.

Therapy with May was different than it had been with Miss Callahan. Maybe the psychiatric community as a whole had changed its beliefs about the treatment patients should receive, or maybe it was just May's personal style that was different. Whatever the case, while we still dug around in my past a lot, she answered any questions I asked with direct answers. She treated me as an equal and a friend rather than a patient. Believing that relationships are based on give-and-take, I felt unworthy of her friendship, since my self-image had plummeted, leaving me to believe I had nothing to give. A child wandering around in a woman's body was how I saw myself. To expect anyone to respect my opinion or take me seriously seemed unrealistic. Since I looked down on myself, I expected others to do the same.

"It feels like there are all these people inside my head," I told May. "They fight all the time. I wish they would shut up. All the conflict makes me tired."

"Who do you think these people are?" she asked.

Her question made me squirm with embarrassment. "Well, sometimes I get strong messages that sound like Grandma, and at other times, I swear I hear my mother. But there's also this fearful little girl. I think maybe she causes the dizziness. When she's afraid, she makes me dizzy. Then the mother angrily tells her to shut up and behave. Grandma tells her, 'Tsk, tsk, just settle down. There's nothin' to be skeered of.' I guess they're all just parts of me, but when I try to get some thoughts into the mix, Mother and Grandma squelch them. If I think about flying in a plane, for example, the little girl says she's too scared. Grandma says that folks weren't meant to fly anyway, and Mother says, 'Yeah, and you'll crap, too, if you eat regular.'"

As May listened, her usual bright, cheerful expression took on a look of excitement, as though she were about to let me in on a great secret.

Giving a delighted laugh, she said, "You don't realize how normal you are. We all have these different personas or influences that determine our thought life and, consequently, our behavior. There's a parent who will be nurturing or criticizing. You got a double whammy with two who are critical. We also have a child, who will either be free or adapted. That child is the source of our emotions. Then there's an adult, whose job it is to give an objective appraisal of reality and referee between the two should conflict arise. It sounds as though the adapted, fearful child and the critical parents are dominating the reasoning, reality-based adult in you."

"So I don't know about being normal," I replied pensively, "but I sure am crowded."

She worked hard with me and used every therapy technique she knew. That they didn't work was not her fault. If nothing else, her constant encouragement did make me feel better about myself. She even offered to spend the night in a motel with me to observe a night-terror episode. The very idea of putting her out like that was unthinkable. She challenged that I was worth it, whether I thought so or not, but sheer pride and embarrassment prevented me from taking her up on her offer.

When I became pregnant again, I was surprised but not as panicked as with the pregnancy with Simon. The new child within me grew, and at the usual four-month mark, it kept me mindful of its presence with frequent kicks and movement. At five months, it stopped. There were no warning signs of a miscarriage, so it was a shock when it died in utero.

Dr. Miller ordered a scan that confirmed that the baby had indeed died, and he wanted to perform a dilation and curettage as soon as I felt comfortable with the idea. After weeks of grieving, I thought I had reconciled and accepted the loss and believed I was ready to take the necessary steps to put the whole painful experience behind me. Dr. Miller was on vacation again, so I had to make an appointment with an unfamiliar doctor. Anxiety about going through this procedure without Dr. Miller rapidly built up.

Jerry accompanied me to the hospital, and once there, I tried, oh, how I tried, to go through with the surgery. Stripping down and putting on a surgical gown was required. But emotional paralysis took over mind and body, and I couldn't get further than removing my blouse.

The doctor, a young, dark-haired man, gently coaxed and cajoled me while Jerry paced, snorted, and pulled at his moustache. Unable to go forward or backward, I sat, shuddering and crying.

"Barbara, it's up to you," the doctor said. "This isn't an emergency, so you can do it now or later. The only risk to you is that if you wait too long, infection could set in."

My brain jammed, and I couldn't make a decision.

"Just get this the hell over with," Jerry growled. "I'm not going to sit here all day, watching you cry, and the doctor has better things to do. Why didn't you tell me you were this way before we got married?"

It struck me as being futile to remind him that I had told him I was "this way" in as much detail as I was able, but he hadn't heeded my warning. Oddly enough, Jerry's anger zapped energy into my brain. Wordlessly but resolutely, I put on my blouse and walked out. He was furious! The certainty that, this time, our marriage was surely doomed enveloped me. How could he bear being stuck with someone like me? I was a coward and a baby. I became angrier and more defensive than ever. Seeking consolation, I told myself it was OK; I'd just stop depending on him, and then he couldn't hurt me anymore. And with that thought, I closed off more feeling for my husband.

When Dr. Miller returned, I went to see him…alone.

"Well, Barb," he greeted me, "how's it going? Any bleeding or unusual discharge yet?"

"No, and that's what makes this so hard. I've seen no signs that I'm losing this baby, and surgically removing its little body from mine feels like an abortion. I can't do this."

He sat on his stool, rolled closer to me, and reached for my hands. He took them gently but firmly in his own and said, "I can assure you the baby has died. I'm sorry, but it's true. You're in no immediate physical danger, so if you want to wait for proof, you can do that. I'll wait for you."

There it was again: compassion and acceptance without anger or pressure. I loved this man.

"What procedure would you use when you do *it?*" I humbly asked.

"Well, believe it or not," he answered, "there are several ways we can go."

"Several ways!" I exclaimed. "I asked the other doctor what the alternatives were, and he said there weren't any."

"Oh, him." Dr. Miller laughed, waving a hand dismissively. "I hear you really gave him a rough time. Cynthia told me all about it. She said she was so proud of you for not letting yourself be railroaded. Ya done good, kid. Yes, several ways. The one I recommend is the insertion of a small cylinder-shaped piece of dried seaweed into the vaginal opening. It absorbs all the tissue, and then all I have to do is remove it. I can do the insertion today, and you should come in first thing tomorrow to have it cleaned out."

Once again, I marveled at the difference in doctors. Since they're only human beings, I wondered if we patients expected too much of them. My own expectations had been uniformity in opinion and method of treatment. How wrong I'd been. Whatever had made me uncomfortable and caused such a bad experience with the other doctor had served me well. Something had told me to wait. Sure, I'd felt lousy, but I had been right. Dr. Miller affirmed that my instinct had been good and that I'd had the right to use it, which was something I needed to know and believe. But with my lack of emotional health, was my instinct always trustworthy?

CHAPTER FORTY-SIX

Courage is fear holding on a minute longer.

—George S. Patton

"Jerry, do you really believe you're a Christian?" I asked one night several weeks after the loss of the baby.

"Yeah, of course I do." His answer held a tone of indignation. "I went to Catholic schools all my life and went to mass every Sunday. I believe in God and all that; yeah, I'm a Christian. Why do you ask?"

"Well, do you believe that God works in your life? I mean, do you believe he isn't just stuck up there in heaven but is right in your heart, watching and caring for you? Disapproving of your behavior at times but always loving you?"

He kind of snarled at that. "I believe in prayer, if that's what you mean. Why?"

"I want to go back to church. I *need* to go back to church; I need the fellowship. Even with our friends, I feel lonely and need to walk with the Lord again."

When we were first married, I went to church alone. Sometimes the kids would go, but Jerry wouldn't. After the first miscarriage, I told him I needed him to go with me, and for a while, he went every week. But when one of the women there criticized his teaching style, he refused to continue, and I stopped going as well.

Pressing him further, I tried bargaining with him. "Look, we can go back to our old church for a while and give it another chance. If you don't like it, May's husband will be pastoring his own church soon, and we can go there instead. It's an Episcopal church, which is supposed to be like a Catholic church. Maybe you'd feel more comfortable there. What do you think?"

"I'd rather just wait, if it's all the same to you," he tartly replied.

So as soon as Fred became the priest there, we started attending St. Joseph's Episcopal Church. We enjoyed active roles there and grew in the Lord with Christians more mature than ourselves. The smaller congregation especially appealed to me. Potlucks were frequent, and under May's tutelage, combined with the ultrarelaxed atmosphere, I learned how to potluck with the best of 'em. Still not socially comfortable, I was sure the others thought me a little on the quirky side, but they fully embraced me, no questions asked.

Age had stripped away most of the white paint on the old church building, creating gray ghostlike shapes in the weathered wood on the exterior walls. The small steeple was still intact, with a noisily functioning bell. Repairs of one kind or another were constantly needed, along with volunteers to make those repairs; hence it was that Jerry was on the church roof when I called there one Saturday.

"Hello," a man panted heavily into the phone. "May I help you?"

"Hi, Art. It's Bobbie. Is Jerry available?"

"Hey, Bobbie. He's on the roof. Can I give him a message?"

"Uh, no. That's probably not a good idea. Can you ask him to come down for just a minute? I won't keep him long."

"OK, hang on."

Apprehension prowled around my gut as I waited for Jerry to get to the phone. Heavy, booted footsteps announced his approach.

"Yeah, what's up?" he asked brusquely.

The reason for the call needed to be eased into. "Well, it's the darnedest thing...Remember how I thought I had the flu? I just came from seeing Dr. Camara, and it turns out it's not the flu after all. I'm, uh, pregnant."

By now people found it hard to believe we were practicing the dubious art of birth control, but we really were. Simon was sixteen months old, and I'd had concerns about his being an only child. So news of another baby wasn't all that alarming to me.

Jerry had left teaching when he'd found out he could make more money in carpentry. The change in jobs meant a change in medical insurance, so I couldn't have Dr. Miller as my obstetrician. My instincts and I had to find another doctor to deliver the baby... if the baby made it.

My first choice turned out to have too busy a practice to cater to my emotional needs, so I turned to Cynthia for advice, since she worked with so many OB-GYNs. She enthusiastically recommended Dr. Suzanne Regul at the Center for Life in Santa Clara. She was a threefold blessing: a woman, a mother, and a Christian.

Dr. Regul preferred the Lamaze method of childbirth and alternative birthing rooms for her patients. Avoiding the usual large, scary, and sterile hospital delivery room sounded great to me. It didn't seem to be a good idea to reveal my problems with panic and agoraphobia to her. I feared that if she knew the whole truth about me, she'd feel the alternative birthing room was too risky and refuse to deliver there. To her, I wanted to appear every inch the normal, carefree, expectant mommy.

During this pregnancy, a refreshing relaxation was born out of the fellowship I enjoyed in a new Bible study I'd been attending apart from St. Joseph's. A new flame burned in my heart for the Lord, which was brought about by the prayers of the people in the group. A few of them were new Christians, and one woman in particular had a past to which I could relate. All of them were down-to-earth and real; there were no holier-than-thou attitudes, which helped me feel at ease.

After attending this study several weeks without Jerry, I went home one night and announced that I wasn't going back.

"Not going back?" he asked, surprised. "You love that study. All I've heard from you since you started is about how great it is and how great the people are."

"I know. But I had to go places a long time by myself when I was single, and I don't want to do it anymore. They're all married couples, so if you go, I'll go. If you don't, I won't, either."

The next Monday night, Jerry was meeting and shaking hands with Scott, Steve, John, and Rick at the Bible study. God took my shabby presentation and blessed it.

There were several similarities between Steve and Linda Spence, the hosts of the study, and Jerry and me. They had been married before and had only recently become Christians. The children they had were from her previous marriage. Steve was a carpenter like Jerry, and Linda was considered to be somewhat of an airhead like me. A friendship with them grew quickly.

The church that Steve and Linda belonged to appealed to me. Why I was drawn to it, I couldn't explain, but drawn I was. Jerry emphatically refused to change churches, so I went to Spring Valley Church alone when, for whatever reason, he planned to skip church that Sunday. The pastor had an animated style that really stirred me up and taught the Bible like no one I'd ever heard.

Whereas I had previously claimed to love the Lord, it was again a selfish love. I only cared about what he could do for me: heal me, make me feel good, and love me unconditionally. A new style of love crept up on me as I decided to live more according to what he wanted from me. A desire to deserve the blood he'd shed for me grew in my heart. His word was what I wanted to exemplify my life. However, the phobia problem kept getting in the way.

My weakness and what I perceived as a lack of faith brought agony to my heart. Buckets of tears were cried over the fact that I wasn't the gracious witness for Christ I wanted to be.

Even though I admired the behavior of the women at Spring Valley Church, I couldn't relate to them. The feelings of inferiority continued to plague me and cause me to ask myself what they had that I didn't. My conclusion was that they simply had more faith, so I prayed to develop more faith.

While I was sure God appreciated my motivation, he was apparently trying to accomplish something in my life that I didn't recognize yet. Unhappiness about my life in general continued. Incessantly, I prayed for healing but did not feel healed, so I adopted the belief that perhaps the anxiety disorder and all that went with it were to be the thorn assigned to my side. That brought little comfort.

In desperation, I asked Pastor Mills to visit me at home. When he arrived, I explained my problem as best I could. His response horrified me.

"Unconfessed sin," was his cavalier explanation. "There must be some unconfessed sin getting in the way of your prayer; just repent and believe. That's all."

His words crushed me. "Pastor, I have confessed my sins. God knew about them all along anyway, but I have confessed. I've prayed for forgiveness and told him how sorry I am for everything. None of that has gotten rid of the dizzy spells or the fear. Would you tell a person with diabetes or cancer that he or she merely suffers from unconfessed sin or weak faith?"

With a pompous look, he replied, "Of course not! That's ridiculous."

"Yes, yes, it certainly is." I refrained from telling him I thought *he* was pretty ridiculous as well.

Pastor Mill's attitude drastically altered my opinion of him. Once again, I had bared my soul to someone only to have it stomped on. Instead of comfort, he'd tried to feed me a heaping spoonful of shame.

By that time, Jerry was also attending Spring Valley, so despite my disenchantment with Pastor Mills, I continued going there. I seriously doubted that Jerry and the kids would agree to yet another change in churches, and I wouldn't have blamed them. The loving, kind people at St. Joseph's had made it hard to leave there, but we had felt that the Lord was moving us and had wanted to do what we perceived as his leading.

During this transition, our wonderful Samuel Thomas was born. His name was chosen because Samuel means "asked of God" and Thomas means "the worker."

His birth was a far cry from what I'd planned. I didn't get the desired calm, peaceful, alternate birthing room, but I got the one that was safe and necessary for everyone's peace of mind. We didn't know that Sam had decided to enter the world face first. During the last stages of labor, Dr. Regul performed a routine internal examination and couldn't feel Sam's head. She frantically ordered a scan, which revealed a possible abnormality or deformity. All I knew was that the pain was more intense than with any labor I'd experienced before.

An enormous fear snatched away the world around me. A gurney flew me into a delivery room as ceiling lights rushed by overhead in blurs. Doctors charged through doors, shedding coats and flinging them haphazardly in the air. I was vaguely aware that the room was filling up with pediatricians, anesthesiologists, and additional obstetricians to assist Dr. Regul. The scene became a standing-room-only affair while I repeatedly whimpered, "Please let my baby be OK; please let my baby be OK." And he was.

Due to the pressure on his little face while making his way through the birth canal, he was far from a beautiful baby, but he was fine and whole, weighing in at nine pounds one ounce. He was so bruised and pitiful looking that when a nurse placed him in my arms, I laughingly told him, "You poor, little, ugly thing, I promise to make this up to you. Even when you're a big boy, I'll leave you out of the dishwashing rotation."

"You better hope he forgets that." The nurse laughed with me. "He has a lot of witnesses to what you just promised him."

My body was completely exhausted, but my heart was relieved as I held him close and nuzzled his cheeks. Because he was my seventh baby, I had worried that I might have run out of love. My worry was completely unfounded. As with all his brothers and sisters, my heart overflowed with instant and complete devotion.

All too soon, a nurse eased Sammy out of my arms to take him to the nursery. Jerry stood up and prepared to leave.

Lifting my eyes from Sammy's face, I put in a request. "Before you head for home, would you run over to the store and bring me a Coke and pack of cigarettes?"

"What?" he snapped sharply. "I've had a hard day and need a drink. I'm going home to get as drunk as possible." No hug, no kiss, no expression of concern...just the retreating back of a plaid flannel shirt.

Shocked indignation prevented any response. Unable to believe my ears, I simply lay back against the pillows, feeling stung and thirsty and craving a cigarette. A phone call brought Paula to the rescue, wielding caffeine and nicotine, and when the nurse brought Sammy back for his first feeding, those hurt feelings and anger took a hike. His face and head had already lost that scrunched appearance, and cradling his sweetness made everything else unimportant. He seemed to like me OK, too.

Shortly after Sammy's first birthday that next February, we had a particularly heavy rainy season. It wasn't a good time for carpenters. Jerry was laid off more days than he worked, so he quit and tried his hand at other jobs, none of which paid well.

We were committed to my staying home to raise the children, but when Jerry decided to start his own business, it became obvious that I would have to work outside the home for a while. We set a goal of one year for me to work. If the business was not supporting us by that time, I would stay home again, and Jerry would find something else. Neither of us was happy about this turn of events. That old, paralyzing fear seized me as I contemplated going back into the world with my phobias. Doubt that I'd be able to hold down a job without making a fool of myself by either fainting or running out the door in a panic still reigned.

Placement through temporary-employment agencies always appealed to me. To me, the phrase "temporary employment" meant that I had the freedom to quit the job without guilt. The agency I signed on with placed me in the sales office of a construction company. The building phase of a medical-office complex had been completed; it was time to sell the finished product. A few doctors had already purchased units and begun their practices there. It fell to me to collect their monthly payments and handle any sales calls.

It was easy for me to function well in my position since most of the time I was alone. A groundkeeper-maintenance man popped in occasionally, but other than that, I had the place to myself.

Dizziness also popped in occasionally, but it was not severe enough to make me flee with no thought of returning, as was my usual pattern. Besides, we needed the money.

It was easy to delude myself into thinking that since I was holding down a job, I was getting better. The truth was I had merely exchanged one safe place for another. The office became my second home. Whenever there was a break in my regular routine, like going to a store alone, I had to face the fact that I was still unwell emotionally.

The time for my yearly physical rolled around and spread a black cloud of panic over my head, the same level of panic I always felt when confronted with any situation I perceived as threatening. Dr. Regul called me to ask why I hadn't yet come in. By then I had shared with her my problems with anxiety.

Stalling, I told her, "I'm just not ready. Maybe I should see a therapist first to help prepare myself. I wish with all my heart that I could find a doctor who could explain what goes on in my body when the dizziness and panic attacks hit. If only I could understand."

"Well, I know of a doctor near here who's married to a psychiatric therapist," she offered. "Perhaps between the two of them, they could treat both the physical and the emotional…join forces, so to speak. How does that sound?"

"Sounds promising. It just might be what I've prayed for. Now we're getting somewhere."

She gave me the names and phone number, and I called for an appointment with great enthusiasm.

Dr. Grieg was a kind man, but disappointment cut through me like a knife as it became clear that he was content to let me go on as I had. The very label I had longed for turned against me. As soon as he heard "anxiety attacks" and "agoraphobia," he stopped considering a physical ailment of any kind and referred me back to the psychiatric community, which, in this case, was his wife.

And so my counseling with Margo Grieg began. Back into my childhood, we went, rehashing and reliving my history.

"Maybe when you don't hate the people from your past any longer," she suggested during a session, "you won't have these symptoms."

I was astonished. "Hate them? I don't hate them. Hate and resentment have passed. I just want to get well. I'm angry, and hate that I seem to be suffering for their mistakes, but I don't hate them as people."

"Even your father?" she countered.

My father had died years before from an alcohol-related, bleeding stomach ulcer.

"Yes, even my father," was my honest reply. "Not too long ago, I saw a man walking down the road who looked so much like him I almost lost control of my car. Then relief flooded over me as I realized it was just a man, just like my father was just a man. Like any other man, he committed sinful acts, but he's God's responsibility, not mine. That he wasn't able to fight his sinful nature in time to prevent the awful thing he did to me is not my problem. Hating him would be futile, a waste of time. So I don't hate; I hurt. I hurt terribly. I just want to be normal. I've been told for years that the reason I suffer from agoraphobia and anxiety is because of my childhood. Sure, those circumstances make me mad, but the people involved couldn't help themselves. They acted out of their own emotional problems. I bear them no ill will; I just want to get on with my life."

"I must say," she conceded, "that does make sense. Anger at the situation is different from anger directed at the people."

Margo and I hung in there together for a time, but as usual, there were no great or new revelations. The secret of wellness continued to elude me as I went back and forth between her and Dr. Grieg.

Even though I insisted that Valium was the only medication I tolerated well, Dr. Grieg replaced Valium with an antidepressant drug that made me so sleepy I could barely function.

"Margo," I pleaded one day, "can you please convince your husband to put me back on Valium? This stuff he prescribes puts me in la-la land. I can't take it."

"Yeah, I know what you mean," she responded. "I have Ménière's disease. When we fly somewhere, he prescribes the same medication for me, and I miss out on half our vacation because I sleep through it."

"Ménière's disease? What's that?"

"It's a disease of the inner ear," she explains. "In fact, I wanted to ask you to pray for me. It's been bad lately, and we're due to go on a trip. I don't want my ear to act up to the extent I can't enjoy myself. When it does, my equilibrium goes out of whack, and I feel like I'm drunk."

"Hmm, sounds familiar," I quipped. "Can I recommend a good psychotherapist to you?"

"Getting back to you, Bobbie." She switched gears on me. "I've been meaning to ask if you and Jerry would consider changing churches. I know a small group of Christians who have started a church called North Valley Community. They're all young couples dedicated to raising healthy Christian children. I won't knock Spring Valley and Pastor Mills too much, except to say that I've counseled people from that church, and if you start there with a poor self-image, you end up with a lower one. I think you'd find the love and acceptance you need at North Valley. I'll give you the name and number of a gal I know there who would be happy to tell you more."

After talking at length with Patti Close, one of the founders of North Valley, we did start attending there. Everything she said about this church appealed to me. Teaching replaced preaching, as the Bible was studied as a group with no denominational slant or side of fries. Foundationally, the sole purpose of these people was to learn it and then live it.

And live it they certainly did. The admiration and love I felt for the women there knew no bounds. They set examples of parenting and womanhood that I gladly and gratefully mimicked. Their acceptance and inclusion of me into their lives was like a warm hug. They all had special gifts and talents that they shared with me, and I flourished in their company.

People generally speak negatively about lives lived in a rut. In my case, I loved a rutted life. It was a predictable, familiar, and nonchallenging comfort zone. When someone, or something, threw anything outside my routine into my rut, it was a boulder thrown into my path. The jury summons that came in the mail was just such a boulder. I could get over or maybe around it, but one thing I knew for sure…I couldn't get through it. Barely able to even enter a courthouse, I certainly couldn't be held captive in a jury box. Additionally, I was convinced that the courthouse in San Jose would be much bigger and more frightening than the one in Fairfield. Frantically, I tried to think of a way out.

Margo had already gone on her trip, which left me with a feeling of helpless abandonment. Unwilling to face his predictable ridicule, I couldn't go to Jerry with my dismay.

Aside from a few small challenges, life had been going along fairly well. Daily I'd go to my office to play office manager, go home to play with my two adored toddlers, and then play at pretending I was a normal, functional, capable woman. Now this!

That critical parent voice mocked me. "Look at you, little Miss Hotshot. You think you're doing so well. What makes you think you'd get off so easy? Think you can do this? Think you can control yourself long enough to be a good citizen and do your civic duty? Ha!"

Shame and panic reduced me to nothing. Over and over, I berated myself. *Why can't I take these things in stride?*

With trembling hands, I called Patti's husband, Don, for an appointment. As he was a licensed therapist, I hoped he could help.

Once in session with him, I explained that I'd been agoraphobic for almost twenty years and that a summons for jury duty had me scared to death. He agreed that under the circumstances, my presence in a courtroom would definitely not further the cause of justice.

As our session got underway, he didn't ask me the usual questions about my childhood and waved aside my attempts to offer such information as being unimportant. He didn't care to hear about my past pain, the buried scream, or any of the things that held so much interest to previous therapists. He merely asked me one question as he handed me a hastily written letter to the court.

"Tell me, Bobbie, when was it that you decided to become phobic?"

CHAPTER FORTY-SEVEN

Nothing is more desirable than to be released from an affliction, but nothing is more frightening than to be divested of a crutch.

—James A. Baldwin

I ndignation and rage yanked me out of the chair and onto my feet. "What do you mean? Being phobic isn't a choice I've made. How can you say such a thing?"

My furious response was wasted on him. His dark-brown eyes calmly appraised me as he said, "You've paid for an hour of my time. There're no exchanges and no returns, so you might as well get your money's worth and use me."

Curious but still angry and defiant, I sat back down. As it turned out, he practiced a completely different kind of therapy than I'd previously known. His primary goal, it seemed, was to determine how and when I adopted agoraphobia to protect myself. It was a struggle for me to grasp that anyone would deliberately make that choice. As we delved deeper, however, a new understanding evolved.

He explored other areas of my life not dealt with before. He administered a written test to determine if my diet was a contributing factor to the anxiety and dizziness. He pointed out that a proper diet is absolutely essential for people suffering from stress-related illnesses. Studies had shown that a great number of people who had been brought to emergency rooms because of suicide attempts were invariably deficient in protein. The recommended prescription for these people was the diet common for hypoglycemia sufferers: high in protein and low in sugar and caffeine.

He also requested that I list the levels of anxiety I experienced on a daily basis, ten being totally out of control and one being totally calm. He instructed me to grade everything in between, along with the event causing rises of an anxiety level. This test clearly showed that most mornings I awoke at a level of five. Not good. Don likened these levels to a mainspring in a watch.

Leaning forward, with his elbows supported on his knees, Don tilted his dark head. As always when he went into his listen-up-this-is-important-don't-miss-a-word-as-I-educate-you mode, he clasped his hands together with both index fingers aimed at me.

"When I go to bed at night, I put my watch on the nightstand. After sitting there the eight or nine hours that I sleep, it completely winds down. In the morning, I can safely give it ten good winds to get it going again. However, if the watch has only wound down to a five and I wind it the usual ten times, eventually the spring will burst. The mainspring wasn't made to take that much tension, and neither are you."

As I squirmed in my chair, my eyes sought an object on which to focus while I digested this analogy.

"If you wake up in the morning at zero anxiety," he continued, "and the events of the day take you to level six, that's OK. Chances are you'll get back to zero with a good night's sleep, but waking up at a five? You wind up in the out-of-control range, and the part of the brain that defends you steps in and yells to your emotional and physical operating systems, 'Shut down on this woman before she kills us all!'"

Turning my eyes to meet his, I confided, "Killing us all doesn't sound like such a bad idea. I won't do myself in, of course, but not having to live like this anymore certainly is appealing sometimes. Life is wasted on me, since I'm too scared to live it. I'm so tired of fighting this, tired of fighting Jerry about it."

Don flopped back in his chair and covered his face with his hands in frustration. "Look, I can't stress enough that this is curable...you are curable. Various phobias have always existed. Agoraphobia just happens to be the new kid on the block, so it isn't as readily recognized by society at large. My plan of attack for you is relaxation, prayer, and desensitization. Your mind has chosen phobic behavior as a means of protecting you, its host. Other people react to stress with chronic back pain, headaches, or ulcers. These emotionally induced illnesses get these people off the hook in tension-provoking situations. People have different reasons for adopting illness as a guardian, but in reality, they're more in control than they give themselves credit for."

He turned his chair aside to toss his clipboard on the desk behind him. "It comes as no surprise that your mind would choose agoraphobia."

"Really?"

"Really," he replied. "Yours is not just a matter of stress; you're battling past trauma as well."

Sarcastically, I joked, "Lucky me, the last thing a woman wants to hear is that she's ordinary."

Tears of frustration burned but didn't fall. The scream was given a warning to stay suppressed. Ever since it had taken up residence inside me, it had collected my fears and tears as souvenirs. Each episode of disappointment, each thwarted attempt to find answers and a cure, added to its sad treasure trove. The burial of these pitiful mementos was mandatory. How else could I maintain the disguise of a friendly, sometimes shy, sometimes wisecracking, capable woman? Loving my children was the only real, visible quality I possessed.

Don exuded an infectious confidence in his ability to help me. A bit of cautious hope renewed itself. First I needed to get unscared enough to do as he prescribed.

As a tool to help me relax, he started me on a meditation routine. I'd sit in an easy chair, while he talked to me in a soft, soothing voice, and plant peaceful images in my mind. He taped our sessions so that I could take the tapes home to play and learn to relax on my own.

"OK, Bobbie," he said during one taping, "I want you to think of a place where you feel at peace."

As I reclined with my eyes closed, my mind went in search of any place it considered a safe haven of peace. Tears flowed in unchecked rivulets down my cheeks and dripped from my chin. The concept of a place free of anxiety created a mournful longing in me. "I'm sorry, but there is no place like that for me."

"That's all right," he comforted, handing me a tissue. "If you can't think of a current place, how about a place from the past? Was there ever a place you went to relax?"

"It doesn't matter when?"

"Not at all."

"'Cause, there was one place when I was a kid living with Grandma. Our backyard was a series of hills leading to the base of Mount Diablo. Just before you reached the sharp incline of the mountain, there was a royal-oak tree with a sizably large, odd hump growing at the base of the trunk. It looked like a lone branch had thought to grow on its own but had changed its mind and turned back to rejoin the original tree. To me, as a small child, that growth looked like a buffalo. I always called it *my* buffalo tree. Whenever my mother came to visit and once again refused to take me with her when she left, I'd run to that tree, climb on that buffalo, and pretend it would carry me off to a place where no one could hurt my feelings. From that tree, I could see for miles around and look down on the farmhouse, where everyone else was; I could daydream about all kinds of stuff. Everything always felt better after I sat there."

"Fine," Don said. "Just close your eyes, and in your mind, I want you to go meet the Lord at that tree. Concentrate on how much he loves you. Feel how safe you are at your tree with him. Look out all around you and then look up...see the clouds lazily drifting by. Put a problem on each of those large, fluffy, white clouds, and let the breeze and God's love for you take them drifting away. Let it all go."

At home, this visualization became a daily routine, and for the first time in countless years, I experienced a zero anxiety level.

Then, during a session with Don, an extraordinary thing happened.

"What's the matter, Bobbie?" he asked. "You're a little squirmy. You don't look relaxed at all. What's going on at the tree?"

"You know how it's usually just me and the Lord at the tree? Today it's not just us. A couple of other people are there."

"Who are these people?"

"Wait...wait!" My voice was barely above a whisper. "More have just come. Why...they're all me! I see three-year-old me, eight- or nine-year-old me, teenage me, and—you know how you always tell me to imagine myself as the woman the Lord created me to be? Well, today she's there, too. He's sitting on the hump and cradling her in his lap. The others are just milling aimlessly around."

"This is OK," Don said reassuringly. "Now I want you to go to that three-year-old child. Tell her that everything has turned out fine. Comfort her and nurture her, because she's still with you, crying out fearfully. Tell all of those guilt-ridden, hurting Bobbies that they're all OK; the woman you are today will take care of them."

Sinking further into my meditative state, I silently spoke to each of these Bobbies, each representing a painful time in my life. I assured them that they would be fine. The entire experience was very strange.

Since we rarely discussed my past, Don only inquired about a certain time or event if it just happened to crop up in my meditation.

"You have such a soft, gentle side," he said one day. "I always appreciate your sharing it with me. It's seldom that you let down that witty guard enough to let me in. I sense it costs you dearly when you do. A dozen alarms must go off. I'm looking forward to the day I can greet you as a friend, give you a hug, and know that you're comfortable with your feelings at last."

My sudden, obviously uncomfortable reaction to that prompted him to ask, "Aren't you accustomed to hugging? Didn't little Bobbie get enough hugs?"

A deep sigh launched itself from my toes. "Not from men. I'm sorry if I act standoffish. It's not intentional. You're right; hugging men isn't comfortable."

Tears rolled down my cheeks as I told him about Uncle Pokey. "Unfortunately, I only saw him when the kid swap was executed at his house once a year."

"You mean he's the only man who has ever expressed nonsexual affection for you?"

"Yep, all the other significant males in my life, until recently, either punched me or only offered sexual attention."

Don leaned back in his chair, narrowed his eyes, and caressed his chin thoughtfully. "Would you consider it possible that Skeeter is the one who decided to become phobic?" He leaned forward, eyes widened with potential discovery. "Let's look at the whole picture. Skeeter only had one month a year to feel loved and cherished. She grew into young Bobbie without anyone to care for or protect her. Teenage Bobbie had some terrifying experiences with both parents. Young woman Bobbie, struggling to become adult Barbara, had a frightening experience happen to her, with no explanation to offset the belief that no matter what happened, she had no one to take care of her. Skeeter adopted phobic behavior as a means of guarding herself, along with each subsequent person you became."

"That's not hard to believe at all," I told him. "I can't remember a time when I didn't know—not just feel but know—that I was strictly on my own. But now what will convince Skeeter to drop this behavior?"

"It's going to be a day-by-day process. You've been impacted by Skeeter's belief for over twenty years; changing it won't happen overnight. When panic threatens to overcome you in a store, for example, look around you at all the other people. Remind her that you're just one of those people. Be the mother to Skeeter she needs; assure her you're looking out for her. Use the visualization tapes as often as you can. They'll act as a tool to subdue some of that anxiety. Also, desensitization is helpful. We'll go into that another day."

"This is a lot of information to consider," was my response. "I guess I need to do something with it, but what?"

He relaxed back into his chair again and grinned. "Well, you could write a book about your experience with panic and the unexplained dizzy spells. It could be useful, not only for yourself but also for others."

Rolling my eyes at him, I countered, "First of all, I'm not a writer. Second, I wouldn't read a book on panic disorder unless it offered some solutions and explanations. When and if I ever have something useful to say, maybe I will share my experience in book form. Who knows?"

That "something useful" popped up quite unexpectedly.

Leaving Don's office, I set out to do some grocery shopping. The trip through the store, selecting the items I needed, passed uneventfully. However, while I was waiting for the cashier to ring up my groceries, the floor suddenly rolled under my feet. Efforts to ignore it and concentrate on my newly learned relaxation techniques failed. Of their own volition, my feet demanded to flee the scene. Attempts to lock them into place and stick it out didn't work. That old, familiar numbness grew in my feet and climbed to my face. Terror jammed my brain.

Embarrassed, I mumbled to the cashier, "Excuse me, I'm not feeling well. I need some air, but I'll be right back in to pay for my groceries."

As steadily as possible, I made my way outside to collapse on a bench near the exit. Out of concern, the checker sent a bag boy after me with a cup of water. He was very solicitous, which only added to my discomfort. An explanation was in order, I felt, but I didn't have one.

Finally forcing myself to go back into the store, I shakily wrote out a check. My whole being was still poised and ready for flight... from what to where, I didn't know.

"What seems to be the matter, sweetie?" the checker asked. "Ear problem?"

"I don't really know," I admitted. "Occasionally I just get dizzy."

Through her gum cracking, she declared with a knowing look, "Well, you might check in with a doctor to see if you have an ear infection. My mother had one recently, and she acted the same way you just did. Said she thought we were having an earthquake and started runnin'."

After thanking her, I meekly followed the bagger to my car. When I arrived home, I called one of the doctors I'd met while working at Jackson Medical Center's sales office, an ear, nose, and throat doctor by the name of Alvin Nickel.

"Dr. Nickel, is there anything in your realm of medicine that would include dizziness, loss of equilibrium, nausea, and disorientation?"

"Why, yes, as a matter of fact, those symptoms indicate you might have Ménière's disease," he replied. "Let me connect you with my receptionist to schedule testing for you."

After making the appointment, I dug out an old home medical encyclopedia from our bedroom closet. Finding Ménière's disease, I read, "Attacks of Ménière's disease usually occur past middle age and are most common in elderly persons. The disease is rare among children but may appear at any age. During an attack, the patient will become dizzy (vertigo), hear strange ringing or other noises in the ears (tinnitus), may have trouble hearing and become nauseated, vomit, and sweat profusely. The person may become so unbalanced as to fall to the ground."

At first I read the definition of Ménière's with mild interest and curiosity, and then something leaped from the pages that knocked the wind out of me with the impact of its revelation: "Sedatives, such as phenobarbital, help calm the patient, who may become emotionally disturbed as the result of continued dizziness and nausea."

Tears splatted on the pages of the book as I sat on the edge of the bed and demanded of my closet door, "When did I decide to become phobic indeed?"

Reaching for the phone, I called directory assistance for Pleasant Hill, California. "Yes, operator, I'd like the number for a physician. Dr. Donald K. Fisher, please."

My shaking hands managed to dial the number she gave me. "Dr. Fisher, you probably won't remember me. You knew me as Bobbie Elling when I was your patient."

Understandably, his memory had tucked me away, but he listened patiently as I highlighted our history for him, along with the subsequent health issues. Then I presented him with the question. "Why wouldn't you have diagnosed me as having Ménière's disease at that time?"

"Oh, my dear." He sighed sadly. "Back in 1965, we knew so little about that disease. We thought it only hit the elderly, and you were so young. I am so very, very sorry."

"I didn't call to make you sorry." It was my turn to console him. "I just so badly needed confirmation. I don't blame you at all. I guess it's all a matter of the time in which we're born. For example, at one time an attack by Indians was an ever-present health threat. So while I have unexplainable panic attacks over misunderstood dizzy spells, I can be grateful that, well, at least I don't have to worry about being attacked by Indians."

The explanation for the dizzy spells and resulting anxiety attacks finally came through the tests administered by Dr. Nickel.

The thought of facing another bout of Jerry's ridicule and impatience with my fears was less than appealing, but going alone was out of the question. Besides, he wanted to know the cause of my anxious behavior, too, so he eagerly accompanied me to Dr. Nickel's for the tests. I'd built up such a bad case of anticipatory anxiety that I was a trembling wreck by the time we got there.

The general hearing tests passed uneventfully, but the test specifically for Ménière's was startling, one I'd never forget. A technician laid me on a cold metal table, turned me onto my left side, and squirted water into my right ear. My body took off for the ceiling. My arms flailed about in an attempt to grab anything that would prevent me from falling up…yes, up. This test generated exactly what I experienced as a panic attack.

"Help, help me. I'm floating away. Everything's blurry and spinning."

"Good, you're doing great," the technician declared.

The floating, spinning sensation eased a bit. Shakily and sarcastically, I replied, "Oh, sure, store clerks and dentists love it when I do this."

Torture Man, the technician, softly chuckled as he turned me to the right and shot water into my left ear. Tension knotted my muscles as I waited for all the horrible sensations to begin, but nothing happened.

"I don't feel anything. Am I doing something wrong?"

Again the soft chuckle. "No, you're not doing anything wrong, but your inner ear is. Let me take these test results to the doctor. He'll be right with you."

Jerry and I waited, and soon Dr. Nickel came in, beaming. "Congratulations, my dear," he said with a broad smile. "You're not crazy; you're sick."

We were astonished!

"You mean that all this time, for all these years, I've had a perfectly legitimate medical reason for the dizzy spells?"

"That's exactly what I mean," Dr. Nickel assured. "So how are you with this new information?"

Shock and wonder overwhelmed me. "I don't know. A little angry and resentful but so relieved that I'm not mentally deficient. Suddenly the past twenty years don't seem to matter as much. I mean, after all, I did make it through."

Dr. Nickel enfolded me in his arms and gave me a tight squeeze. "And you made it through just fine."

Questions flooded through my mind and out my mouth. Would Valium suppress symptoms? Were there periods of time when a person would be symptom-free, like a remission state? The answers to these questions were yes.

All the way home, my mind chanted, *I'm not crazy; I'm not crazy.* All those years had been a terrible mistake.

For several weeks, I vacillated between fury and relief. On the one hand, I was angry at every doctor and therapist I'd ever seen. Dr. and Margo Grieg were on a first-name basis with Ménière's disease, and because they hadn't explored that as a possibility in me, they had fed my phobic behavior. On the other hand, and that was some big hand, I was grateful that the doors leading to information and answers to twenty-year-old questions were opening.

CHAPTER FORTY-EIGHT

History, despite its wrenching pain, cannot be unlived but
if faced with courage, need not be lived again.

—*Maya Angelou*

At our next session, I told Don, "After quite an emotional battle, my rage and resentment have been outweighed by gratitude for all the blessings in my life. But I'm determined that if I can prevent anyone else from being victimized by a medical misdiagnosis, I'll do it."

"But, Bobbie," Don asked, "how does knowing you have Ménière's disease help you? What good is that information to you in regard to your phobic condition?"

"I'll try to give you an analogy," I replied pensively. "Say I'm alone in my two-story house that has so many doors that when I'm upstairs, almost anyone could walk in without my knowing. Let's further say I've just gotten out of the shower and hear a noise downstairs. My brain hollers out to the defense mechanism in my brain, 'All right, send out the adrenaline troops while I go through my noise-identification files. Danger may be eminent!' Once my brain has identified that the sound is Sammy clanking around with my antique, metal cream pitcher, my defense mechanism yells, 'OK, everyone stand down; there's no cause for alarm!' and I relax. Now if I get dizzy in a store or bank or wherever, knowing I have a medical condition causing it, my brain won't need to send out alarms. There's a logical explanation, so there's no need for crippling fear."

"Well, that's all fine and good," he conceded. "But we still need to reprogram Skeeter, because it's sad but true: you are phobic. Now that we know why, we need to work more on relaxation techniques next week."

"Don, before I go, I need to ask you a question. For the past twenty years, when I'd see a doctor about the problem I have, every doctor has always, without exception, referred me to the psychiatric side of medicine. I need to know, and you as a therapist need to know, what about referral the opposite direction? After I've received treatment from the psychiatric community without any positive effect, why hasn't any psychiatrist referred me back to the physiological side of medicine? It makes me sad to think there are other people like me who have a legitimate physical problem who will never know it. Once they start seeing psychiatrists, who won't admit defeat and won't consider other causes for a particular set of symptoms, they'll never be cured."

Don solemnly answered, "It's a sad truth, but I imagine you're right. The ratio of referral from therapists to doctors is probably small. Considering your history, though, assuming that you needed emotional healing is understandable."

One door leading to enlightenment had opened, and I gratefully stepped through it. But God had even more doors for me to walk through.

Jerry and I had been attending a support-and-share group at our church, and we were reading a book in which the author offered some gentle criticism and advice for ladies who ran from one self-help class to another. He maintained that they were gaining knowledge, and good knowledge at that, but when were they going to slow down and actually apply it to their lives? This really started me thinking. Flitting from study to study wasn't my style, nor was attending seminars and classes. But what about all the psychotherapy in which I'd been involved? I'd been in and out of one kind of therapy or another for twenty years! Wasn't it time that I stepped out on faith and applied what I'd learned?

At my next session with Don, I shared my new belief. "You know, Don, for many years, I've prayed to be healed of this phobic-anxiety thing, and on many occasions, my faith has really taken a beating, because I wasn't getting any better. I've asked for and received prayer from others, and again, seemingly nothing happened. So now I'm wondering, what if God has healed me, but I haven't been leading a healed life? What if all I have to do is claim the healing he has already provided?"

"That's a nice thought," Don replied. "Where are you going with all this?"

With an impish grin, I laid a shock on him. "Home! I'm going home. I'm grateful for all you've taught me, but there's more to know about myself outside a therapist's office. I'm going to find it and use it, along with all the other information I've gathered so far."

Jerry wasn't exactly overjoyed with my quest to find more pieces of the dizziness-with-ensuing-panic puzzle. Or was it panic with ensuing dizziness?

A noteworthy puzzle piece was unearthed when I attended a four-hour seminar on premenstrual tension. What an eye-opener! The symptoms listed for sufferers of this syndrome were dizziness, nausea, irritability, an inability to cope emotionally, and a temporary increase in anxiety. Dr. Nickel and my general practitioner, Dr. Camara, both confirmed that PMT sufferers with Ménière's disease definitely had a hard time of it. The fluid retention common to PMT would increase the symptoms of Ménière's.

More enlightenment came when a run-of-the-mill ear infection sent me to see Dr. Camara. Sitting behind his incredibly cluttered desk, he scrutinized my chart. "Let's see now; according to my notes, you're allergic to penicillin. Any allergies to other medications that you know of?"

"Yes, I have a reaction to the ingredient in most Novocains. My dentist has to use one particular type when he works on my teeth."

Dr. Camara looked up sharply. "What kind of reaction do you have?"

The mental image of my last dental-chair experience made me laugh. "You'd have to see it to believe it. Most of those gum-numbing shots propel me from lying down to flying straight up and running full speed for the door. The shot abruptly pitches me forward."

That put an ear-to-ear grin on his face. "Barbara, do you know what that medication is? It's epinephrine, a form of adrenaline. For someone prone to panic attacks, additional adrenaline is the last thing you need."

Most people aren't quite so delighted to find they have certain allergies and diseases, but I was floating on a cloud. That cloud wasn't one of those gray, gloomy ones, either; my cloud was white and fluffy, with a wondrous silver lining, a platform for dancing with joy. Filled with elation, I wanted to run up and down the streets, yelling, "I'm not crazy! Never have been; never will be. Hey, kids, your mother is not the looney tune she has thought she was."

Jerry was understandably angry about all the money, time, and heartache spent over this misdiagnosed illness.

"But the blessings, Jerry," I'd argue. "I share your feelings about twenty years of my life being seemingly wasted, but were they really? I've raised three and a half children, considering I didn't have the privilege of raising Paula for most of her life, and am raising two more. I've had wonderful friends, and most of all, God has shown me he loves me. Just think, a year ago I knew nothing and had no hope. I prayed for his guidance, and he said loudly and clearly, 'It's about time you turned to me. Now I'm going to show you how I do things.' And he did them perfectly. The Bible says that he helps us in our troubles so that we are able to help others by using the same help we have received from God."

Jerry continued to scowl as I went on. "I'm sorry these things happened, too, and the only comfort here is that maybe God allowed this to happen so he could use me to further his will in someone else's life. You can bet I'm going to be on the lookout for anyone who complains of dizziness and anxiety so I can share my experience with them in hopes that it'll be beneficial."

More answers and challenges were to come as I was forced to face the fact that despite the Ménière's diagnosis, I still battled panic attacks.

CHAPTER FORTY-NINE

Hope is like the sun, which, as we journey toward it, casts the shadow of our burden behind us.

—*Samuel Smiles*

With more labels and information, I dragged Skeeter down the road to reconciliation with these illnesses and syndromes. Accomplishing things that were so ordinary for other people was a thrill for me. Skeeter wasn't always as happy about growing as I was and continued to raise a fuss now and then. Grocery shopping, medical appointments, or even trips to the bank continued to challenge me, but whatever the distance, I'd go as far as I felt God with me. If on some days I could only make it from the front door to the end of the driveway, I'd give myself permission to turn back and vow to make it farther the next day.

Each successful trip to anywhere brought elation. If that strong sense of dread rolled over me, I'd mentally get in touch with little Skeeter and treat her like I would Simon or Sammy. Whenever they were fearful, I held them and reassured them that I loved them and would protect them and encourage them. Skeeter certainly deserved the same nurturing, and she responded pretty well.

We all have a Skeeter inside us. Yours has a different name, but that little kid is inside us all. He or she may be playful or, like mine, timid, fearful, and unsure if anyone will take care of him or her when times are rough.

Also, as kids do, Skeeter sought out peers but without much luck. After living the life of a phobic person for twenty years, I knew there must be more phobics in the world but had encountered only four: three women and one man. Amazing! Statistically, at that time 20 percent of the nation's population was agoraphobic.

One of the women adamantly told me she would talk to me about anything but agoraphobia. Even after becoming fairly close friends, she would not discuss her phobic problem. One day I asked her if she would answer just one question.

"Maybe," she said cautiously.

"Well, the question is this," I said. "If more people were agoraphobic and the public at large knew more about it, do you think you'd be phobic at all? I mean, what if you were in a store and could say, 'Excuse me, I need to step outside for a moment; I'm phobic and feeling a bit anxious.' If they knew what you were talking about, would you feel better?"

"OK," she responded with a laugh. "I'll answer that. If, and that's a big *if*, I could be comfortable admitting I was having an anxiety attack, I probably wouldn't have it."

One of the other self-confessed phobic women claimed to be cured. Quite the crusader on behalf of people with agoraphobia, she worked with a psychiatrist by taking his patients on desensitization excursions. My outing with her was a ride from San Jose to Oakland on Bay Area Rapid Transit. During that ride, she offered a few symptom-control tips and insights.

"There's some real physical activity going on in the brain during an attack," she explained. "But when the amygdala or the hippocampus send out alarm signals, you can confuse or sidetrack them by using other parts of your brain to focus on something else. For example, if you start feeling panicky while standing in line at a store, do some math."

"The whattala and hippo-who? What the heck are those?"

She laughed. "Sorry. The amygdala is a section of the brain that processes emotions. It dictates memory storage and determines the size of an emotional response in any situation. It's sort of like posttraumatic stress. If the amygdala decides that, based on the memory of a similar situation, an event is something to fear, it prepares your body for an emergency and sets up your fight-or-flight plan. The hippocampus is next door to it and also deals with memory and emotions."

Another tool she used was wearing a rubber band on her wrist; when panic struck, she snapped it. According to her, pain also confused the amygdala enough to short-circuit anxiety.

Sexual intercourse was another useful prevention. I didn't see that as very practical in most situations, but it did explain a lot about previous behavior on my part.

And while I couldn't argue the logic in exercising to burn off adrenaline, I failed to see how a person could suddenly jump out of a dental chair to do jumping jacks. It did offer an explanation for the urge to run or walk when anxiety hit.

She also stressed good dietary practices, which made a lot of good sense. Full-blown panic attacks caused frequent urination and diarrhea, both of which caused loss of vitamins and electrolyte imbalance.

What I fed my mind, as well as my body, began to get more consideration. It also made sense that if physically we are what we eat, then that must surely apply to our emotional and mental state as well. Watching lighthearted programs on television rather than suspenseful ones lessened tension in my mind. That was in keeping with Philippians 4:8 that says "Fill your minds with those things that are good and deserve praise: things that are true, noble, right, pure, lovely, and honorable."

The man I mentioned would only talk to me on the phone. He stated firmly that he would never publicly reveal his agoraphobia or anxiety issues for fear of losing his job. How sad but understandable.

He had other encouraging information to share with me, though. He had poked around and found out about discoveries unearthed by forensic psychiatrists at Stanford in California. They had studied brain-tissue samples, and the results had proved that a chemical imbalance existed that contributed to the problem of anxiety and the malfunctioning of certain receptors in the brain, which caused the symptoms of agoraphobia.

It was exciting and comforting to know that the medical profession no longer took a blasé attitude toward this disease. Without widespread public awareness, however, these discoveries didn't alleviate the embarrassment of the sufferer nor remove the stigma of mental illness.

A lot of social issues were coming out of the closet, but not those pertaining to mental illness. There were many television shows, movies, books, and magazine articles on child molestation, alcoholism, child and domestic abuse, drug abuse, and homosexuality. In addition, there was a strong campaign to enlighten the public regarding AIDS. Mental illness in any form was apparently too tricky to fit into a sitcom script.

Those of us with mental and emotional issues thought it was high time the public be made more keenly aware that there are wonderful, loving, capable people in their midst suffering from a different but no less important and painful affliction. We didn't expect understanding but craved recognition, acceptance, and tolerance.

Over the many years I suffered from a chemical imbalance, I'd sought out hordes of therapists and tried their methods of treatment. However, I began setting a statute of limitations on the amount of time spent trying a particular method of therapy or medication.

Once that statute of limitations had passed without a positive result, a new medical territory was explored. After all, if I'd gone to a doctor who prescribed orange juice three times a day for a headache and after six months I still had the original headache plus a skin rash, I'd have to assume that he or she made a wrong diagnosis and prescribed the wrong treatment. At that point, I would hope he or she would be willing to explore other possibilities. If not, I'd need to take care of myself by seeking another provider.

In the late 1960s, several labels for the high-anxiety issue became popular: territorial apprehension, housewife syndrome, anticipatory apprehension. In 1985, they used panic disorder. They all meant the same thing to me: something was wrong, something that prevented me from functioning like everyone else.

My fearful condition still shamed me and affected every area of my life. It dictated how I dressed, worked, played, and handled or, as was often the case, mishandled relationships.

In time, I stopped judging myself so harshly and instead evaluated myself by the people who loved me. My address book was filled with names of people I admired and respected, and I knew they wouldn't waste precious time on me if I wasn't a quality person of value. Their eyes mirrored a woman I liked.

One of these dear friends had a daughter, who maintained she was losing her mind. She was having dizzy spells and had a hard time functioning at work. She was frightened. Her father confided in Jerry, who told him about me. The father called me, and I shared with him the confusion surrounding the question, am I sick or crazy? Before he took his daughter to a psychiatrist, I urged him to take her to an ear, nose, and throat doctor. Sure enough, she had an inner-ear problem. Not crazy...sick!

What a relief it didn't take twenty years for that young girl to get that sorted out. When health problems aren't properly diagnosed, despair digs deep, ugly emotional scars.

It was encouraging to see ongoing research and development in the area of unwarranted panic. It also amazed me to realize how strong our minds are and how intimidating battered emotions can be. It was also saddening to realize that we lived in such an analytical, intellectual society that made health problems without easy, visible explanations unacceptable.

In the twenty years of living a fearful, phobic life, I raised children, ran a household, held down jobs, and was a contributing community member. These things were done fearfully and in terror most of the time, until I realized that I didn't have to live life as my neighbor or mother or grandma did. I just needed to live my life...period.

Looking back over the most horrible times, I now see my life as a tapestry. It's no more beautiful than yours, to be sure, but it is wonderfully different. Singularly, each of the threads woven through mine is not so spectacular; in fact, some are rather gruesome in color and texture.

The thread representing losing Joe is too terrible to look on by itself. When entwined with the thread of having him in the first place, however, it's lovely beyond compare.

The thread representing giving Kate up for adoption makes me flinch with its ugliness, but when the fact that there is a wonderful young woman out there in the world to whom I gave life is woven around it, it becomes dazzling.

The thread of all those years without my precious Paula is the color of gloom itself. But the thread of our reunion, a true gift from God, is stunning.

There are brilliant hues of delight and joy that represent each of my children. Set against the dark background of a life lived with physical and mental illness, they depict a heart-wrenchingly exquisite picture.

God, the master weaver, has placed before my mind's eye a life tapestry fit to hang in heaven, fit to take into glory with me when I go. Throughout the threads of dark pain and somber sorrow, in with the threads of jewel-toned joys, he has artfully woven brilliant golds and silvers, signifying the blessings he has bestowed on me.

As for the chemical imbalance and subsequent panic attacks, they may not be completely curable, but the symptoms can be managed enough to allow me a productive, satisfying life.

The scream has settled down to a sigh as I meet with my Lord at the buffalo tree.

EPILOGUE

Jerry had been a very good director when teaching theater arts. Director was his favorite role to play. The role of his wife could not be scripted or directed, however, and due to my illness, along with our background and age difference, our marriage bond snapped. No one was surprised.

Many delightful and surprising things happened for me after the divorce. Kate and I found each other, and hugging that sassy, little blonde was pure, undiluted joy.

All seven children have grown up to be fine human beings and good friends. Twelve beloved grandchildren were born to further bless my life, and I found myself doing things I never would have thought possible. The frustrating pursuit of finding the right doctor and the right medication to control my symptoms paid off.

Fly to Florida alone? Me? Yep, that happened. Pack up and move to Oregon? Yep. Drive back and forth between Oregon and California? Yep. Learn to play bass? Did that. Stand behind a microphone before a crowd and sing? Uh-huh. Write a book to hopefully encourage other panic-disordered people? That finally happened, too.

CPSIA information can be obtained
at www.ICGtesting.com
Printed in the USA
LVHW041553100119
603457LV00021B/1175/P